Robert Lowry

Good as Gold

a new collection of Sunday school songs

Robert Lowry, William H. Doane

Good as Gold
a new collection of Sunday school songs

ISBN/EAN: 9783337850968

Printed in Europe, USA, Canada, Australia, Japan

Cover: Foto ©Lupo / pixelio.de

More available books at **www.hansebooks.com**

Good as Gold:

A NEW COLLECTION OF

SUNDAY SCHOOL SONGS.

BY

REV. ROBERT LOWRY AND W. HOWARD DOANE.

GOOD AS GOLD.

GOOD AS GOLD is intended to have an honorable place among the popular Song Books that have preceded it. The steadily increasing confidence with which the Christian public look to this House for the best Sunday School Songs has been carefully kept in view in this compilation.

GOOD AS GOLD is designed to subserve a practical use rather than illustrate a particular theory. The gracefulness of its melodies and the simplicity of its harmonies will commend it to the great mass of singers in the Sunday School.

GOOD AS GOLD gives reverent prominence to the Lord Jesus Christ in His Advent, His Sacrifice, His Resurrection, and His Second Coming. The various phases of Experience and Duty are held forth in song. The aged saint and the little child are remembered with equal care.

GOOD AS GOLD contains a fair proportion of hymns adapted to the International Lessons of 1880 and 1881.

GOOD AS GOLD is not made up of a few shining particles in the midst of a waste of useless matter. The best mode of discovering its treasures is to begin at the beginning and sing the book through.

GOOD AS GOLD.

The Lord's Prayer.

1. Our Father, who art in heaven, | hallowed | be Thy | name; || Thy kingdom come, Thy will be done on | earth, . . as it | is in | heaven;
2. Give us this | day our | daily | bread: || And forgive us our debts, as | we for- | give our | debtors.
3. And lead us not into temptation, but de- | liver | us from | evil; || For Thine is the kingdom, and the power, and the glory, for- | ever. | A- | men.

Gloria Patri.

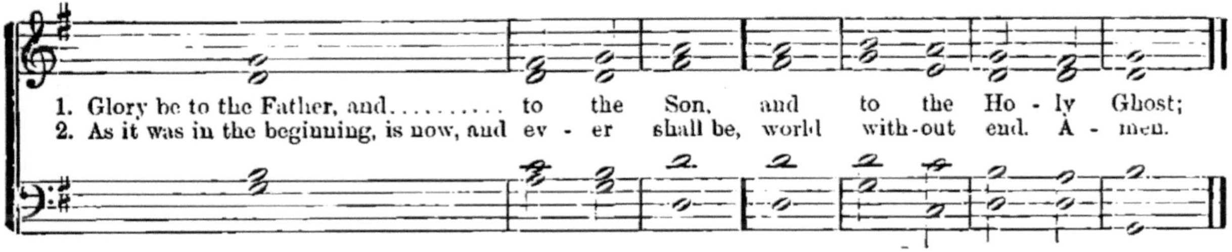
1. Glory be to the Father, and.......... to the Son, and to the Ho - ly Ghost;
2. As it was in the beginning, is now, and ev - er shall be, world with-out end. A - men.

4

It is I.

F. A. Crafts. *Be of good cheer; it is I; be not afraid.*—Mark 6: 50. R. Lowry.

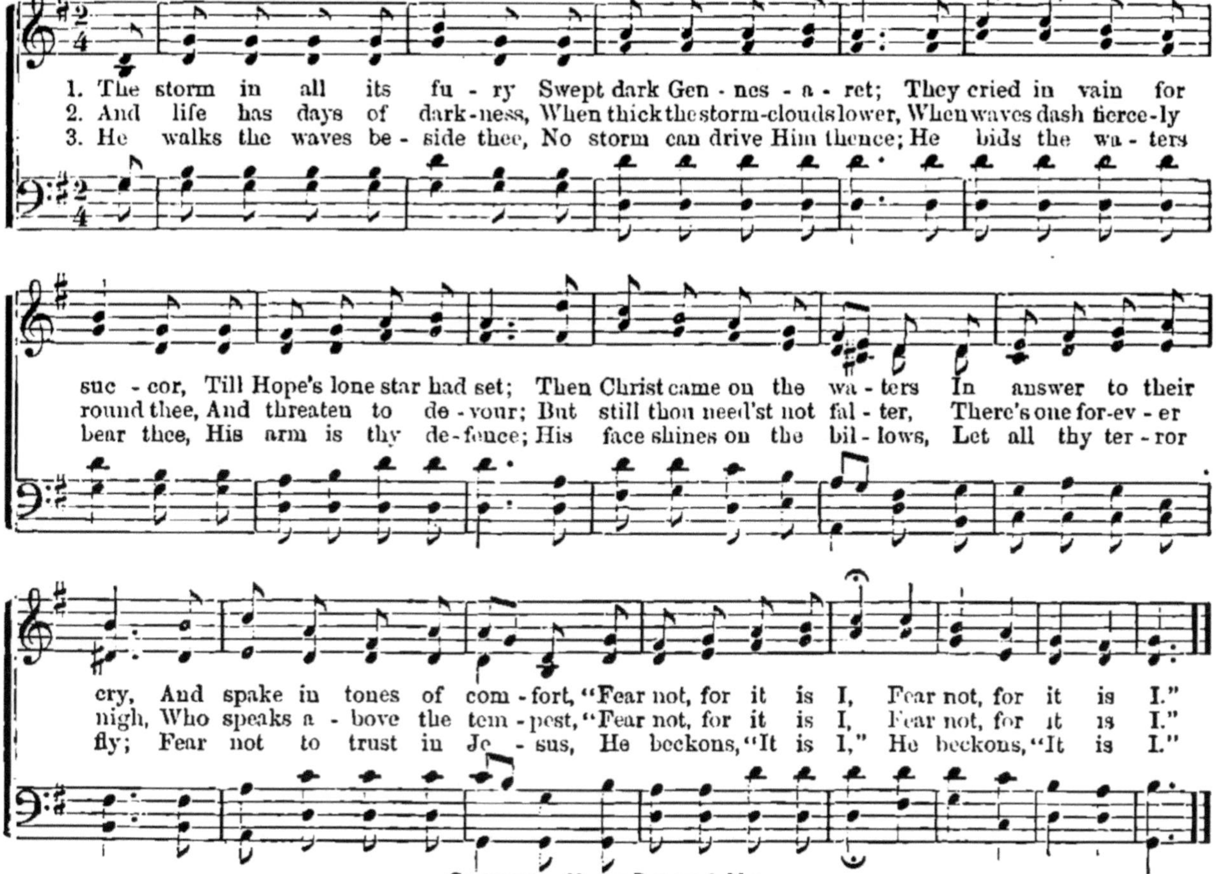
1. The storm in all its fu - ry Swept dark Gen - nes - a - ret; They cried in vain for suc - cor, Till Hope's lone star had set; Then Christ came on the wa - ters In answer to their cry, And spake in tones of com - fort, "Fear not, for it is I, Fear not, for it is I."
2. And life has days of dark-ness, When thick the storm-clouds lower, When waves dash fierce-ly round thee, And threaten to de - vour; But still thou need'st not fal - ter, There's one for-ev - er nigh, Who speaks a - bove the tem - pest, "Fear not, for it is I, Fear not, for it is I."
3. He walks the waves be - side thee, No storm can drive Him thence; He bids the wa - ters bear thee, His arm is thy de - fence; His face shines on the bil - lows, Let all thy ter - ror fly; Fear not to trust in Je - sus, He beckons, "It is I," He beckons, "It is I."

Down at the Cross.

REV. E. A. HOFFMAN. *Ye are complete in him.*—COL. 2: 10. JOHN R. SWENEY.

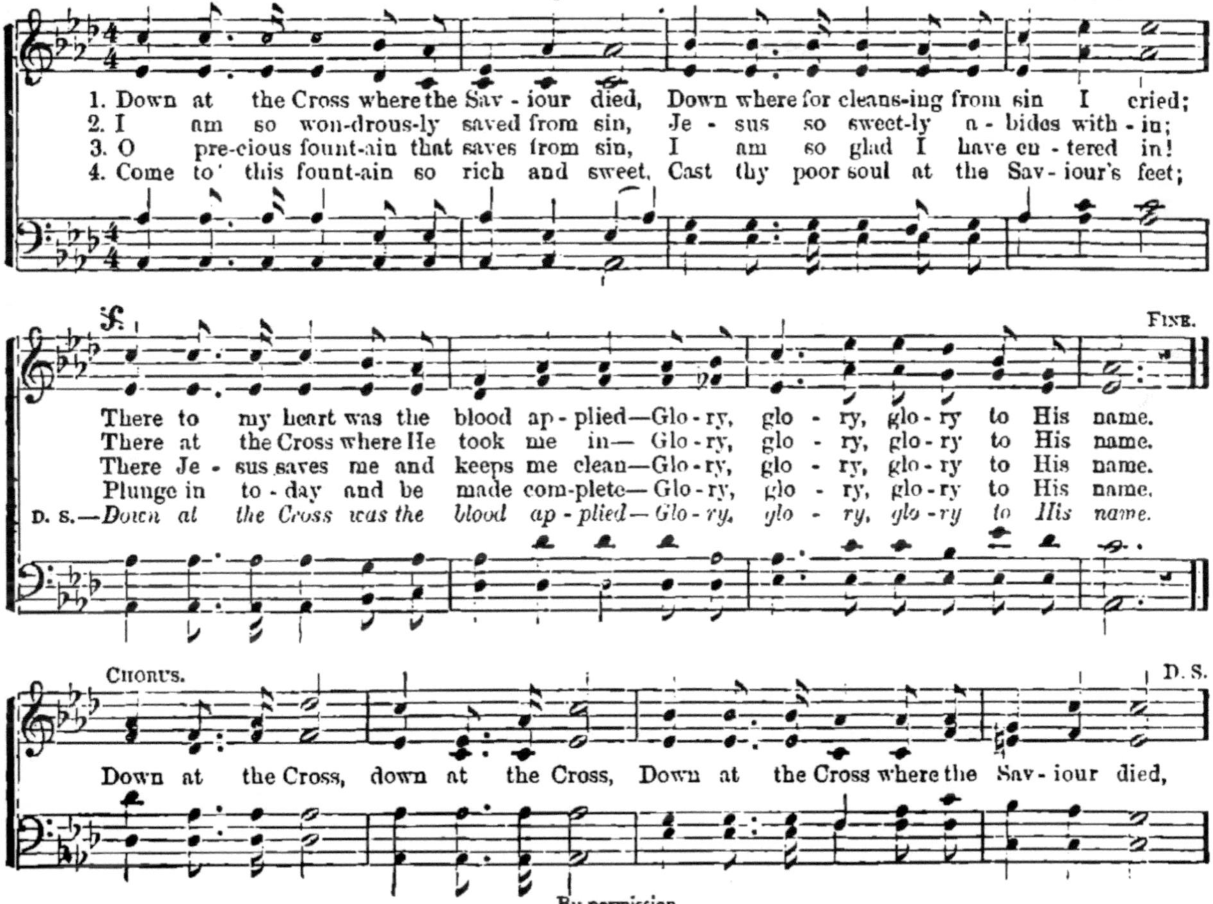
1. Down at the Cross where the Sav - iour died, Down where for cleans-ing from sin I cried;
2. I am so won-drous-ly saved from sin, Je - sus so sweet-ly a - bides with - in;
3. O pre-cious fount-ain that saves from sin, I am so glad I have en - tered in!
4. Come to this fount-ain so rich and sweet, Cast thy poor soul at the Sav-iour's feet;
FINE.
There to my heart was the blood ap - plied—Glo - ry, glo - ry, glo - ry to His name.
There at the Cross where He took me in— Glo - ry, glo - ry, glo - ry to His name.
There Je - sus saves me and keeps me clean—Glo - ry, glo - ry, glo - ry to His name.
Plunge in to - day and be made com-plete—Glo - ry, glo - ry, glo - ry to His name.
D. S.—Down at the Cross was the blood ap - plied—Glo - ry, glo - ry, glo - ry to His name.
CHORUS.
D. S.
Down at the Cross, down at the Cross, Down at the Cross where the Sav - iour died,

By permission.

6 Deeper Love for Thee.

W. H. D. *Let my supplication come before thee.*—Ps. 119: 170. W. H. Doane.

1. Precious Saviour, dear-est Friend, While we bend the knee, Come and give our long-ing hearts Deep-er love to Thee.
2. Come and con-se - crate us now, Seal us ev - er Thine; May we to Thy ho - ly will Ev - ery power re - sign.
3. Trusting as a lit - tle child Help us, Lord, to be, While we ask in sim-ple faith Deep-er love to Thee.
4. Deep-er love, yes, deep-er love, This our constant plea; Deep-er love, yes, deep-er love, Till we're lost in Thee.
Refrain.
O Sav - iour, lov-ing Re-deemer, Sav - iour, precious to me,
Grant me, I pray Thee, More of Thy Spir - it, Draw-ing me clos - er, Clos-er to Thee.

O let Me tell it Once Again.

Mrs. Kate S. Burr. *Preach the gospel to every creature.*—Mark. 16: 15. R. Lowry.

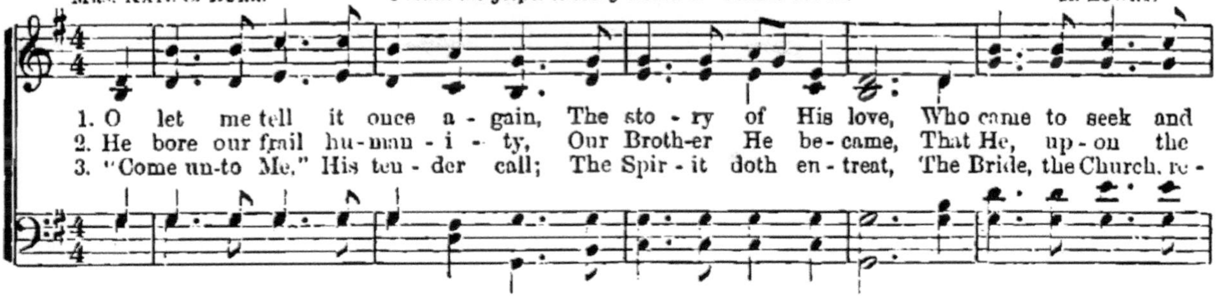
1. O let me tell it once a - gain, The sto - ry of His love, Who came to seek and
2. He bore our frail hu-man - i - ty, Our Broth-er He be-came, That He, up - on the
3. "Come un-to Me," His ten - der call; The Spir - it doth en - treat, The Bride, the Church, re -

Chorus.
save the lost, And guide them safe a - bove. O tell the sto - ry once again, The sto-ry of His love; O
blood-stained cross, Might bear our sin and shame.
ech - oes, Come; Let each the call re - peat.

tell the sto - ry once a-gain, The sto - ry of His love.

4.

For whosoever will may come—
Exhaustless the supply—
And, from life's everlasting fount,
May drink and never die.

We will Follow Jesus.

W. S. *Jesus said unto him, Follow me.*—Matt. 8: 22. Wm. Stevenson.

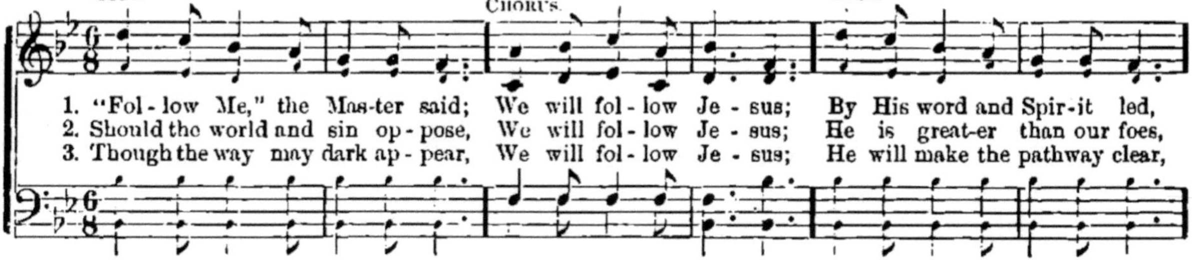
Solo.
Chorus.
Solo.
1. "Fol - low Me," the Mas-ter said; We will fol - low Je - sus; By His word and Spir-it led,
2. Should the world and sin op - pose, We will fol - low Je - sus; He is great-er than our foes,
3. Though the way may dark ap - pear, We will fol - low Je - sus; He will make the pathway clear,

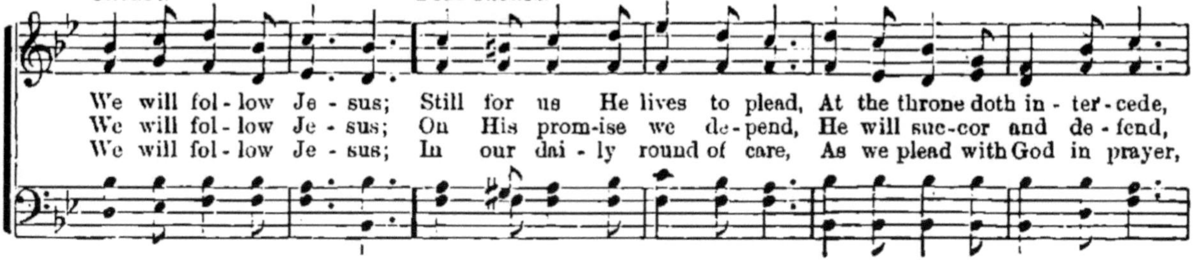
Chorus.
Full Chorus.
We will fol - low Je - sus; Still for us He lives to plead, At the throne doth in - ter - cede,
We will fol - low Je - sus; On His prom-ise we de - pend, He will suc-cor and de - fend,
We will fol - low Je - sus; In our dai - ly round of care, As we plead with God in prayer,

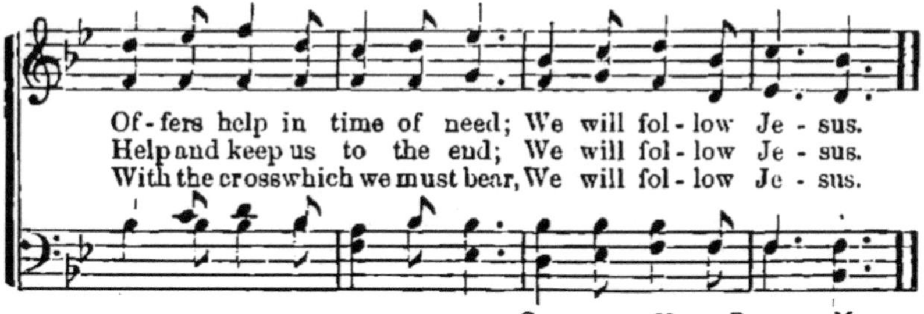
Of - fers help in time of need; We will fol - low Je - sus.
Help and keep us to the end; We will fol - low Je - sus.
With the cross which we must bear, We will fol - low Je - sus.

4.
Ever keep the end in view,
We will follow Jesus;
All His promises are true,
We will follow Jesus;
When this earthly course is run,
And the Master says, "Well done,"
Life eternal we have won!
We will follow Jesus.

Not Forever.

Mrs. Fanny Van Alstyne. *There remaineth a rest to the people of God.*—Heb. 4: 10. W. H. Doane.

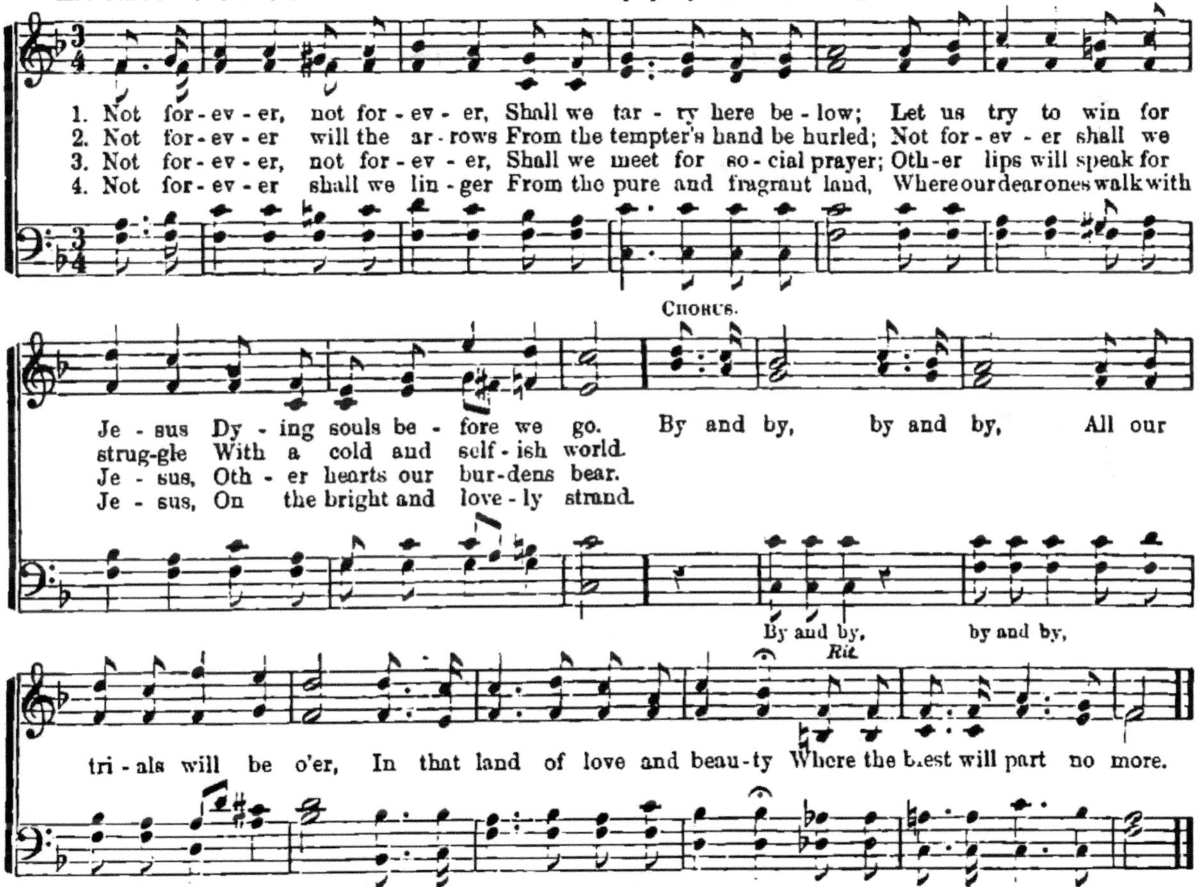
1. Not for - ev - er, not for - ev - er, Shall we tar - ry here be - low; Let us try to win for Je - sus Dy - ing souls be - fore we go.
2. Not for - ev - er will the ar - rows From the tempter's hand be hurled; Not for - ev - er shall we strug-gle With a cold and self - ish world.
3. Not for - ev - er, not for - ev - er, Shall we meet for so - cial prayer; Oth - er lips will speak for Je - sus, Oth - er hearts our bur - dens bear.
4. Not for - ev - er shall we lin - ger From the pure and fragrant land, Where our dear ones walk with Je - sus, On the bright and love - ly strand.
Chorus.
By and by, by and by, All our
By and by, by and by,
Rit.
tri - als will be o'er, In that land of love and beau - ty Where the blest will part no more.

Awake, and Sing.

MARY A. LATHBURY. *The Lord is in his holy temple.*—HAB. 2: 20. M. L. BARTLETT.

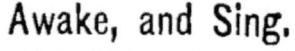

1. The Lord is in His ho - ly tem - ple, Wide as the world its port - als stand, To gath-er
2. His star of prom-ise shines a - bove thee, And lights thee to His tem - ple gates; And then, to
3. Come home, come home! the Father calls thee, And Christ the Shepherd bids thee come; The ten-der
home His ho - ly peo - ple From every age, from ev - ery land.
greet Thy glad home-coming, The King of heaven in pa-tience waits.
lambs His arm shall gath-er, His love their light, His heart their home.
CHORUS.
A-wake, and sing the song of
triumph, O ransomed of the Lord, a - wake! While earth and heav'n their silence break.
Come throng His gates with glad thanksgiving,

By permission.

Cross of Calvary.

S. D. PHELPS, D. D. *There shall be a fountain opened * * * * for sin and uncleanness.*—ZECH. 13: 1. R. LOWRY.

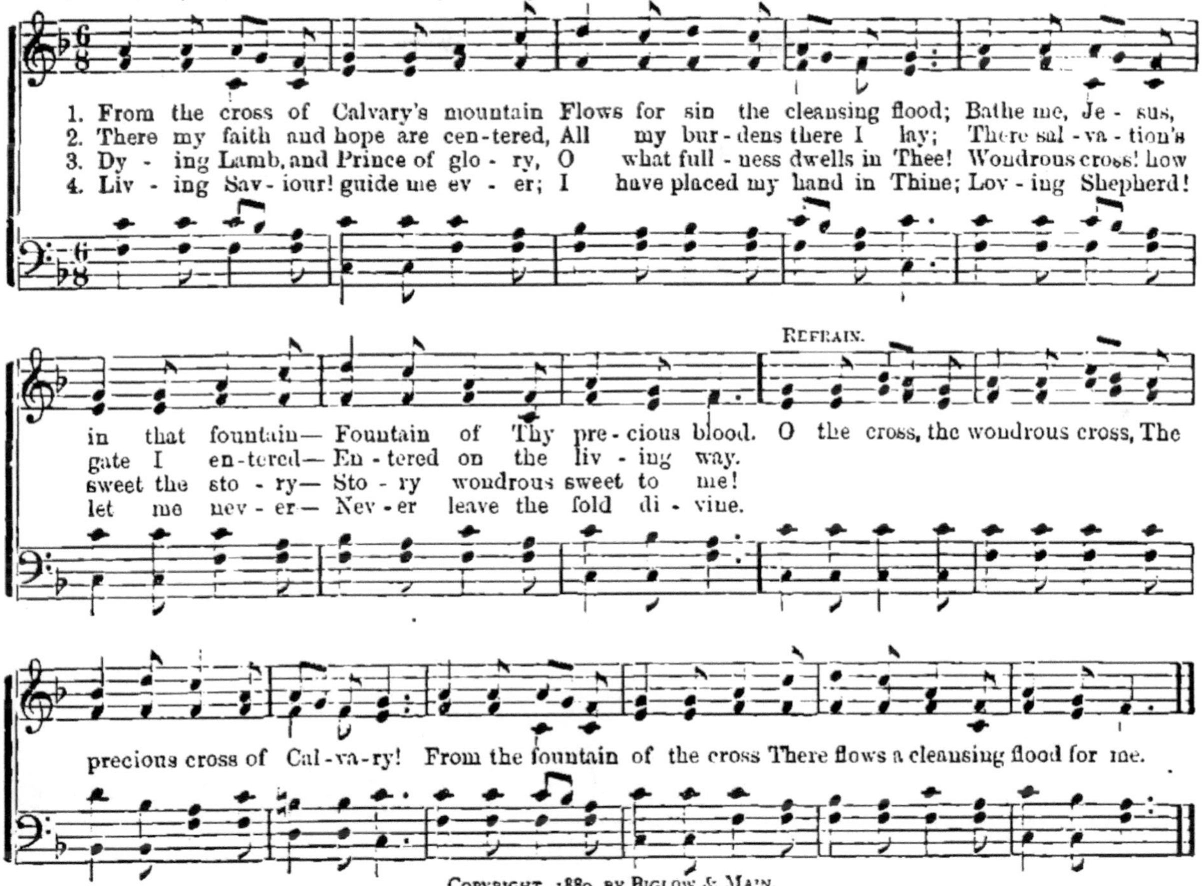
1. From the cross of Calvary's mountain Flows for sin the cleansing flood; Bathe me, Je - sus,
2. There my faith and hope are cen-tered, All my bur-dens there I lay; There sal - va - tion's
3. Dy - ing Lamb, and Prince of glo - ry, O what full - ness dwells in Thee! Wondrous cross! how
4. Liv - ing Sav - iour! guide me ev - er; I have placed my hand in Thine; Lov - ing Shepherd!
in that fountain— Fountain of Thy pre - cious blood.
gate I en-tered— En - tered on the liv - ing way.
sweet the sto - ry— Sto - ry wondrous sweet to me!
let me nev - er— Nev - er leave the fold di - vine.
REFRAIN.
O the cross, the wondrous cross, The precious cross of Cal-va-ry! From the fountain of the cross There flows a cleansing flood for me.

When Jesus comes to Bethany.

W. H. D. —*went out of the city into Bethany.*—Matt. 21: 17. W. H. Doane.

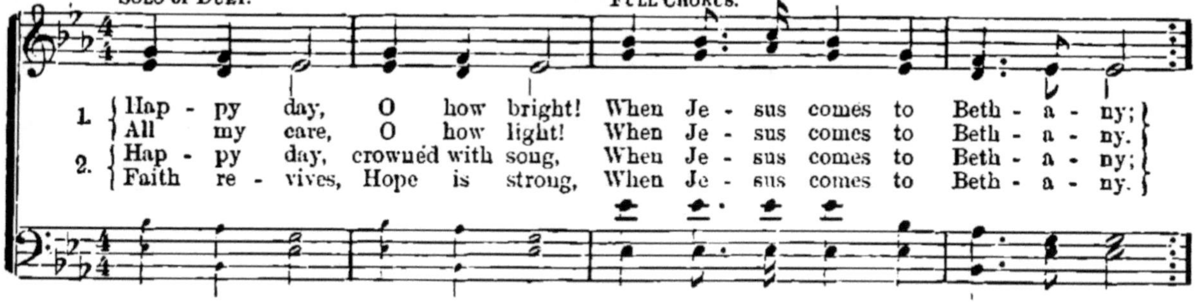
Solo or Duet.
Full Chorus.
1. Hap - py day, O how bright! When Je - sus comes to Beth - a - ny;
All my care, O how light! When Je - sus comes to Beth - a - ny.
2. Hap - py day, crownèd with song, When Je - sus comes to Beth - a - ny;
Faith re - vives, Hope is strong, When Je - sus comes to Beth - a - ny.

Refrain.
Touched by Him the tears of woe Melt a - way in smiles of glad - ness; O my soul, 'tis

heaven be - low When Je - sus comes to Beth - a - ny.

3 Happy day, O how blest!
When Jesus comes to Bethany;
Holy calm fills my breast
When Jesus comes to Bethany.

4 Happy day, ever dear,
When Jesus comes to Bethany;
Not a cloud, not a fear,
When Jesus comes to Bethany.

EVEN ME.

1 Lord, I hear of showers of blessing
Thou art scattering full and free—
Showers the thirsty land refreshing;
Let some droppings fall on me—
Even me.

2 Pass me not, O God, my Father!
Sinful though my heart may be;
Thou might'st leave me, but the rather
Let Thy mercy light on me—
Even me.

3 Pass me not, O gracious Saviour!
Let me live and cling to Thee;
For I'm longing for Thy favor;
While Thou'rt calling, O call me—
Even me.

4 Pass me not, O mighty Spirit!
Thou canst make the blind to see;
Witnesser of Jesus' merit,
Speak some word of power to me—
Even me.

Mrs. Elizabeth Codner.

PASS ME NOT.

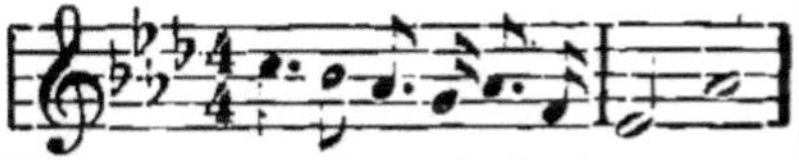

1 Pass me not, O gentle Saviour,
Hear my humble cry:
While on others Thou art smiling,
Do not pass me by.
CHO.—
Saviour, Saviour, hear my humble cry;
While on others Thou art calling,
Do not pass me by.

2 Trusting only in Thy merit,
Would I seek Thy face;
Heal my wounded, broken spirit,
Save me by Thy grace.

3 Thou the Spring of all my comfort,
More than life to me,
Whom have I on earth beside Thee?
Whom in heaven but Thee!

Fanny J Crosby.

HE LEADETH ME.

1 He leadeth me! O blessed thought!
O words with heavenly comfort fraught!
Whate'er I do, where'er I be,
Still 'tis God's hand that leadeth me.
REF.—He leadeth me, He leadeth me,
By His own hand He leadeth me;
His faithful follower I would be,
For by His hand He leadeth me.

2 Lord, I would clasp Thy hand in mine,
Nor ever murmur nor repine—
Content, whatever lot I see,
Since 'tis my God that leadeth me.

Rev. J. H. Gilmore.

LABAN.

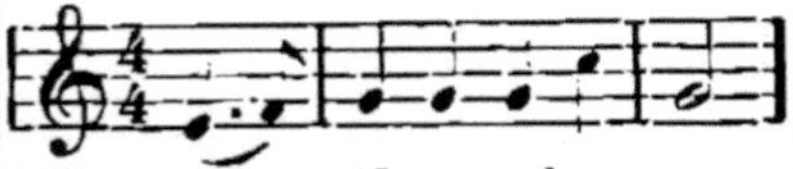

1 My soul, be on thy guard;
Ten thousand foes arise:
The hosts of sin are pressing hard
To draw thee from the skies.

2 O watch, and fight, and pray;
The battle ne'er give o'er;
Renew it boldly every day,
And help divine implore.

3 Ne'er think the victory won,
Nor lay thy armor down;
Thy arduous work will not be done
Till thou obtain thy crown.

4 Fight on, my soul, till death
Shall bring thee to thy God;
He'll take thee, at thy parting breath,
Up to His blest abode.

George Heath.

BETHANY.

1 Nearer, my God, to Thee,
Nearer to Thee!
E'en though it be a cross
That raiseth me,
Still all my song shall be,
Nearer, my God, to Thee,
Nearer to Thee!

2 Though, like the wanderer,
The sun gone down,
Darkness be over me,
My rest a stone,
Yet in my dreams I'd be
Nearer, my God, to Thee,
Nearer to Thee!

3 There let my way appear
Steps unto heaven;
All that Thou sendest me
In mercy given;
Angels to beckon me
Nearer, my God, to Thee,
Nearer to Thee!

Mrs. Sarah F. Adams.

14 Blessed Saviour, Hear and Help me.

Dr. C. R. Blackall. *Hear me, O Lord, hear me.*—1 Kings 18: 37. W. H. Doane.

1. Je - sus, teach me truth di - vine, Take my heart and seal it Thine; Feed me from Thy plenteous
2. Je - sus, keep me night and day, Hear and help me when I pray; Guard me from the power of
3. Je - sus, Thou my friend in - deed, Show me now what most I need; Bless and make me more like

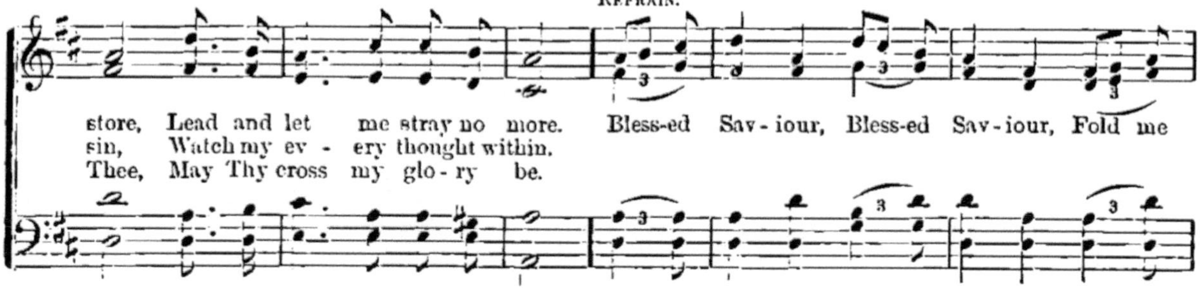
Refrain.
store, Lead and let me stray no more. Bless-ed Sav - iour, Bless-ed Sav - iour, Fold me
sin, Watch my ev - ery thought within.
Thee, May Thy cross my glo - ry be.

in Thy arms of love; Bless-ed Sav-iour, Bless-ed Sav-iour, Draw me near Thy throne a - bove.

O Come to the Saviour.

REV. F. W. FABER. *According to his mercy he saved us.*—TIT. 3: 5. R. LOWRY.

1. O come to the mer - ci - ful Sav - iour who calls you, O come to the Lord who for - gives and for - gets; Tho' dark be the for - tune on earth that be - falls you, A
2. O come then to Je - sus, whose arms are ex - tend - ed To fold His dear children in clos - est em - brace; O come, for your ex - ile will short - ly be end - ed, And
3. Then come to the Sav - iour, whose mer - cy grows bright-er The long-er you look at the depths of His love; And fear not, 'tis Je - sus, and life's cares grow light - er While

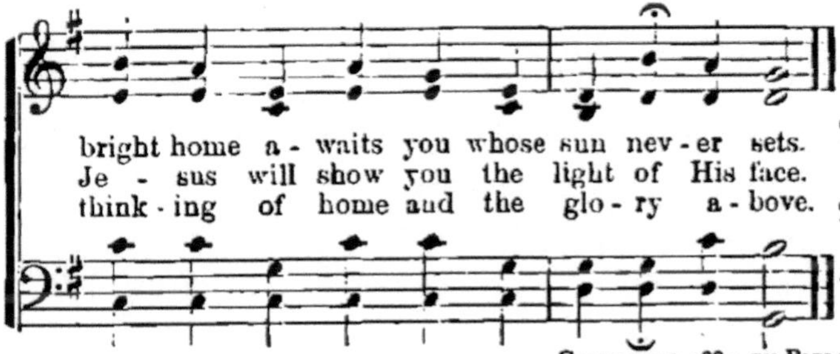
bright home a - waits you whose sun nev - er sets.
Je - sus will show you the light of His face.
think - ing of home and the glo - ry a - bove.

Hope in God.

1 While Thou, O my God, art my Help and Defender,
No cares can o'erwhelm me, no terrors appall;
The wiles and the snares of the world will but render
More lively my hope in my God and my All.

2 To Thee, dearest Lord, will I turn without ceasing,
Though grief may oppress me, or sorrow befall,
And love Thee till death, my glad spirit releasing,
Secures to me Jesus, my God and my All.

REV. WILLIAM YOUNG.

16 The Song of the Soul.

Rev. Henry A. von Dulsem. *And they sung a new song.*—Rev. 5: 9. T. C. O'Kane.

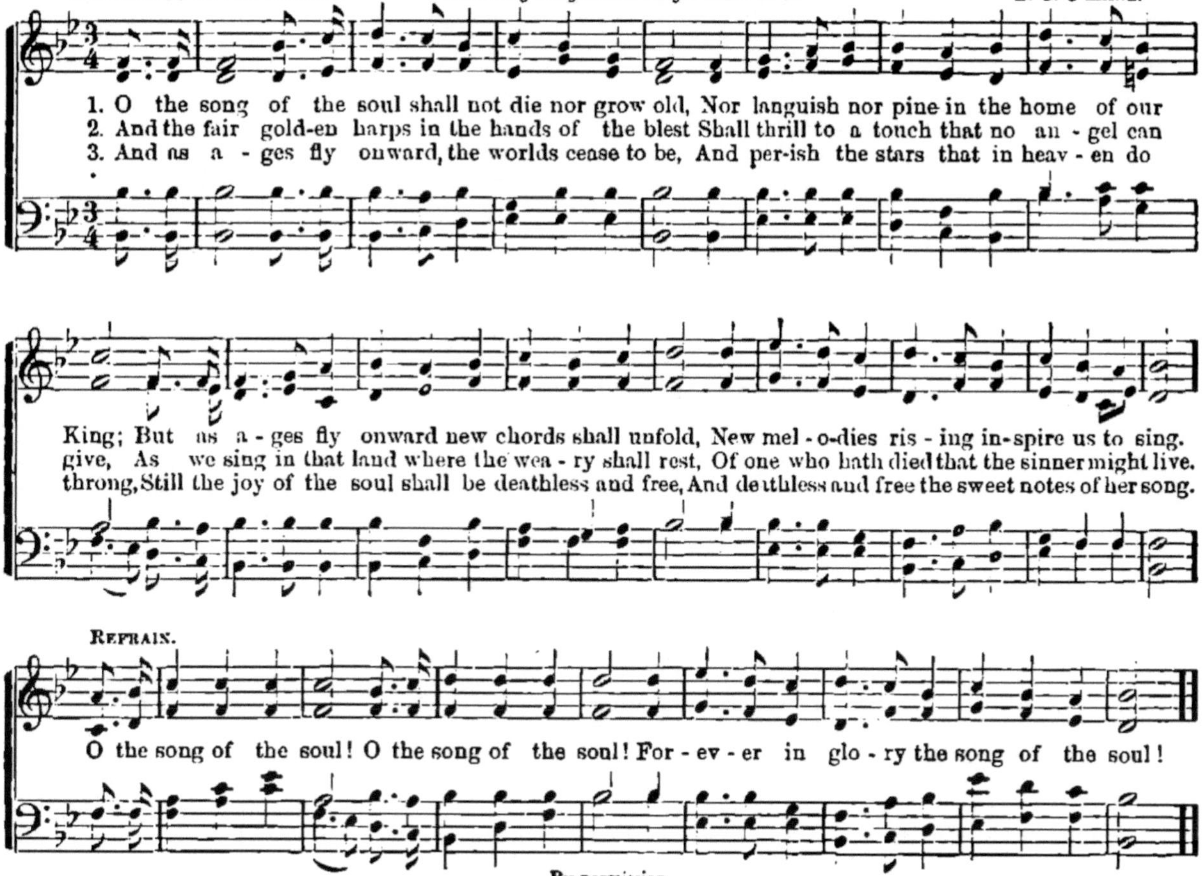
1. O the song of the soul shall not die nor grow old, Nor languish nor pine in the home of our King; But as a - ges fly onward new chords shall unfold, New mel - o-dies ris - ing in-spire us to sing.
2. And the fair gold-en harps in the hands of the blest Shall thrill to a touch that no an - gel can give, As we sing in that land where the wea - ry shall rest, Of one who hath died that the sinner might live.
3. And as a - ges fly onward, the worlds cease to be, And per-ish the stars that in heav - en do throng, Still the joy of the soul shall be deathless and free, And deathless and free the sweet notes of her song.
Refrain.
O the song of the soul! O the song of the soul! For - ev - er in glo - ry the song of the soul!

By permission.

Weary Wanderer, Stop and Listen.

GRACE J. FRANCES. *And they all with one consent began to make excuse.*—LUKE 14: 8. HUBERT P. MAIN.

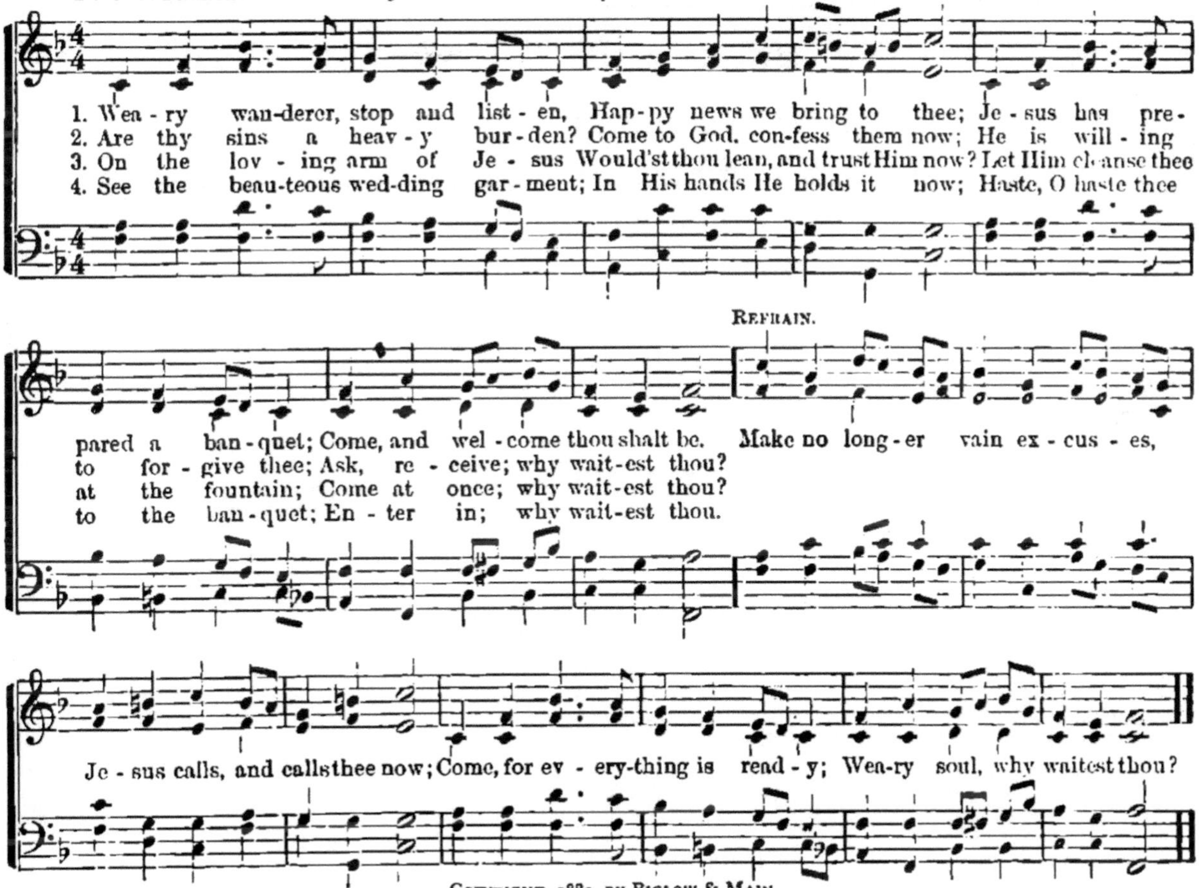
1. Wea - ry wan-derer, stop and list - en, Hap - py news we bring to thee; Je - sus has pre-
2. Are thy sins a heav - y bur - den? Come to God, con-fess them now; He is will - ing
3. On the lov - ing arm of Je - sus Would'st thou lean, and trust Him now? Let Him cleanse thee
4. See the beau-teous wed-ding gar - ment; In His hands He holds it now; Haste, O haste thee
REFRAIN.
pared a ban - quet; Come, and wel - come thou shalt be. Make no long - er vain ex - cus - es,
to for - give thee; Ask, re - ceive; why wait-est thou?
at the fountain; Come at once; why wait-est thou?
to the ban - quet; En - ter in; why wait-est thou.
Je - sus calls, and calls thee now; Come, for ev - ery-thing is read - y; Wea-ry soul, why waitest thou?

18 What is all the World to Me?

R. L. *Lo, I am with you alway.*—MATT. 28: 20. R. LOWRY.

1. What is all the world to me, With my Saviour near me? What is all the mirth I see, With my Lord to cheer me?
2. How can sense be - guile my soul, When my Sav - iour loves me? How can sin my heart con - trol, When my Lord ap - proves me?
3. Why should du - ty dark ap - pear, If my Sav - iour sends me? Why should dan-ger give me fear, If my Lord be - friends me?
4. All my way I trust to Him, Je - sus now re - ceives me; All my way till sight grows dim, Je - sus nev - er leaves me.
CHORUS.
"Lo! I am with you al - way, Lo! I am with you al - way;" O precious is that word! Promise sweet of Je - sus.

The Sinner's Friend.

Anon. W. H. Doane.

Greater love hath no man than this, that a man lay down his life for his friends.—John 15 : 13.

1. I've found a friend, O such a friend! He loved me ere I knew Him; He drew me with the
2. I've found a friend, O such a friend! He bled, He died to save me; And not a - lone the
3. I've found a friend, O such a friend! All power to Him is giv - en To guard me on my
4. I've found a friend, O such a friend! So kind and true and ten - der; So wise a coun - sel -
cords of love, And thus He bound me to Him; And round my heart still close - ly twine Those
gifts of life, But His own self, He gave me; Naught that I have my own I'll call, I'll
on - ward course, And bring me safe to heav - en; E - ter - nal glo - ries gleam a - far, To
lor and guide, So might - y a de - fend - er; From Him who loves me now so well, What
ties which naught can sever, For I am His and He is mine. For ev - er and for ev - er.
hold it for the giv - er; My heart, my strength, my life, my all, Are His, and His for ev - er.
nerve my faint en - deav - or: So now to watch, to work, to war— And then to rest for ev - er.
power my soul shall sev - er? Shall life or death, shall earth or hell? No; I am His for ev - er.

Come, Sinner, Come!

WILL. ELLSWORTH WITTER. *Come unto me all ye that labor and are heavy laden.*—MATT. 11 : 28. H. R. PALMER.

1. While Je - sus whispers to you, Come, sin - ner, come! While we are pray-ing for you,
2. Are you too heav - y lad - en? Come, sin - ner, come! Je - sus will bear your bur - den,

Come, sin - ner, come! Now is the time to own Him, Come, sin - ner, come!
Come, sin - ner, come! Je - - sus will not de - ceive you, Come, sin - ner, come!

Now is the time to know Him, Come, sin - ner, come!
Je - sus can now re - deem you, Come, sin - ner, come!

By permission.

3.

O hear His tender pleading,
Come, sinner, come!
Come and receive the blessing,
Come, sinner, come!
While Jesus whispers to you,
Come, sinner, come!
While we are praying for you,
Come, sinner, come!

Holy Trinity. 21

R. L. *Holy, holy, holy, Lord God Almighty.*—Rev. 4: 8. R. Lowry.

Ho - ly Trin - i - ty! Glo - ry be to God the Fa - ther! Ho - ly Trin - i - ty!
Glo - ry be to God the Son! Ho - ly Trin - i - ty! Glo - ry to the Ho - ly
Spir - it! God ev - er - last - ing, Three in One! A - men, A - men, A - - - men.

Jesus is Here.

W. S. *Jesus himself drew near.*—LUKE 24: 15. WM. STEVENSON.

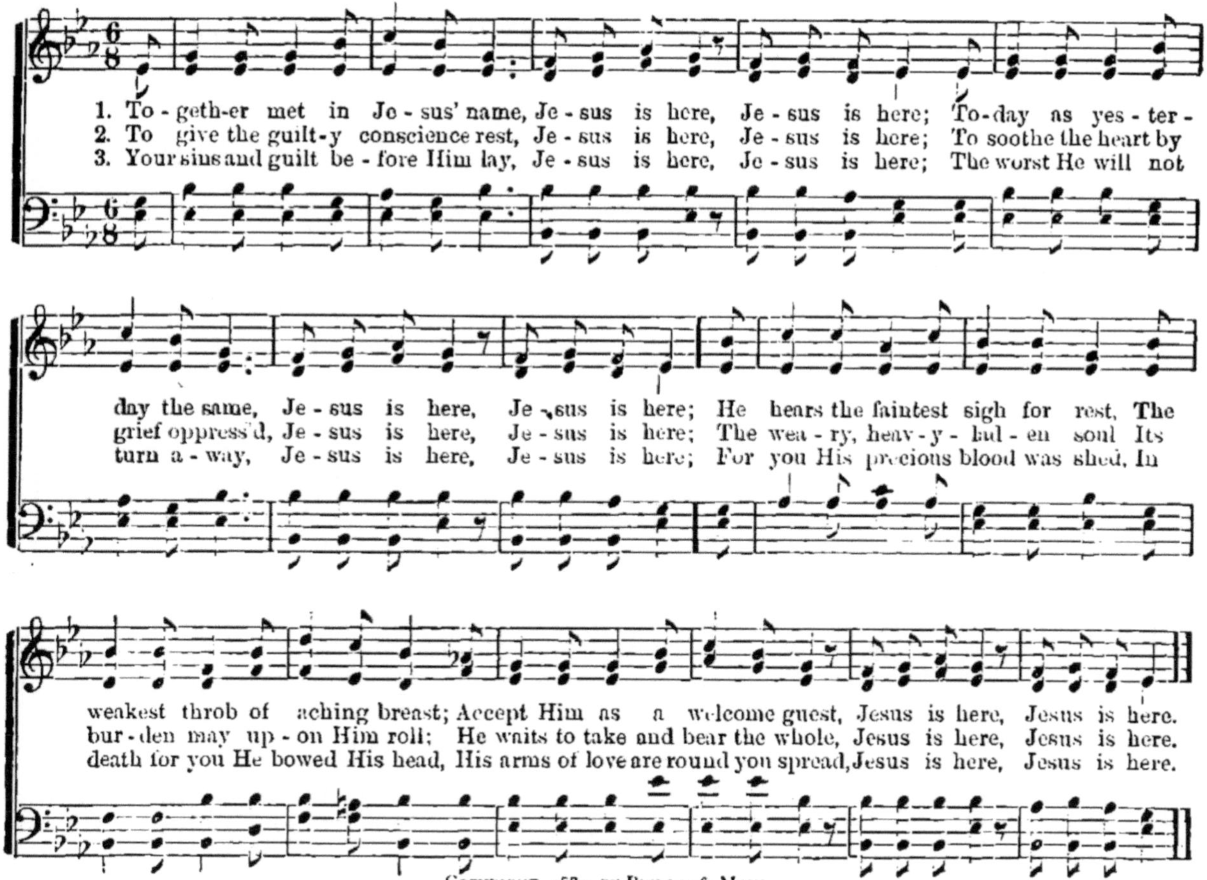
1. To-geth-er met in Je-sus' name, Je-sus is here, Je-sus is here; To-day as yes-ter-
2. To give the guilt-y conscience rest, Je-sus is here, Je-sus is here; To soothe the heart by
3. Your sins and guilt be-fore Him lay, Je-sus is here, Je-sus is here; The worst He will not
day the same, Je-sus is here, Je-sus is here; He hears the faintest sigh for rest, The
grief oppress'd, Je-sus is here, Je-sus is here; The wea-ry, heav-y-lad-en soul Its
turn a-way, Je-sus is here, Je-sus is here; For you His precious blood was shed, In
weakest throb of aching breast; Accept Him as a welcome guest, Jesus is here, Jesus is here.
bur-den may up-on Him roll; He waits to take and bear the whole, Jesus is here, Jesus is here.
death for you He bowed His head, His arms of love are round you spread, Jesus is here, Jesus is here.

Turn Away.

Mrs. Jessie Glenn. *Turn ye unto him.*—Isa. 31: 6. W. H. Doane.

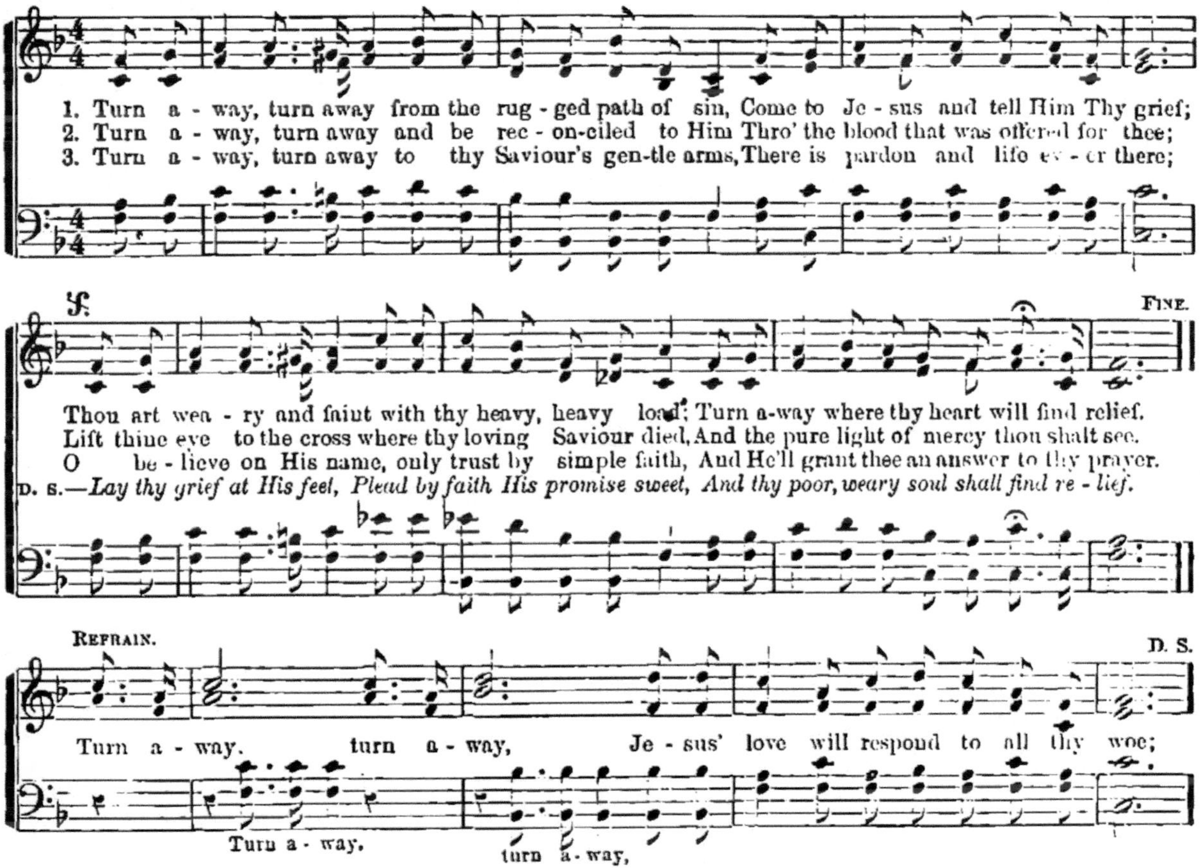
1. Turn a - way, turn away from the rug - ged path of sin, Come to Je - sus and tell Him Thy grief;
2. Turn a - way, turn away and be rec - on-ciled to Him Thro' the blood that was offered for thee;
3. Turn a - way, turn away to thy Saviour's gen-tle arms, There is pardon and life ev - er there;
Fine.
Thou art wea - ry and faint with thy heavy, heavy load; Turn a-way where thy heart will find relief.
Lift thine eye to the cross where thy loving Saviour died, And the pure light of mercy thou shalt see.
O be - lieve on His name, only trust by simple faith, And He'll grant thee an answer to thy prayer.
D. S.—*Lay thy grief at His feet, Plead by faith His promise sweet, And thy poor, weary soul shall find re - lief.*
Refrain.
D. S.
Turn a - way, turn a - way, Je - sus' love will respond to all thy woe;
Turn a - way, turn a - way,

24 Everything for Jesus.

Mrs. Annie S. Hawks. *Glorify God in your body and in your spirit.*—1 Cor. 6: 20. R. Lowry.

1. Do ev - ery - thing for Je - sus, Nor seek an hour's re - prieve, But give Him all thy
2. Bear ev - ery - thing for Je - sus, Oft suf - fer - ing or wrong; The pa - tient soul grows
3. Share ev - ery - thing with Je - sus, For thou art not thine own; The pain, the joy, the
serv - ice From morn till si - lent eve; How much to do for Je - sus, O
strong - er; The way will not be long; Bear ev - ery - thing for Je - sus, And
con - flict, Is not for thee a - lone; Share ev - ery - thing with Je - sus, Each
nev - er, nev - er ask; 'Tis ev - ery-thing for Je - sus—This light - ens ev - ery task.
count the loss but gain, Since by His grace He frees us, And shat - ters ev - ery chain.
want, each woe, each care; In ev - ery-thing He sees us, And hears our ev - ery prayer.

Still of Jesus.

FANNY J. CROSBY. *A name which is above every name.*—PHIL. 2: 9. HENRY TUCKER.

1. Still of Je - sus, on - ly Je - sus, I am thinking all day long, And the liv - ing, cleansing Riv - er, Thro' my spir-it flowing ev - er, Is the bur-den of my song.
2. Still of Je - sus, on - ly Je - sus, And the rap - ture of my soul, When He said, My life I gave thee, Dost believe that I can save thee, Then thy faith has made thee whole.
3. Still of Je - sus, on - ly Je - sus, He a - lone my song shall be; O my love is deep-er, pur - er, Faith is brighter, hope is sur - er, And the name more sweet to me.
4. Still of Je - sus, on - ly Je - sus, With my lat - est breath I'll sing; Then in realms of end-less glo - ry, While I sing redemption's sto-ry, Nobler strains shall praise my King.
CHORUS
O'er and o'er, o'er and o'er, Still my song is Je - sus, O'er and o'er, o'er and o'er, Still my song is Je - sus.
O'er and o'er, o'er and o'er
O'er and o'er, o'er and o'er,

26 Oft I hear my Saviour say.

MRS. FANNY J. VAN ALSTYNE. *Lean upon the Lord.*—MICAH 3: 11. W. H. DOANE.

Tenderly.
1. Oft I hear my Sav - iour say, Lean on Me, Lean on Me; I will smooth thy rug - ged
2. Thou art weak, I know it all; Lean on Me, Lean on Me; Trust, and thou shalt nev - er
3. Art thou wea - ry? would'st thou rest? Lean on Me, Lean on Me; Anguish once my soul op -
way; Lean, my child, on Me; Mine's a love that can - not die, More than
fall; Lean, my child, on Me; Thou dost need my con - stant care, I will
pressed; Lean, my child, on Me; For thy life my own I gave, I have
earth - ly friend am I, I have heard thy ev - ery sigh; Lean, my child, on Me.
hear and an - swer prayer, Teach thee how the cross to bear; Lean, my child, on Me.
tri - umphed o'er the grave; I, the Lord, am strong to save; Lean, my child, on Me.

Follow Me.

Mrs. Kate S. Burr. *If any man will serve me, let him follow me.*—John 12 : 26. R. Lowry.

1. "Follow me;" in life's fair morning Hear that kind in-vit-ing voice; Follow where the Saviour lead-eth, Early make His paths thy choice.
2. "Follow me;" yes, walk with Je-sus, Thro' this vale of grief and tears, To His ten-der love con-fid-ing All the cares that cloud thy years.
3. "Follow me;" thro' death's low portal His own hand shall lead thy way Up to realms of light and beau-ty, Shin-ing with e-ter-nal day.
Refrain.
"Follow me;" 'tis Je-sus call-eth; "Follow me," no more to roam; "Follow me;" His hand shall safely Lead thee to thy heavenly home.

The Praise of Jesus' Name.

FANNY J. CROSBY. *Show forth the praises of him who hath called you.*—1 PET. 2: 9. CHESTER G. ALLEN, M. D.

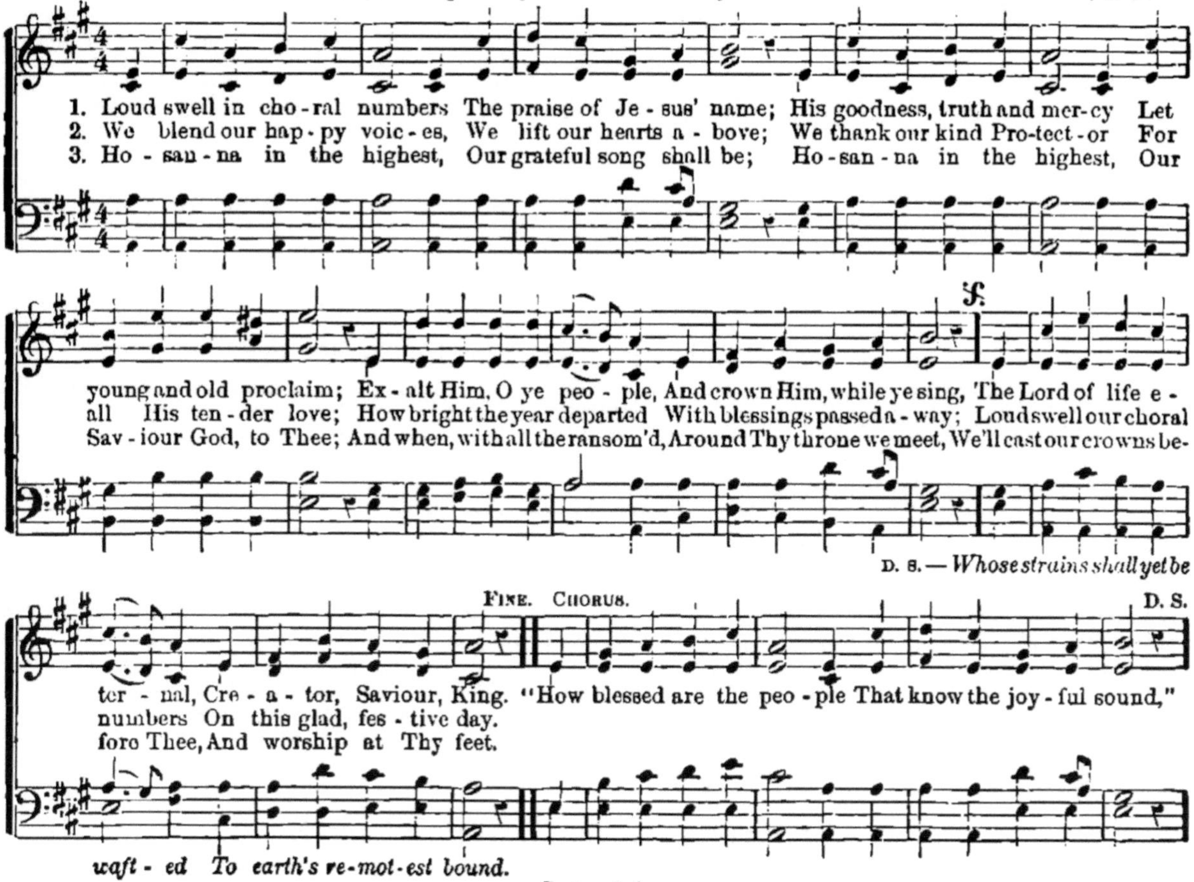
1. Loud swell in cho-ral numbers The praise of Je-sus' name; His goodness, truth and mer-cy Let young and old proclaim; Ex-alt Him, O ye peo-ple, And crown Him, while ye sing, The Lord of life e-ter-nal, Cre-a-tor, Saviour, King.
2. We blend our hap-py voic-es, We lift our hearts a-bove; We thank our kind Pro-tect-or For all His ten-der love; How bright the year departed With blessings passed a-way; Loud swell our choral numbers On this glad, fes-tive day.
3. Ho-san-na in the highest, Our grateful song shall be; Ho-san-na in the highest, Our Sav-iour God, to Thee; And when, with all the ransom'd, Around Thy throne we meet, We'll cast our crowns be-fore Thee, And worship at Thy feet.
FINE. CHORUS.
"How blessed are the peo-ple That know the joy-ful sound,"
D. S.
D. S.—Whose strains shall yet be waft-ed To earth's re-mot-est bound.

By permission.

ARRANGED.

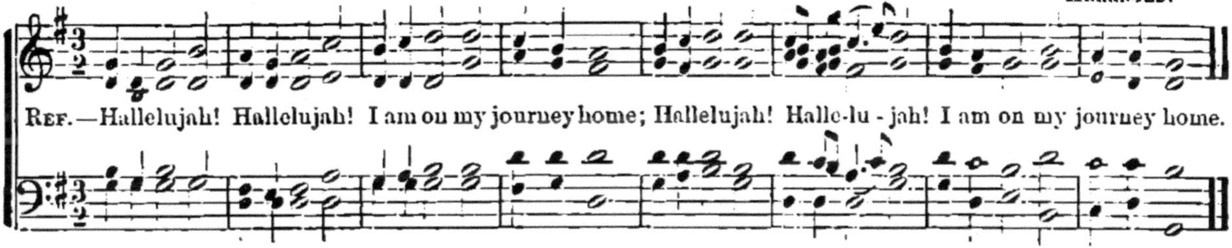
REF.—Hallelujah! Hallelujah! I am on my journey home; Hallelujah! Halle-lu - jah! I am on my journey home.

Hasting Onward.

1 This is not my place of resting,—
Mine's a city yet to come;
Onward to it I am hasting—
On to my eternal home.

2 In it all is light and glory,
O'er it shines a nightless day;
Every trace of sin's sad story,
All the curse, has passed away.

3 There the blessed Shepherd leads us
By the streams of life along,—
On the freshest pastures feeds us,
Turns our sighing into song.

4 Soon we pass the desert dreary,
Soon we bid farewell to pain;
Never more are sad or weary,
Never, never sin again.

Horatius Bonar, D. D.

Hark! the Sound.

1 Hark! the sound of holy voices
Chanting at the crystal sea,
Hallelujah, hallelujah,
Hallelujah, Lord, to Thee!

2 Multitude, which none can number,
Like the stars in glory stand,
Clothed in white apparel, holding
Palms of victory in their hand.

3 They have come from tribulation,
And have washed their robes in blood,—
Washed them in the blood of Jesus;
Tried they were, and firm they stood.

4 Love and peace they taste forever,
And all truth and knowledge see
In the Beatific Vision
Of the Blessed Trinity.

Bp. Christopher Wordsworth.

Time, Thou Speedest.

1 Time, thou speedest on but slowly,
Hours, how tardy is your pace!
Ere with Him, the High and Holy,
I hold converse face to face.

2 Here is naught but care and mourning;
Comes a joy, it will not stay;
Fairly shines the sun at dawning,
Night will soon o'ercloud the day.

3 Onward then! not long I wander
Ere my Saviour comes for me,
And with Him abiding yonder,
All His glory I shall see.

4 O the music and the singing
Of the host redeemed by love!
O the hallelujahs ringing
Thro' the halls of light above!

Catherine Winkworth. Tr. from
Rev. Johann Georg Albinus.

Hallelujah!

1 Hallelujah! song of gladness,
Song of everlasting joy;
Hallelujah! song the sweetest
That can angel-hosts employ.

2 Hallelujah! church victorious,
Thou may'st lift this joyful strain;
Hallelujah! songs of triumph
Well befit the ransomed train.

3 Hallelujah! let our voices
Rise to heaven with full accord;
Hallelujah! every moment
Brings us nearer to the Lord.

4 But our earnest supplication,
Holy God, we raise to Thee;
Bring us to Thy blissful Presence,
Let us all Thy glory see.

Anon.

30 'Tis the Blessed Hour of Prayer.

FANNY J. CROSBY. —*went into the temple at the hour of prayer*..—ACTS. 3: 1. W. H. DOANE.

1. 'Tis the bless - ed hour of prayer, when our hearts low - ly bend, And we gath - er to
2. 'Tis the bless - ed hour of prayer, when the Sav - iour draws near, With a ten - der com -
3. 'Tis the bless - ed hour of prayer, when the tempt-ed and tried To the Sav - iour who
4. At the bless - ed hour of prayer, if we firm - ly be - lieve That the bless-ing we
Je - sus, our Sav - iour and Friend; If we come to Him in faith, His pro-tec-tion to share,
passion His chil - dren to hear; When He tells us we may cast at His feet ev - ery care,
loves them their sor-row con-fide; With a sym-pa-thiz-ing heart He re-moves ev - ery care;
ask for we'll sure - ly re - ceive, In the full-ness of de - light we shall lose ev - ery care;
FINE.
CHORUS.
D. S.
What a balm for the wea - ry! O how sweet to be there! Blessed hour of pray'r, Blessed hour of pray'r;
D. S.—*What a balm for the wea - ry! O how sweet to be there!*

The Name of Jesus.

REV. W. O. CUSHING. *Far above * * * * every name that is named.*—EPH 1: 21. HUBERT P. MAIN.

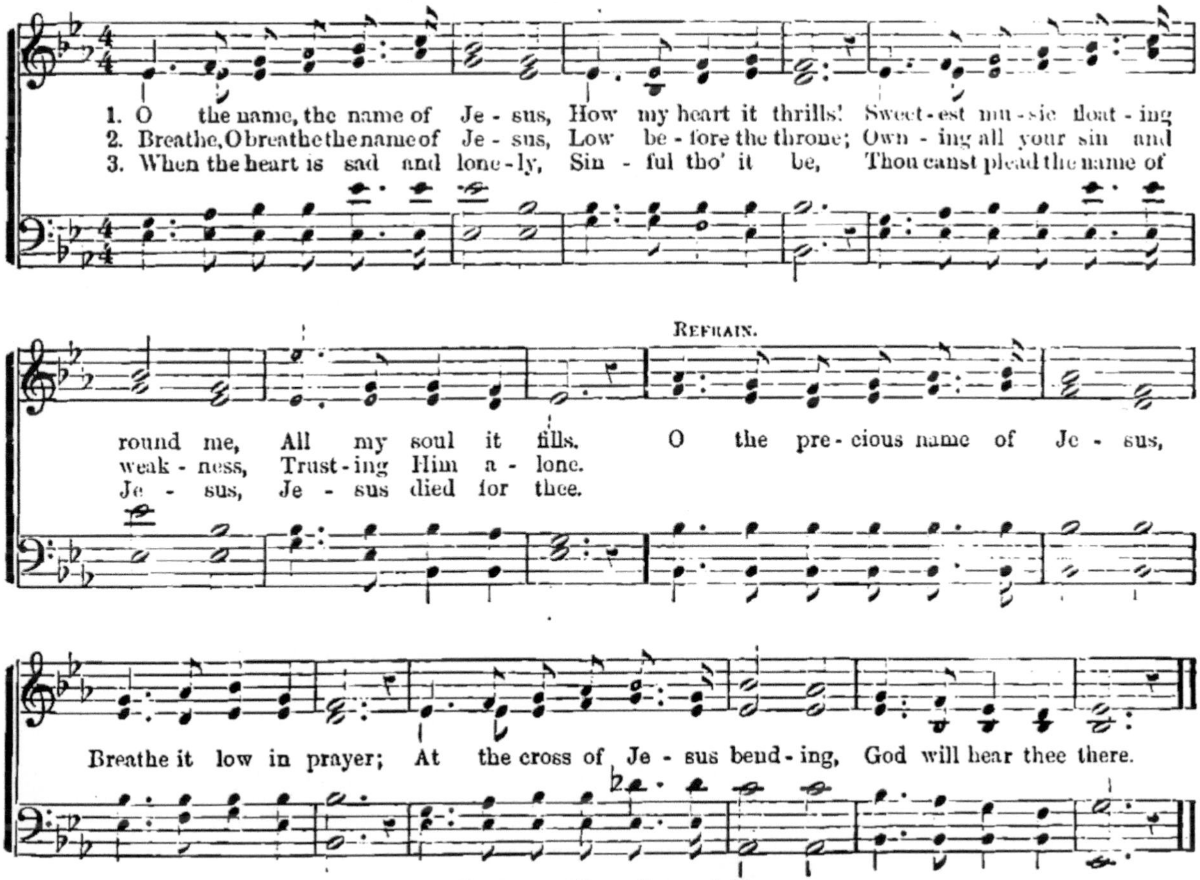
1. O the name, the name of Je - sus, How my heart it thrills! Sweet - est mu - sic float - ing round me, All my soul it fills.
2. Breathe, O breathe the name of Je - sus, Low be - fore the throne; Own - ing all your sin and weak - ness, Trust - ing Him a - lone.
3. When the heart is sad and lone - ly, Sin - ful tho' it be, Thou canst plead the name of Je - sus, Je - sus died for thee.
REFRAIN.
O the precious name of Je - sus, Breathe it low in prayer; At the cross of Je - sus bend - ing, God will hear thee there.

O to be Something.

C. B. Stout. *Whether we live, we live unto the Lord.*—Rom. 14: 8. R. Lowry.

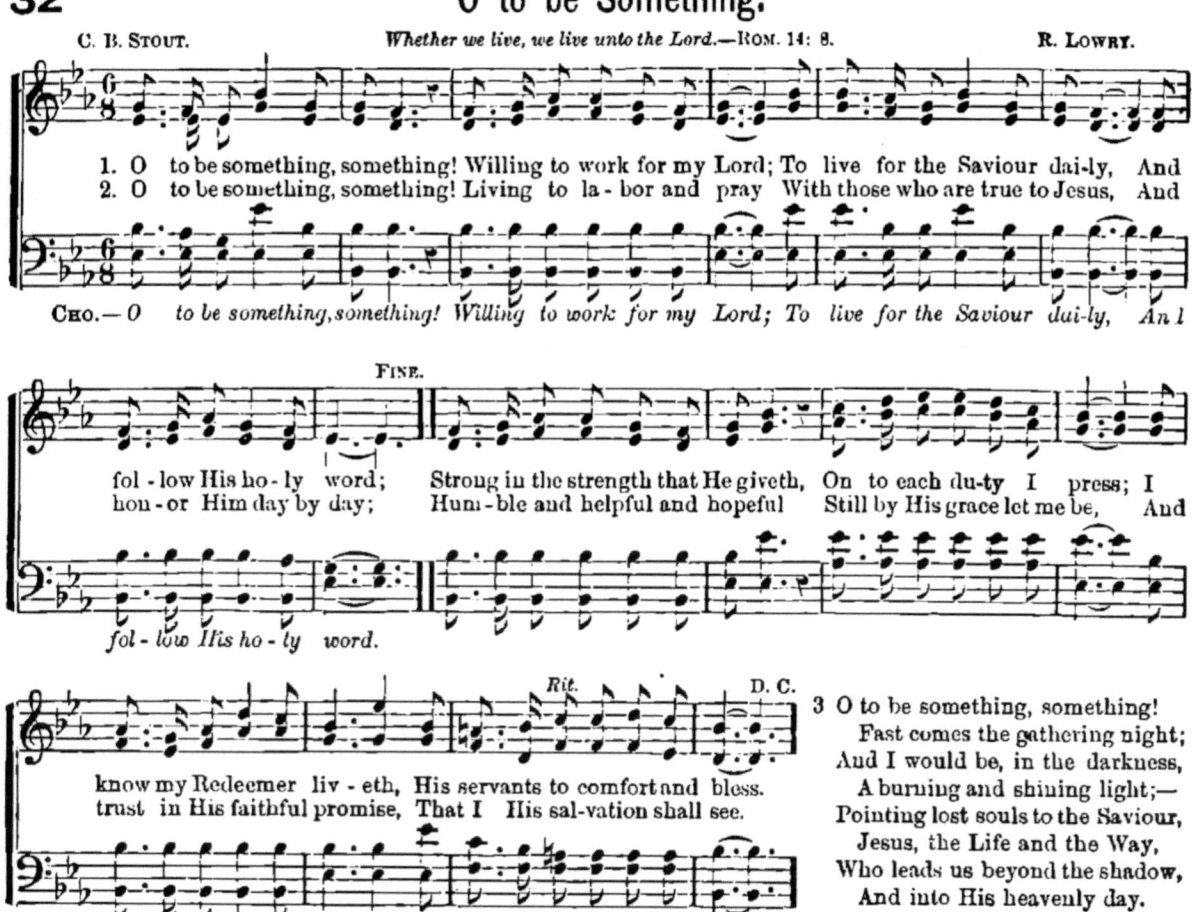

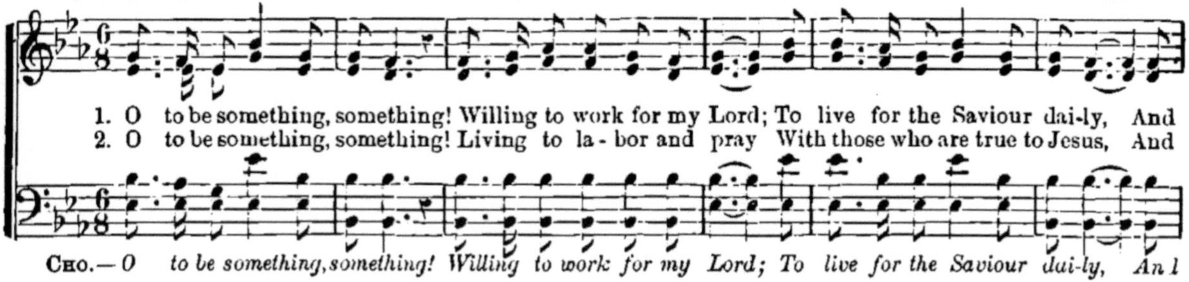
1. O to be something, something! Willing to work for my Lord; To live for the Saviour dai-ly, And
2. O to be something, something! Living to la - bor and pray With those who are true to Jesus, And
Cho.—O to be something, something! Willing to work for my Lord; To live for the Saviour dai-ly, And

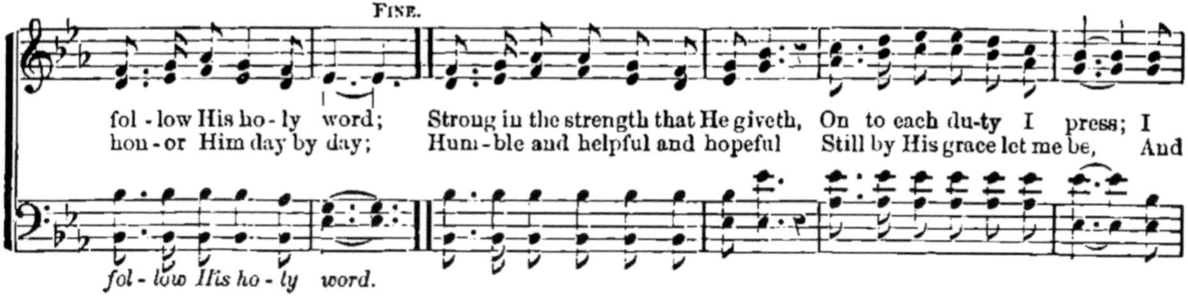
Fine.
fol - low His ho - ly word; Strong in the strength that He giveth, On to each du-ty I press; I
hon - or Him day by day; Hum - ble and helpful and hopeful Still by His grace let me be, And
fol - low His ho - ly word.

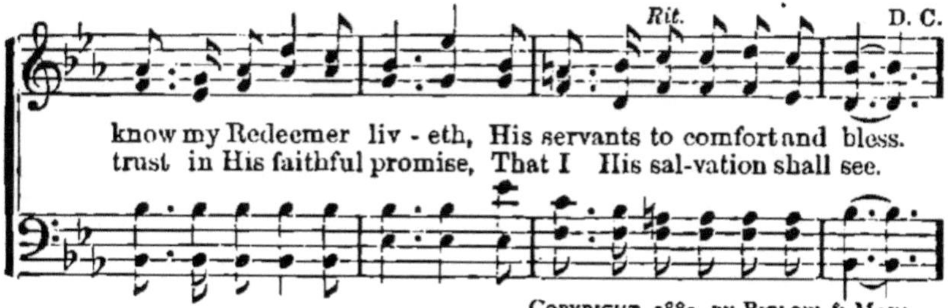
Rit.
D. C.
know my Redeemer liv - eth, His servants to comfort and bless.
trust in His faithful promise, That I His sal-vation shall see.

3 O to be something, something!
Fast comes the gathering night;
And I would be, in the darkness,
A burning and shining light;—
Pointing lost souls to the Saviour,
Jesus, the Life and the Way,
Who leads us beyond the shadow,
And into His heavenly day.

Does the Anchor Hold?

C. L. CLIFFORD. *Which hope we have as an anchor of the soul, both sure and steadfast.*—HEB. 6: 19. W. H. DOANE.

1. Does the anch-or hold, my broth-er? Is it firm be-neath thy feet? Canst thou trust thy soul to its keep-ing now, Tho' the bil-lows round thee beat?
2. Does the anch-or hold, my broth-er? Is it fast to Christ the Rock? When the thunders roll, and the lightnings flash, Will it stand the last great shock?
3. Does the anch-or hold, my broth-er? What a welcome thine will be! Thou hast fought the fight, thou hast kept the faith, There's a crown laid up for thee.
REFRAIN.
O the sky is brighter, brighter grow-ing, And my heart with joy o'er-flow-ing; Yes, the anchor holds, and I am trusting, It will hold for ev-er-more.

34 Behold, what a Wonder!

ALEXANDER CLARK, D. D. *The Lord your God, that hath dealt wondrously with you.*—JOEL 2: 26. HUBERT P. MAIN.

1. Be - hold, what a won - der! A deathless soul un - der The bond-age of sin to re - main,
2. By great mer - cy on - ly, To lost ones and lone-ly, Low down in their pris-on and pain,
3. The crim - son stain whit-ens, The scar-let stain lightens, Like spots un - der snow or the rain,
4. What full-ness of bless-ing! Be - liev-ing, con - fessing,—Lo, whit - er than wool ev - ery stain!
By faith rise and sev - er The fet-ters for - ev - er, Thro' the blood of the Lamb that was slain.
The light of life ris - es Till glo - ry sur - pris - es, Thro' the blood of the Lamb that was slain.
When hearts for transgression Make humble con - fes - sion, Thro' the blood of the Lamb that was slain.
'Tis more than sal - va - tion, 'Tis God's new cre - a - tion, Thro' the blood of the Lamb that was slain.
REFRAIN.
The blood of the Lamb, O Spir-it, ap - ply, It cleanses and bless - es a - gain and a - gain;

Behold, what a Wonder!—Concluded.

The peace of the cov - e - nant now rat - i - fy, Thro' the blood of the Lamb that was slain.

Rise, Sun of Righteousness.

Mrs. K. S. Burr. *Shall the sun of righteousness arise with healing in his wings.*—Mal. 4: 2. R. Lowry.

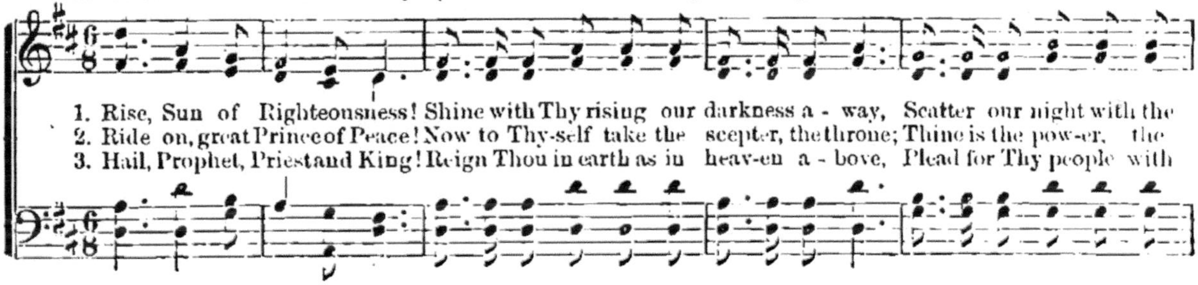
1. Rise, Sun of Righteousness! Shine with Thy rising our darkness a - way, Scatter our night with the
2. Ride on, great Prince of Peace! Now to Thy-self take the scepter, the throne; Thine is the pow-er, the
3. Hail, Prophet, Priest and King! Reign Thou in earth as in heav-en a - bove, Plead for Thy people with

dawn-ing of day; Thine is the kingdom, come quickly, we pray: Rise, shine, Thy peo - ple bless!
glo - ry Thine own; Thou hast redeemed us, Thy blood doth a-tone: Haste, haste earth's glad re - lease!
pleadings of love, Teach Thou the nations, the wayward re - prove, And full re-demp-tion bring.

Purify Me.

Mrs. Kate Smiley. *Purify your hearts.*—James 4: 8. W. H. Doane.

1. Pu - ri - fy me, pu - ri - fy me, Now by grace di - vine; Help me to say, lov-ing-ly say,
2. Pu - ri - fy me, cleanse me anew, Cleanse from every stain; Searcher of hearts, try me as gold,

Refrain.
Lord, Thy will is mine. Now, blessed Re - deem - er, At Thy throne I bend;
Till no dross re - main.

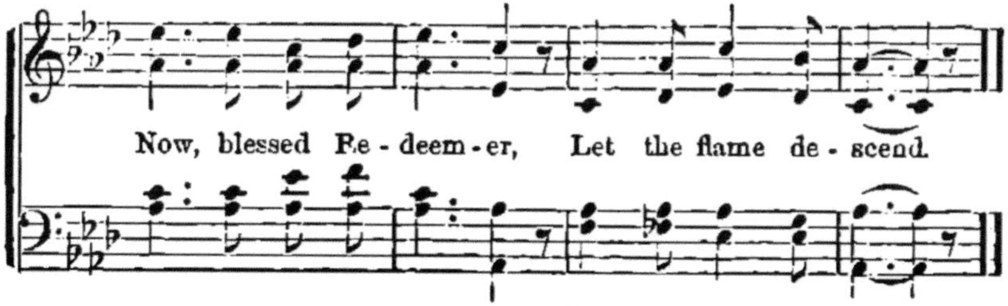
Now, blessed Re - deem - er, Let the flame de - scend.

3 Purify me, Lord, as Thou wilt,
Bind my soul to Thee;
Trusting I'll pass under Thy rod,
If 'tis best for me.

4 Purify me, so shall I rise
Earthly care above;
Purify me, then shall my soul
Taste Thy perfect love.

Jesus is My Saviour.

R. L. —*went on his way rejoicing.*—Acts. 8: 39. R. Lowry.

1. My soul is hap-py all day long— Je-sus is my Sav-iour; And all my life is full of song— Je-sus died for me.
2. My heav-y load of sin is gone— Je-sus is my Sav-iour; At His dear cross I laid it down— Je-sus died for me.
3. I heard the voice of mer-cy call— Je-sus is my Sav-iour; I sim-ply trusted, that was all— Je-sus died for me.
4. Now will I tell it all a-round— Je-sus is my Sav-iour; How sweet a blessing I have found— Je-sus died for me.
Chorus.
Hal-le-lu-jah! Hal-le-lu-jah! To the lov-ing Lamb for sin-ners slain; Hal-le-lu-jah! Hal-le-lu-jah! To the Lamb who lives a-gain.

38 At the Palace Gate.

Ella Dale. *They shall enter into the king's palace.*—Psa. 45: 15. W. H. Doane.

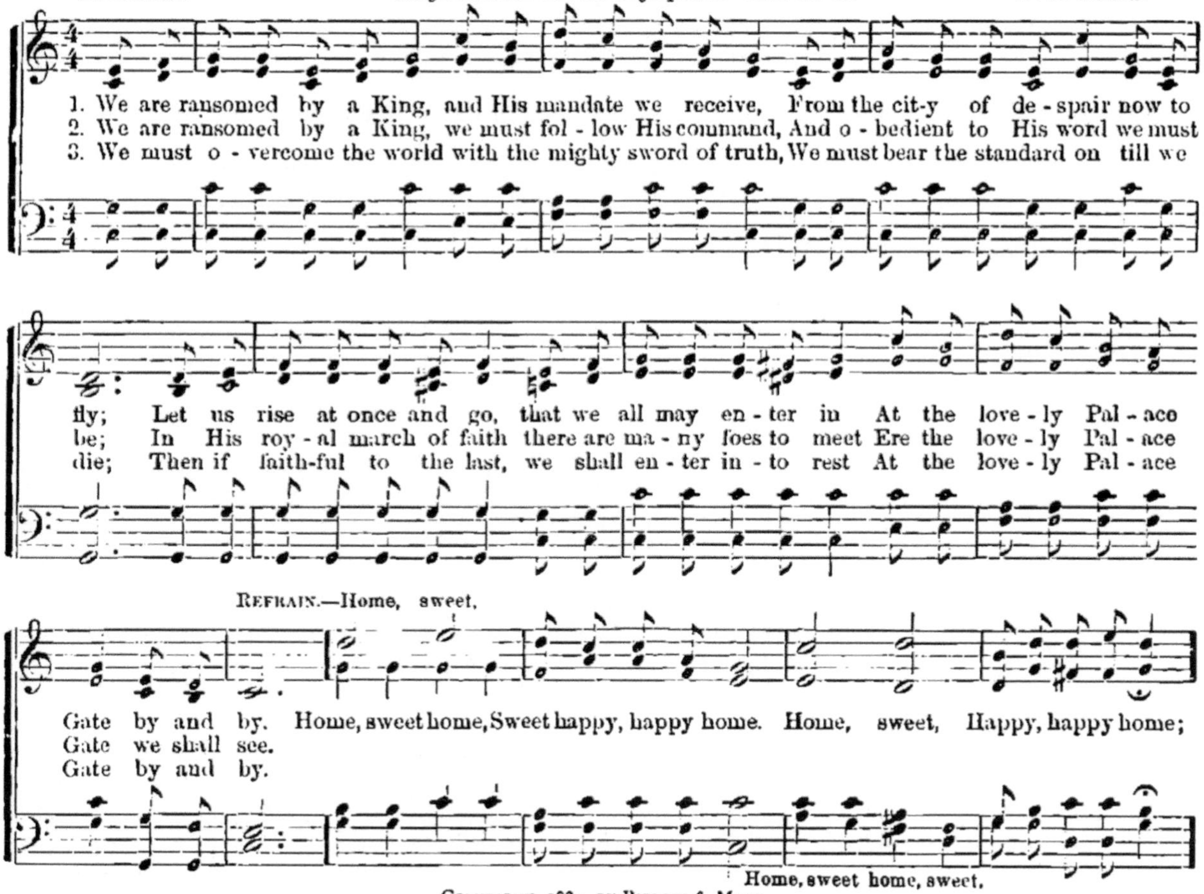
1. We are ransomed by a King, and His mandate we receive, From the cit-y of de - spair now to
2. We are ransomed by a King, we must fol - low His command, And o - bedient to His word we must
3. We must o - vercome the world with the mighty sword of truth, We must bear the standard on till we
fly; Let us rise at once and go, that we all may en - ter in At the love - ly Pal - ace
be; In His roy - al march of faith there are ma - ny foes to meet Ere the love - ly Pal - ace
die; Then if faith-ful to the last, we shall en - ter in - to rest At the love - ly Pal - ace
Refrain.—Home, sweet,
Gate by and by. Home, sweet home, Sweet happy, happy home. Home, sweet, Happy, happy home;
Gate we shall see.
Gate by and by.
Home, sweet home, sweet.

What a shout of joy will ring, When we hail our Saviour King, At the love - ly Pal - ace Gate by and by.

Rise, glorious Conqueror, Rise.

MATTHEW BRIDGES. *Lift up ye heads, O ye gates, * * * * and the king of glory shall come in.*—Ps. 24 : 7. R. LOWRY.

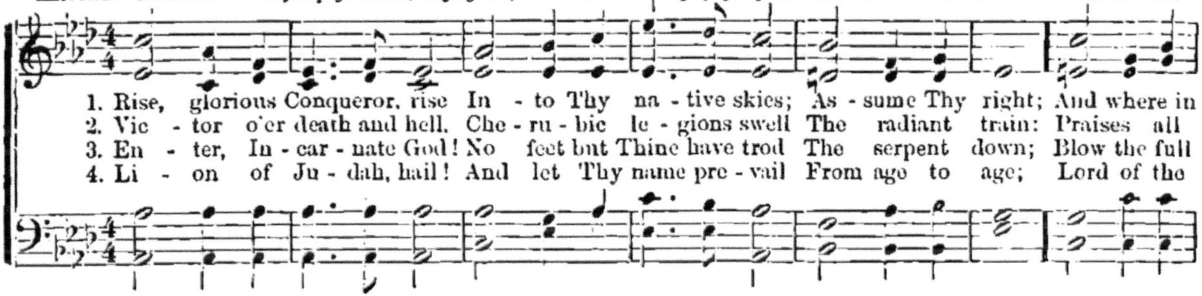
1. Rise, glorious Conqueror, rise In - to Thy na - tive skies; As - sume Thy right; And where in
2. Vic - tor o'er death and hell, Che - ru - bic le - gions swell The radiant train: Praises all
3. En - ter, In - car - nate God! No feet but Thine have trod The serpent down; Blow the full
4. Li - on of Ju - dah, hail! And let Thy name pre - vail From age to age; Lord of the

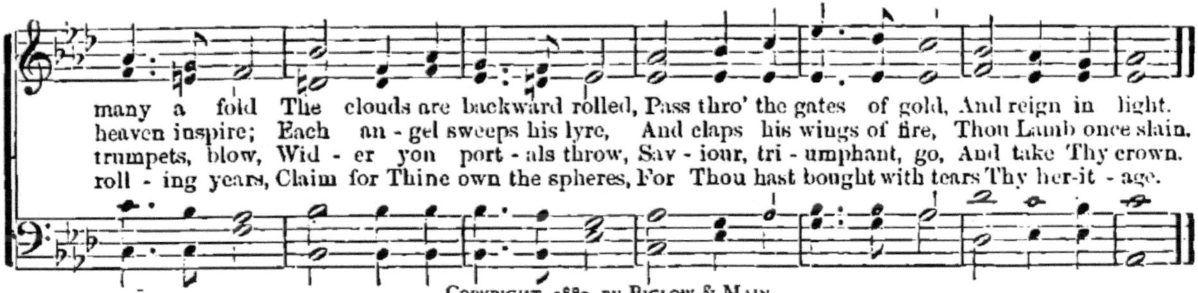
many a fold The clouds are backward rolled, Pass thro' the gates of gold, And reign in light.
heaven inspire; Each an - gel sweeps his lyre, And claps his wings of fire, Thou Lamb once slain.
trumpets, blow, Wid - er yon port - als throw, Sav - iour, tri - umphant, go, And take Thy crown.
roll - ing years, Claim for Thine own the spheres, For Thou hast bought with tears Thy her-it - age.

How Long, O Lord?

JAMES GEORGE DECK. *The bridegroom cometh.*—MATT. 25: 6. R. LOWRY.

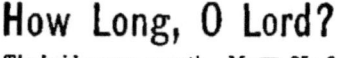

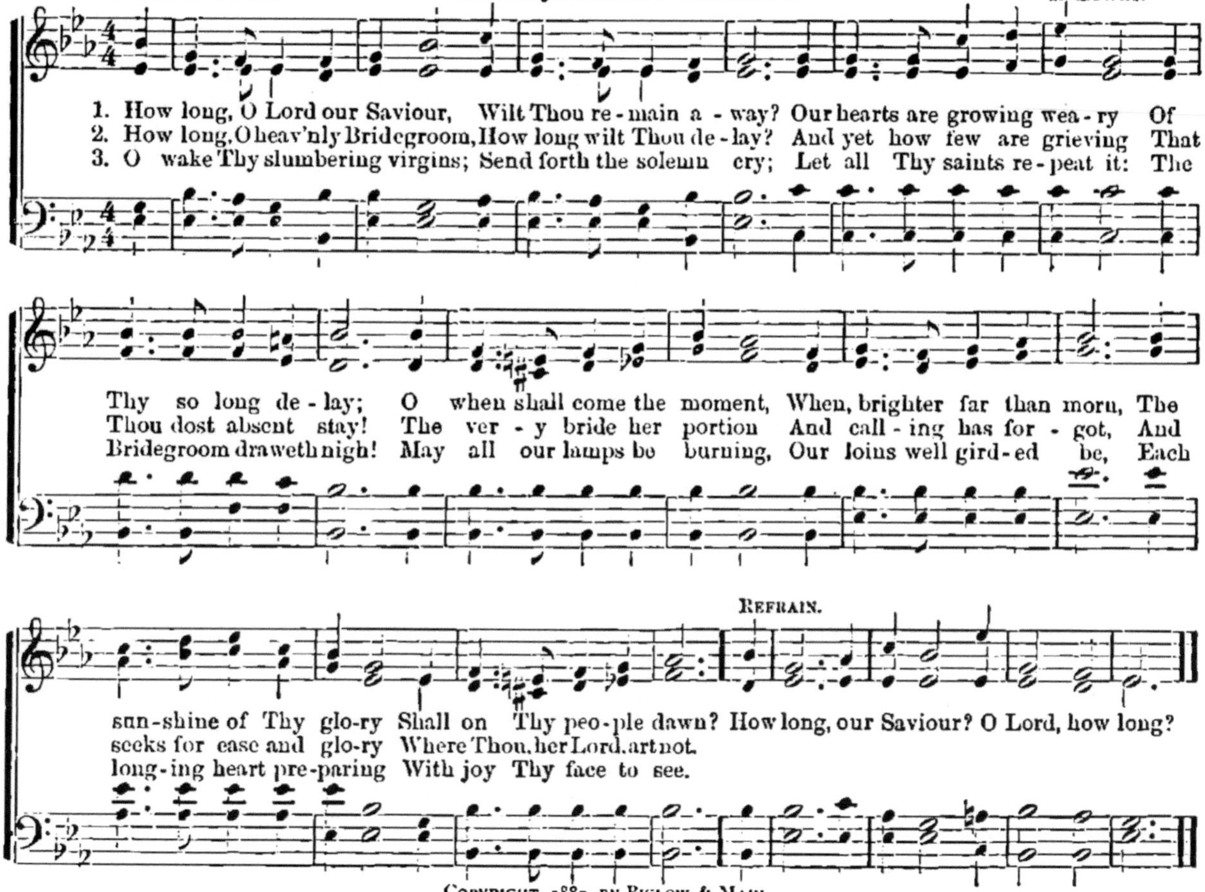
1. How long, O Lord our Saviour, Wilt Thou re-main a-way? Our hearts are growing wea-ry Of
2. How long, O heav'nly Bridegroom, How long wilt Thou de-lay? And yet how few are grieving That
3. O wake Thy slumbering virgins; Send forth the solemn cry; Let all Thy saints re-peat it: The
Thy so long de-lay; O when shall come the moment, When, brighter far than morn, The
Thou dost absent stay! The ver-y bride her portion And call-ing has for-got, And
Bridegroom draweth nigh! May all our lamps be burning, Our loins well gird-ed be, Each
REFRAIN.
sun-shine of Thy glo-ry Shall on Thy peo-ple dawn? How long, our Saviour? O Lord, how long?
seeks for ease and glo-ry Where Thou, her Lord, art not.
long-ing heart pre-paring With joy Thy face to see.

WEBB. 7, 6.

Rejoice, Believers.

1 Rejoice, rejoice, believers,
And let your lights appear;
The evening is advancing,
And darker night is near;
The Bridegroom is arising,
And soon He will draw nigh;
Up, pray, and watch, and wrestle,
At midnight comes the cry.

2 The saints, who here in patience
Their cross and sufferings bore,
With Him shall reign forever,
When sorrow is no more;
Around the throne of glory
The Lamb shall they behold,
Adoring cast before Him
Their diadems of gold.

3 Our Hope and Expectation,
O Jesus, now appear!
Arise, Thou Sun so looked-for,
O'er this benighted sphere!
With hearts and hands uplifted,
We plead, O Lord, to see
The day of our redemption,
And ever be with Thee.

Jane Borthwick. Tr.

Morning Light.

1 The morning light is breaking;
The darkness disappears;
The sons of earth are waking
To penitential tears;
Each breeze that sweeps the ocean
Brings tidings from afar,
Of nations in commotion,
Prepared for Zion's war.

2 See heathen nations bending
Before the God we love,
And thousand hearts ascending
In gratitude above;
While sinners, now confessing,
The gospel call obey,
And seek the Saviour's blessing,
A nation in a day.

3 Blest river of salvation,
Pursue thine onward way;
Flow thou to every nation,
Nor in thy richness stay;
Stay not till all the lowly
Triumphant reach their home;
Stay not till all the holy
Proclaim, "The Lord is come!"

Samuel F. Smith, D. D.

Brief Life.

1 Brief life is here our portion,
Brief sorrow, short-lived care;
The life that knows no ending,
The tearless life, is there;
O happy retribution!
Short toil, eternal rest;
For mortals and for sinners
A mansion with the blest!

2 And there is David's fountain,
And life in fullest glow;
And there the light is golden,
And milk and honey flow;
The light that hath no evening,
The health that hath no sore,
The life that hath no ending,
But lasteth evermore.

3 The morning shall awaken,
The shadows shall decay,
And each true-hearted servant
Shall shine as doth the day;
There God our King and Portion,
In fulness of His grace,
Shall we behold for ever,
And worship face to face.

J. M. Neale, D. D. Tr.

Awake, O Zion.

1 Awake, awake, O Zion,
Put on thy strength divine;
Thy garments bright in beauty,
The bridal dress be thine;
Jerusalem the holy,
To purity restored,
Meek Bride, all fair and lowly,
Go forth to meet thy Lord.

2 The Lamb who bore our sorrows
Comes down to earth again—
No Sufferer now, but Victor,
For evermore to reign;
To reign in every nation,
To rule in every zone;
O wide-world coronation,
In every heart a throne!

3 Awake, awake, O Zion,
The bridal day draws nigh,
The day of signs and wonders,
And marvels from on high;
Thy sun uprises slowly,
But keep thou watch and ward;
Fair Bride, all pure and lowly,
Go forth to meet thy Lord.

Benjamin Gough.

42

See, the Conqueror.

Bp. Christopher Wordsworth. *He led captivity captive.*—Eph. 4: 8. R. Lowry.

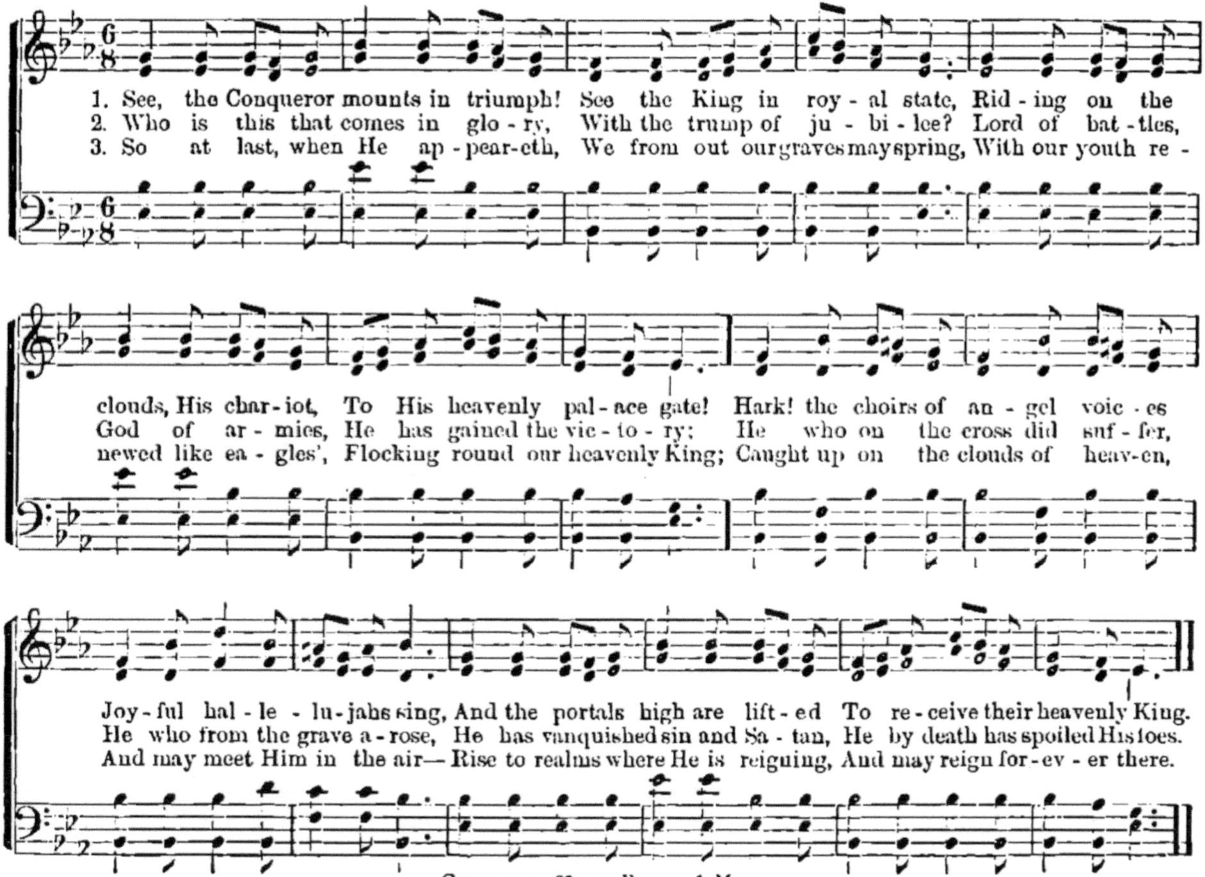
1. See, the Conqueror mounts in triumph! See the King in roy - al state, Rid - ing on the clouds, His char - iot, To His heavenly pal - ace gate! Hark! the choirs of an - gel voic - es Joy - ful hal - le - lu - jahs sing, And the portals high are lift - ed To re - ceive their heavenly King.
2. Who is this that comes in glo - ry, With the trump of ju - bi - lee? Lord of bat - tles, God of ar - mies, He has gained the vic - to - ry; He who on the cross did suf - fer, He who from the grave a - rose, He has vanquished sin and Sa - tan, He by death has spoiled His foes.
3. So at last, when He ap - pear - eth, We from out our graves may spring, With our youth re - newed like ea - gles', Flocking round our heavenly King; Caught up on the clouds of heav - en, And may meet Him in the air— Rise to realms where He is reigning, And may reign for - ev - er there.

Alive in Christ.

REV. ISAAC N. WILSON. *I am the resurrection, and the life.*—JOHN 11: 25. WM. J. KIRKPATRICK.

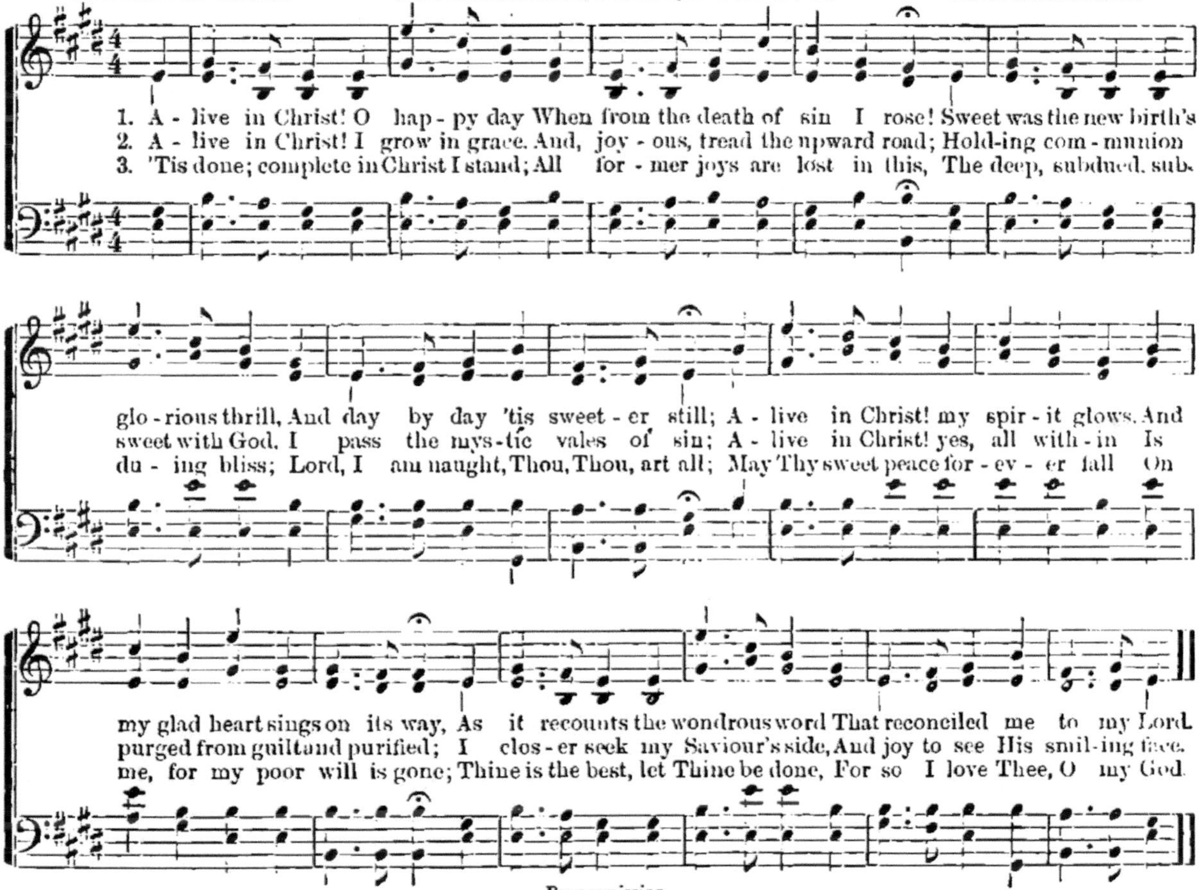
1. A - live in Christ! O hap - py day When from the death of sin I rose! Sweet was the new birth's
2. A - live in Christ! I grow in grace. And, joy - ous, tread the upward road; Hold-ing com - munion
3. 'Tis done; complete in Christ I stand; All for - mer joys are lost in this, The deep, subdued, sub-
glo - rious thrill, And day by day 'tis sweet - er still; A - live in Christ! my spir - it glows. And
sweet with God, I pass the mys - tic vales of sin; A - live in Christ! yes, all with - in Is
du - ing bliss; Lord, I am naught, Thou, Thou, art all; May Thy sweet peace for - ev - er fall On
my glad heart sings on its way, As it recounts the wondrous word That reconciled me to my Lord.
purged from guilt and purified; I clos - er seek my Saviour's side, And joy to see His smil - ing face.
me, for my poor will is gone; Thine is the best, let Thine be done, For so I love Thee, O my God.

By permission.

44

Jesus, the Light of the World.

Fanny J. Crosby. *I am the light of the world.*—John 8: 12. W. H. Doane.

1st.
2d.
1. Shining in darkness by faith we be-hold Je-sus, the Light of the world;
Je-sus, the brightness of glo-ry un-told, Je-sus, the Light of the (Omit.....) world.
2. Shining in darkness thro' tri-als and fears, Je-sus, the Light of the world;
Shining in darkness thro' sor-row and tears, Je-sus, the Light of the (Omit.....) world.
3. Shining in darkness, O In-fi-nite Love! Je-sus, the Light of the world;
Shining in darkness wher-ev-er we move, Je-sus, the Light of the (Omit.....) world.
Refrain.
O walk...... in the beau-ti-ful light That comes with the dew-drops of mer-cy impearled; It
walk in the beauti ful,
shin-eth a-round us by day and by night, 'Tis Je-sus, the Light of the world.

Come, Come and See.

Mrs. Annie S. Hawks. *He saith unto them, Come and see.*—John 1: 39. R. Lowry.

1. O ye who now would view Him, Come, come and see; O ye who nev - er knew Him,
2. If now in youth's bright morning, Come, come and see; Find peace for life's a - dorn - ing,
3. O all ye tempest-tossed ones, Come, come and see; Come, all ye wea - ry, crossed ones,
4. All ye who live to doubt Him, Come, come and see; How can you die with - out Him?
Come, come and see.
Come, come and see.
Come, come and see.
Come, come and see.
Chorus.
See Him in the manger ly - ing, View Him in Gethsem - a - ne, See Him
wounded, bleeding, dy - ing, Christ the Lord, on Cal - va - ry— Dy - ing there for you and me.

46 Christ our King.

DELOSS EVERETT. ——*that your joy might be full.*—JOHN 15: 11. WILLIAM W. CASSEL.

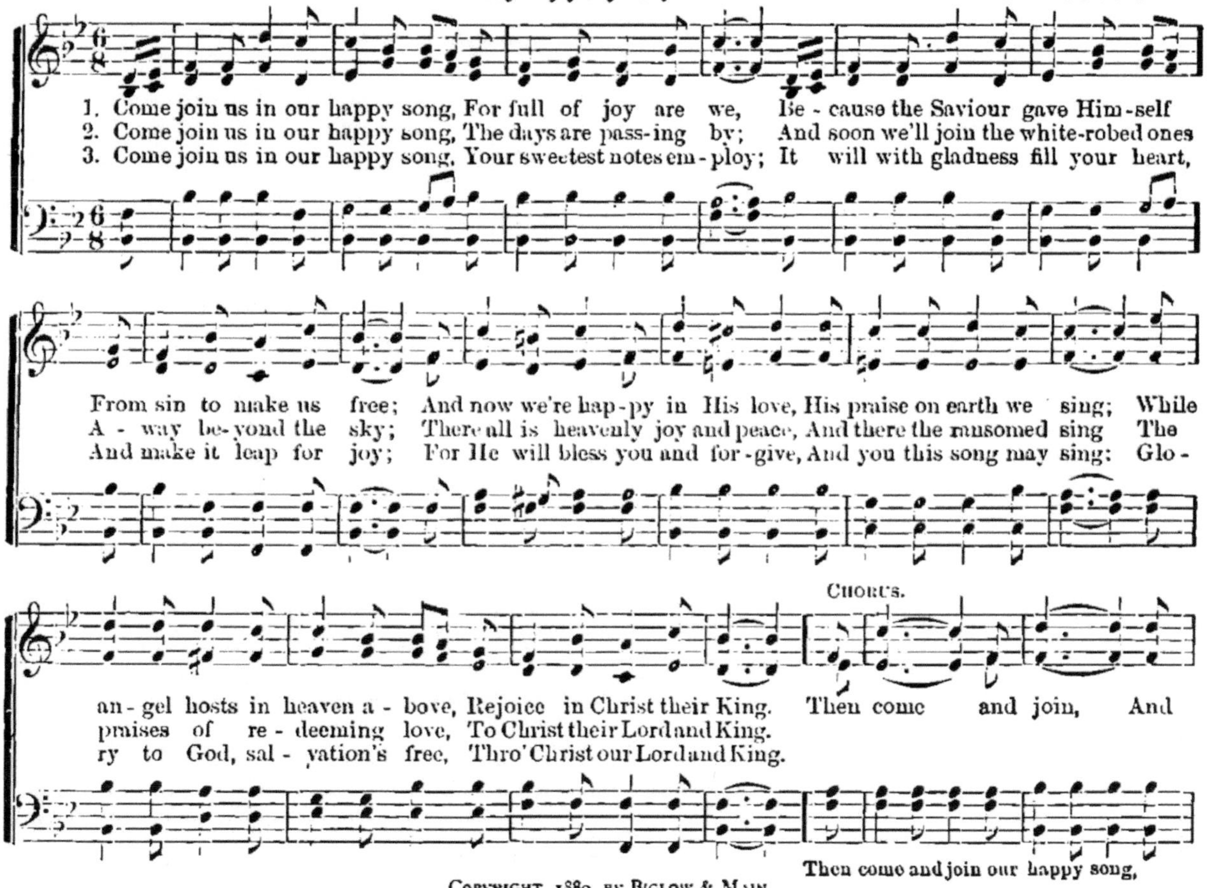
1. Come join us in our happy song, For full of joy are we, Be - cause the Saviour gave Him-self
2. Come join us in our happy song, The days are pass-ing by; And soon we'll join the white-robed ones
3. Come join us in our happy song, Your sweetest notes em - ploy; It will with gladness fill your heart,
From sin to make us free; And now we're hap-py in His love, His praise on earth we sing; While
A - way be-yond the sky; There all is heavenly joy and peace, And there the ransomed sing The
And make it leap for joy; For He will bless you and for - give, And you this song may sing: Glo -
an - gel hosts in heaven a - bove, Rejoice in Christ their King.
praises of re - deeming love, To Christ their Lord and King.
ry to God, sal - vation's free, Thro' Christ our Lord and King.
CHORUS.
Then come and join, And
Then come and join our happy song,

let the cho-rus ring, Till all the nations of the earth Be-lieve on Christ our King.

Lay it Down.

FANNY J. CROSBY. *Cast thy burden upon the Lord.*—Ps. 55: 22. W. H. DOANE.

REFRAIN.
1. { O come, sinner, come, 'tis mercy's call, Here at Jesus' feet;
O come, and repent-ing lay thy all Down at Jesus' feet. }
2. { O come, and believ-ing seek thy rest, Here at Jesus' feet;
Thy heart, with its heavy weight oppress'd, Lay at Jesus' feet. }
O lay it down, lay it down, Lay thy weary

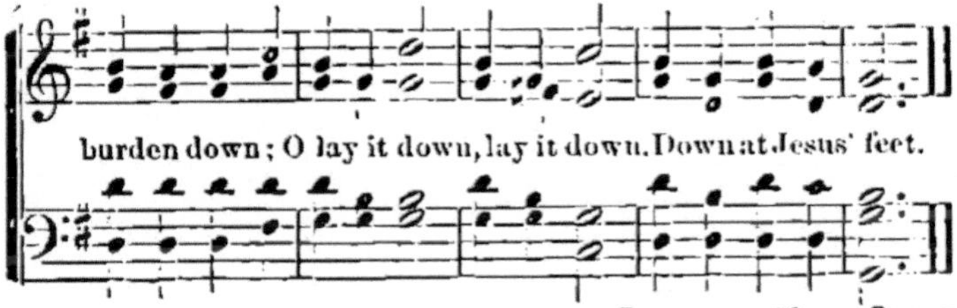
burden down; O lay it down, lay it down. Down at Jesus' feet.

3 O come where thy faith can make thee whole,
Here at Jesus' feet;
O come, and thy weary, troubled soul
Lay at Jesus' feet.

4 O come, bless the Lord, there's room for thee,
Here at Jesus' feet;
Thy burden of guilt, whate'er it be,
Lay at Jesus' feet.

Happy News.

Mrs. N. D. Plume. *I bring you good tidings of great joy.*—Luke 2: 10. W. H. Doane.

1. He has come, our Lord and Saviour, He has come the world to bless; Ev - ery knee shall bow be -
2. Thro' the birth of Christ our Saviour, Love to ev - ery na - tion flows, While the des - ert wastes, re -
3. Thro' the birth of Christ our Saviour, Comes the gentle light of peace; Heav - y souls, oppressed and
4. With the mighty an - gel chorus, Let our humbler songs u - nite, While we hail our great Re -
Refrain.
fore Him, Ev - ery tongue His name con-fess. Happy news, . . . O wonderful sto - ry, Shout it
joic-ing, Bloom and blossom like the rose.
troubled, In His mer - cy find re - lease.
deem-er, On this festive day so bright. Happy news, O wonderful, wonderful sto - ry,
forth to every clime; Happy news, . . . O wonderful sto - ry, Shout it forth to ev-ery clime.
O sweet, Shout it, shout it forth

By permission.

Lead me Every Day.

W. H. D. *Lead me and guide me.*—Ps. 31: 3. W. H. Doane.

1. Je - sus, Thou art call - ing me Ev - ery day, ev - ery day; Thou dost bid me fol - low Thee,
2. Keep me ver - y close to Thee Ev - ery day, ev - ery day; Ver - y hum - ble may I be,

Refrain.
I am com - ing right a - way. Help, O help me, Saviour mine, Lest I wan - der from the way;
Ver - y ear - nest when I pray.

Hold my lit - tle hand in Thine, Lead me ev - ery day.

3 I would love Thee more and more
Every day, every day;
Thinking all Thy mercy o'er,
When I work and when I play.

4 Teach me lessons pure and sweet
Every day, every day;
Thou canst make my willing feet
Strong to run the heavenly way.

The Swelling of Jordan.

How wilt thou do in the swelling of Jordan?—Jer. 12: 5.

Mrs. Georgia Hulse McLeod. R. Lowry.

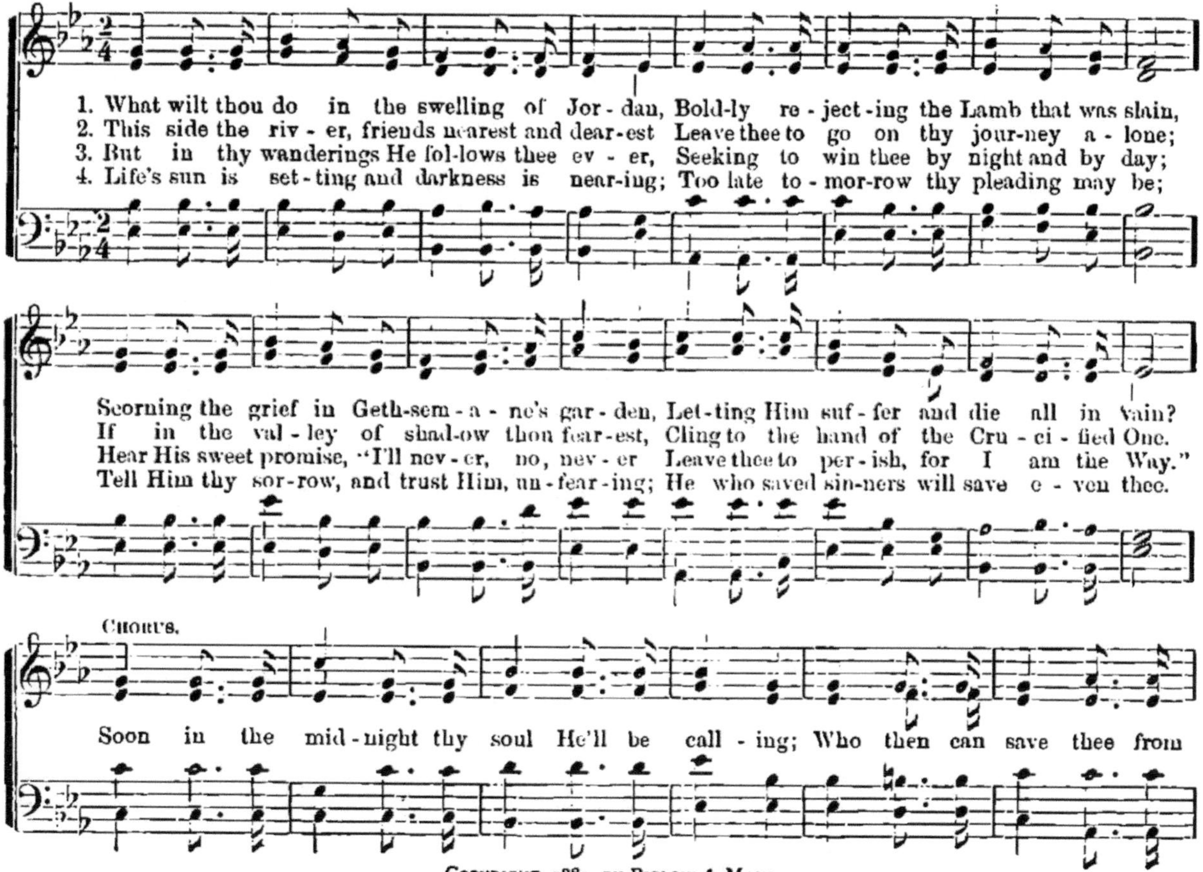
1. What wilt thou do in the swelling of Jor-dan, Bold-ly re-ject-ing the Lamb that was slain,
2. This side the riv-er, friends nearest and dear-est Leave thee to go on thy jour-ney a-lone;
3. But in thy wanderings He fol-lows thee ev-er, Seeking to win thee by night and by day;
4. Life's sun is set-ting and darkness is near-ing; Too late to-mor-row thy pleading may be;
Scorning the grief in Geth-sem-a-ne's gar-den, Let-ting Him suf-fer and die all in vain?
If in the val-ley of shad-ow thou fear-est, Cling to the hand of the Cru-ci-fied One.
Hear His sweet promise, "I'll nev-er, no, nev-er Leave thee to per-ish, for I am the Way."
Tell Him thy sor-row, and trust Him, un-fear-ing; He who saved sin-ners will save e-ven thee.
Chorus.
Soon in the mid-night thy soul He'll be call-ing; Who then can save thee from

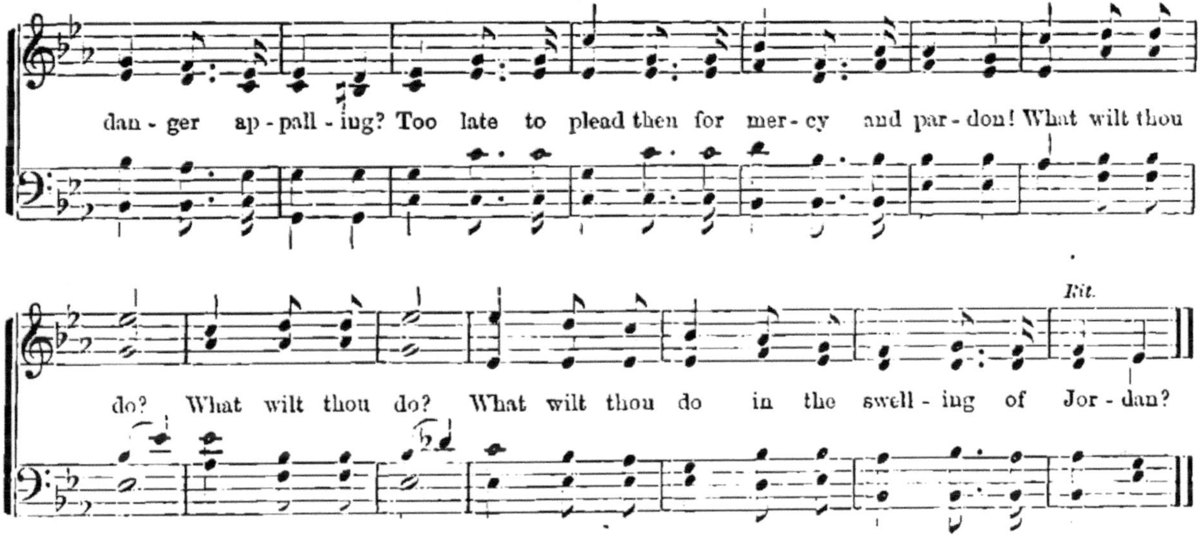
dan - ger ap - pall - ing? Too late to plead then for mer - cy and par - don! What wilt thou
Rit.
do? What wilt thou do? What wilt thou do in the swell - ing of Jor - dan?

To-day the Saviour calls.

Samuel Francis Smith, D. D. *Harden not your hearts.*—Heb. 3: 8. Lowell Mason, Mus. Doc.

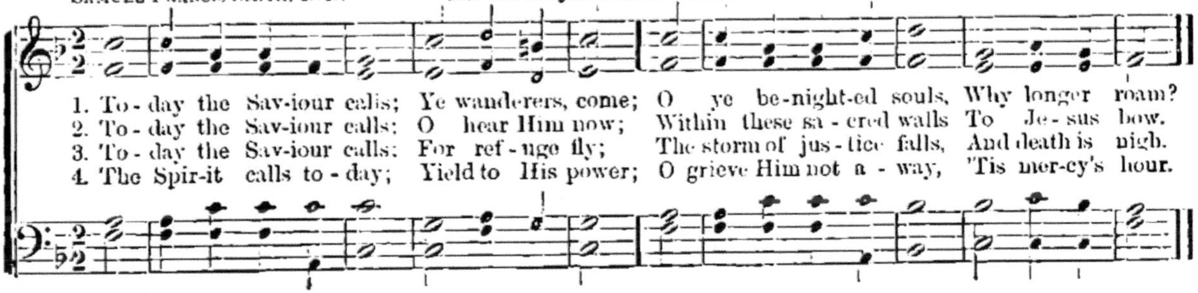
1. To - day the Sav-iour calls; Ye wanderers, come; O ye be-night-ed souls, Why longer roam?
2. To - day the Sav-iour calls: O hear Him now; Within these sa - cred walls To Je - sus bow.
3. To - day the Sav-iour calls: For ref - uge fly; The storm of jus - tice falls, And death is nigh.
4. The Spir-it calls to - day; Yield to His power; O grieve Him not a - way, 'Tis mer-cy's hour.

52 Jesus will Help You.

Wm Stevenson. *Grace to help in time of need.*—Heb. 4: 16. R. Lowry.

1. The Saviour is call-ing you, sin-ner— Urg-ing you now to draw nigh; He asks you by faith to re -
2. Thro' Him there is life in be-liev-ing; Sin-ner, O why will you die? Ac-cept Him by faith as your
3. There's danger in longer de-lay - ing, Swiftly the moments pass by; If now you will come, there is
ceive Him; Je - sus will help if you try.
Sav-iour; Je - sus will help if you try.
mer-cy; Je - sus will help if you try.
Refrain.
Jesus will help you, Jesus will help you, Help you with grace from on
high; The weak-est and poor-est the Sav-iour is call-ing; Je - sus will help if you try.

By permission

Trim thy Lamp.

W. H. D. — *Let your light so shine.*—Matt. 5: 16. — W. H. Doane.

1. Rise and trim thy lamp, O Christian, 'Tis a lamp of light di - vine; In thy soul with heavenly
2. Rise and trim thy lamp, O Christian, Keep it burn-ing bright within; Thou wilt need its beams to
3. Trim thy lamp and trim it quick-ly, Let its rays be bright and clear; Oth-er eyes per-haps are
4. Rise and trim thy lamp, O Christian, Let the world its lus-tre see; By thy dai - ly walk con-
bright-ness, Let its beams of glo - ry shine.
cheer thee Thro' the rug - ged wilds of sin.
wait - ing For its beams their hearts to cheer.
vince them What a Chris-tian life should be.
Chorus.
With the oil of grace so free, Mer-cy fills that lamp for thee; Je - sus lights the sa - cred flame; Hal - le - lu - jah to His name.

I was Lost.

Josephine Pollard.

I have found my sheep which was lost.—Luke 15: 6.

Henry Tucker.

1. I was lost.—in darkness straying, Wand'ring far-ther from the fold; All my weak-ness-es be - tray - ing, Shiv'ring with the bit - ter cold; Torn and bleed - ing, sore - ly wounded By the thorns a - long the way, From the flock, and from the Shepherd, Fool-ish - ly I went a - stray.
2. I was lost,—O sad con - di - tion: I was lost to hope and grace; Ev - ery step was toward per - di - tion, Far - ther from my "hid-ing - place;" I was lost.—and Sa - tan drew me Far a - way from flock and fold; Sin-ners, on - ly sin-ners knew me, They my fee - ble steps con-troled.
3. I was lost,—but Je - sus found me, Found me bleeding and distressed; Put His lov - ing arms a - round me, Drew me clos - er to His breast; Put His name and seal up - on me. Wash'd me clean, and made me whole; Je - sus found me, and re-deemed me, Je - sus saved my guilt-y soul.

I NEED THEE.

1 I need Thee every hour,
Most gracious Lord;
No tender voice like Thine
Can peace afford.
REF.—I need Thee, O I need Thee,
Every hour I need Thee;
O bless me now, my Saviour!
I come to Thee.

2 I need Thee every hour;
Stay Thou near by;
Temptations lose their power
When Thou art nigh.

3 I need Thee every hour,
In joy or pain;
Come quickly and abide,
Or life is vain.

4 I need Thee every hour,
Most Holy One;
O make me Thine indeed,
Thou blessed Son.
Mrs. Annie S. Hawks.

PRECIOUS NAME.

1 Take the name of Jesus with you,
Child of sorrow and of woe—
It will joy and comfort give you,
Take it, then, where'er you go.
CHO.—Precious name, O how sweet!
Hope of earth and joy of heav'n,
Precious name, O how sweet!
Hope of earth and joy of heav'n.

2 O the precious name of Jesus!
How it thrills our souls with joy,
When His loving arms receive us,
And His songs our tongues employ!

3 At the name of Jesus bowing,
Falling prostrate at His feet,
King of kings in heaven we'll crown Him,
When our journey is complete.
Mrs. Lydia Baxter.

HAPPY DAY.

1 O happy that fixed my choice
On Thee, my Saviour and my God
Well may this glowing heart rejoice
And tell its raptures all abroad.
CHO.—
Happy day, happy day,
When Jesus washed my sins away;
He taught me how to watch and pray,
And live rejoicing every day;
Happy day, happy day,
When Jesus washed my sins away.

2 Now rest, my long-divided heart;
Fixed on this blissful centre, rest;
Nor ever from Thy Lord depart,
With Him of every good possessed.

3 High heaven that heard the solemn vow,
That vow renewed shall daily hear,
Till in life's latest hour I bow,
And bless in death a bond so dear.
Rev. P. Doddridge.

FOREST.

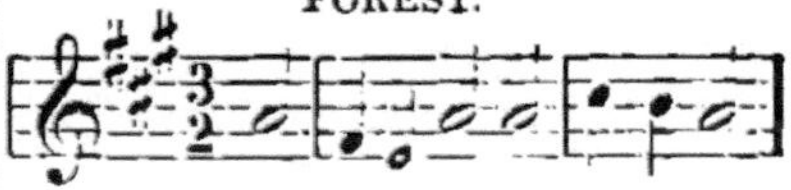

1 O that my load of sin were gone!
O that I could at last submit
At Jesus' feet to lay it down—
To lay my soul at Jesus' feet!

2 Rest for my soul I long to find:
Saviour of all, if mine Thou art,
Give me Thy meek and lowly mind,
And stamp Thine image on my heart.

3 Break off the yoke of inbred sin,
And fully set my spirit free;
I cannot rest till pure within—
Till I am wholly lost in Thee.
Rev. Chas. Wesley.

NEAR THE CROSS.

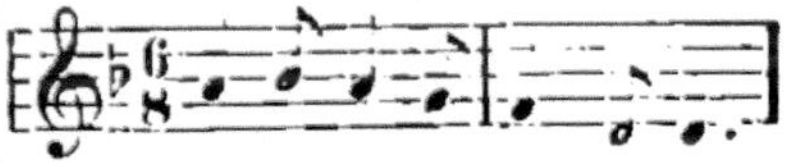

1 Jesus, keep me near the cross,
There a precious fountain,
Free to all, a healing stream,
Flows from Calvary's mountain.
CHO.—In the Cross, in the Cross
Be my glory ever,
Till my raptured soul shall find
Rest beyond the river.

2 Near the cross I'll watch and wait,
Hoping, trusting ever,
Till I reach the golden strand
Just beyond the river.

56 Lift the Royal Standard High.

FANNY J. CROSBY. *Lift up a standard for the people.*—ISA. 62: 10. W. H. DOANE.

1. Lift the roy - al standard high, with a firm and stead-y hand, Lift it high, while our songs we pro-
2. Lift the roy - al standard high in the blaze of gos - pel light, Lift it high with a zeal that will
3. Lift the roy - al standard high, blessed standard of the Lord, Lift it high, now the ranks let us
claim; We are sol - diers of a King, go - ing forth at His command To
show We are read - y with our lives to pro - tect its col - ors bright, And
fill; Lift the roy - al standard high, gath-er quick - ly at the word, O
we pro - claim;
REFRAIN.
fight in a glorious Name. Then lift, then lift the roy - - - al standard high;
shield them against the foe.
come, who so-ev - er will.
Lift it high, lift it high, lift the roy-al standard high;

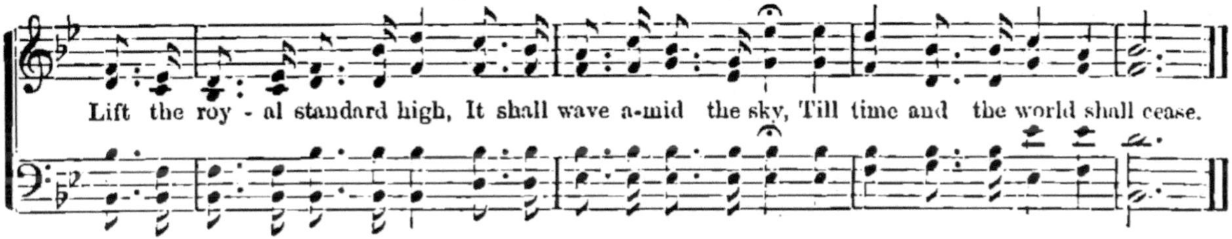
Lift the roy - al standard high, It shall wave a-mid the sky, Till time and the world shall cease.

No, not Despairingly.

ANON. *Out of the depths have I cried unto thee, O Lord.*—Ps. 130 : 1 JOHN R. SWENEY.

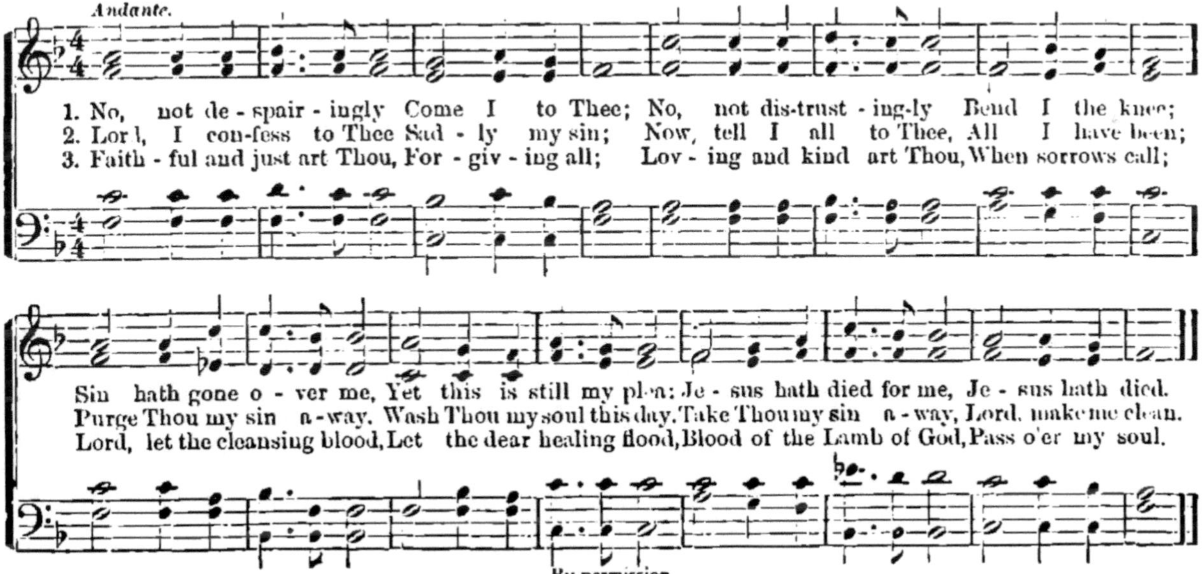
Andante.
1. No, not de - spair - ingly Come I to Thee; No, not dis-trust - ing-ly Bend I the knee;
2. Lord, I con-fess to Thee Sad - ly my sin; Now, tell I all to Thee, All I have been;
3. Faith - ful and just art Thou, For - giv - ing all; Lov - ing and kind art Thou, When sorrows call;
Sin hath gone o - ver me, Yet this is still my plea: Je - sus hath died for me, Je - sus hath died.
Purge Thou my sin a - way, Wash Thou my soul this day, Take Thou my sin a - way, Lord, make me clean.
Lord, let the cleansing blood, Let the dear healing flood, Blood of the Lamb of God, Pass o'er my soul.

By permission.

Our Glad Jubilee.

W. F. S. *Thou crownest the year with thy goodness.*—Ps. 65: 11. Wm. F. Sherwin.

1. Wake, wake the song! our glad ju - bi - lee Once more we hail with sweet mel-o - dy, Bringing our
2. Marching to Zi - on, dear blessed home! Lord, by Thy mer - cy hith - er we come; Guide us, we
3. Yet once a-gain the an-them re-peat, Join ev - ery voice the Mas - ter to greet; Love's sac - ri-
D. C.—Wake, wake the song, &c.
Fine.
hymns of praise un-to Thee, O most ho-ly Lord! Praise for Thy care by day and by night, Praise for the
pray, where'er we may roam, Keep us in Thy fear; Fill ev - ery soul with love all divine, Now cause Thy
fice we lay at His feet, In His temple now; Je - sus, ac-cept the offering we bring, Blending with
D. C.
homes by love made so bright; Thanks for the pure and the soul-cheering light Beaming from Thy word. Then
face up - on us to shine; Grant that our hearts may truly be Thine All the coming year. Then
songs the o-dors of spring; Still of Thy wondrous love we will sing, Till in heaven we bow. Then

By permission.

The Lion of Judah.

Fanny J. Crosby. *The Lion of the tribe of Judah * * * * hath prevailed.*—Rev. 5: 5. W. H. Doane.

1. How sweetly o'er the mountain of Zion, lovely Zi - on, The anthem of a - ges comes sweeping a - long;
2. O happy, happy tidings, the kingdom now is o-pened, The seals are all broken; pro-claim it a - far;
3. Ho - sanna in the highest, all glo-ry ev - er - last-ing, The cross and its ban-ner tri - umphant shall wave;
Fine.
The anthem of the faithful, we hear it, and, re - joic-ing. Our hearts in glad measure keep tune with the song.
From bondage and oppression by Him we are de-liv - ered, The Li - on of Ju - dah, the bright Morning Star.
Ho - san-na in the highest, all glo-ry ev - er - last - ing. The Li - on of Ju - dah His peo-ple will save.
D. S.—Sweet anthem of the faithful, we hear it, and, re-joic - ing. Our hearts in glad measure keep tune with the song.
Refrain.
D. S.
O the Li - on of Ju-dah hath triumphed for - ev - er, O the Li - on of Ju-dah is mighty and strong;

By permission.

60 Look up, O Watchman!

GRACE J. FRANCES. *Watchman, what of the night?*—ISA. 21: 11. HUBERT P. MAIN.

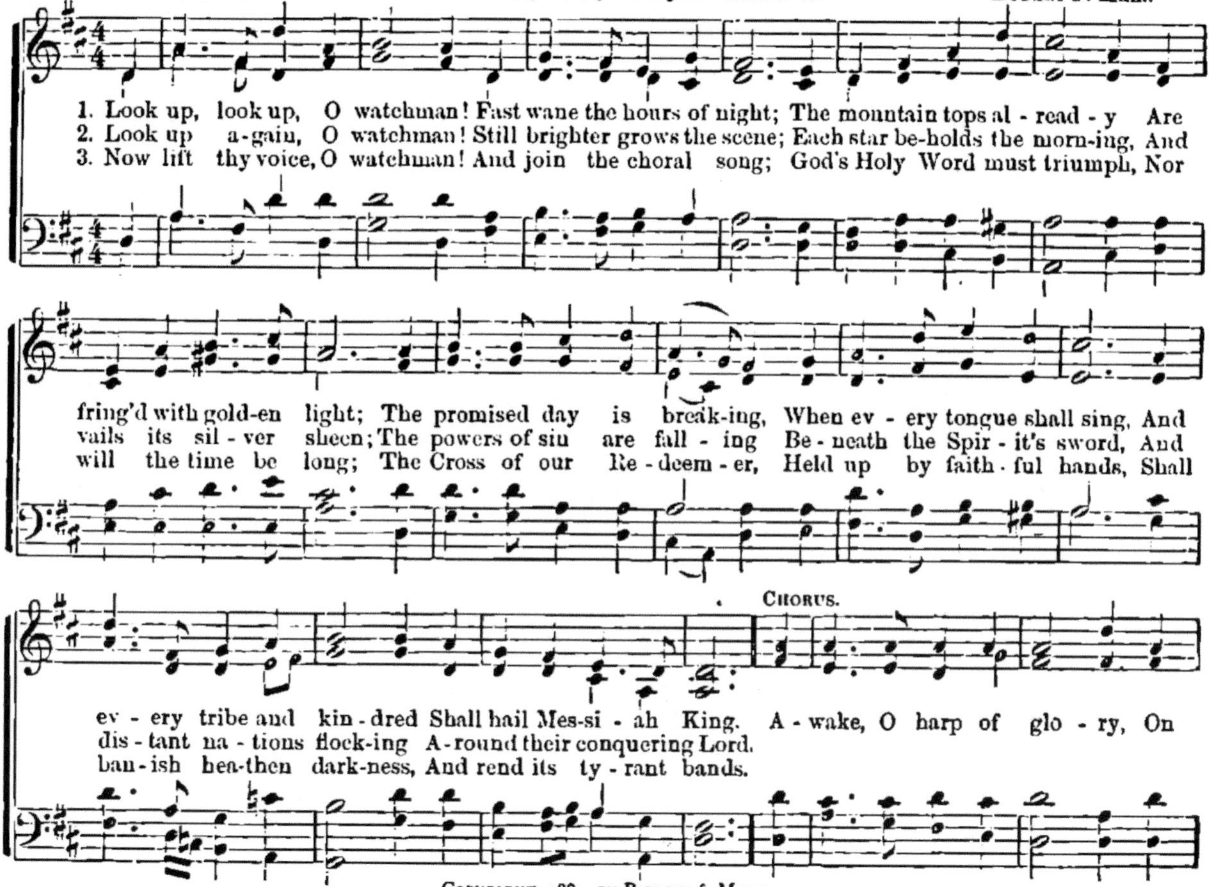
1. Look up, look up, O watchman! Fast wane the hours of night; The mountain tops al - read - y Are
2. Look up a-gain, O watchman! Still brighter grows the scene; Each star be-holds the morn-ing, And
3. Now lift thy voice, O watchman! And join the choral song; God's Holy Word must triumph, Nor
fring'd with gold-en light; The promised day is break-ing, When ev - ery tongue shall sing, And
vails its sil - ver sheen; The powers of sin are fall - ing Be - neath the Spir - it's sword, And
will the time be long; The Cross of our Re - deem - er, Held up by faith - ful hands, Shall
ev - ery tribe and kin - dred Shall hail Mes-si - ah King.
dis - tant na - tions flock-ing A - round their conquering Lord.
ban - ish hea-then dark-ness, And rend its ty - rant bands.
CHORUS.
A - wake, O harp of glo - ry, On

Zi - on's towering hill, And let thy chords ex - ult - ing Send forth a might - y thrill.

What wilt Thou have me to Do?

R. L. *Lord, what wilt thou have me to do?*—Acts 9: 6. R. Lowry.

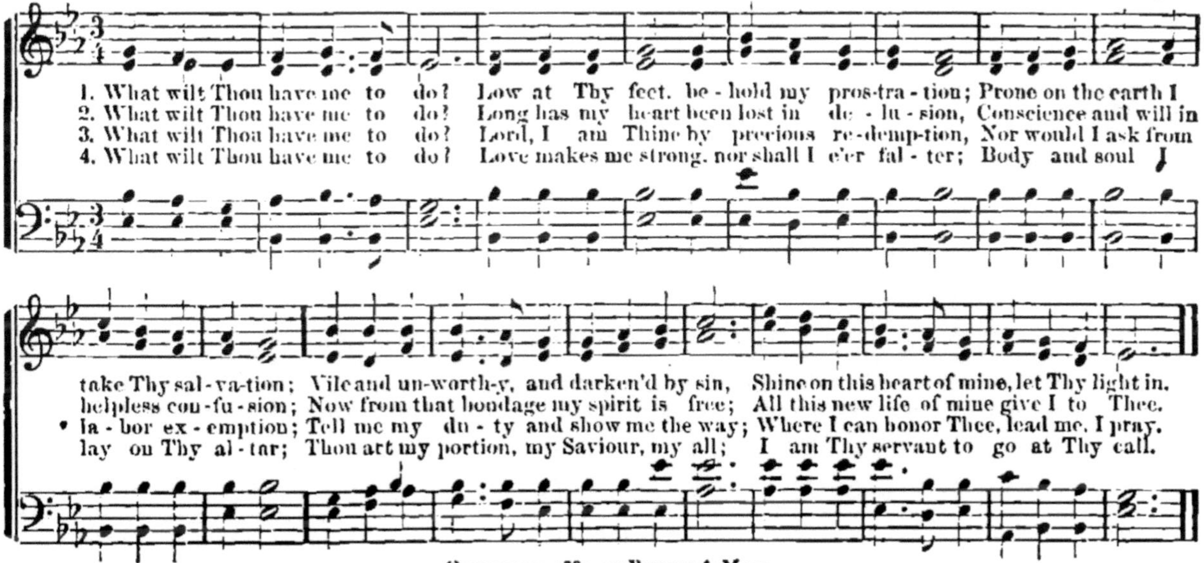
1. What wilt Thou have me to do? Low at Thy feet, be - hold my pros-tra - tion; Prone on the earth I take Thy sal-va-tion; Vile and un-worth-y, and darken'd by sin, Shine on this heart of mine, let Thy light in.
2. What wilt Thou have me to do? Long has my heart been lost in de - lu - sion, Conscience and will in helpless con-fu-sion; Now from that bondage my spirit is free; All this new life of mine give I to Thee.
3. What wilt Thou have me to do? Lord, I am Thine by precious re-demp-tion, Nor would I ask from la - bor ex - emption; Tell me my du - ty and show me the way; Where I can honor Thee, lead me, I pray.
4. What wilt Thou have me to do? Love makes me strong, nor shall I e'er fal - ter; Body and soul I lay on Thy al - tar; Thou art my portion, my Saviour, my all; I am Thy servant to go at Thy call.

62

O Sing the Passing Years.

MARY A. LATHBURY. *The word of the Lord endureth forever.*—1 PET. 1: 25. THEO. F. SEWARD.

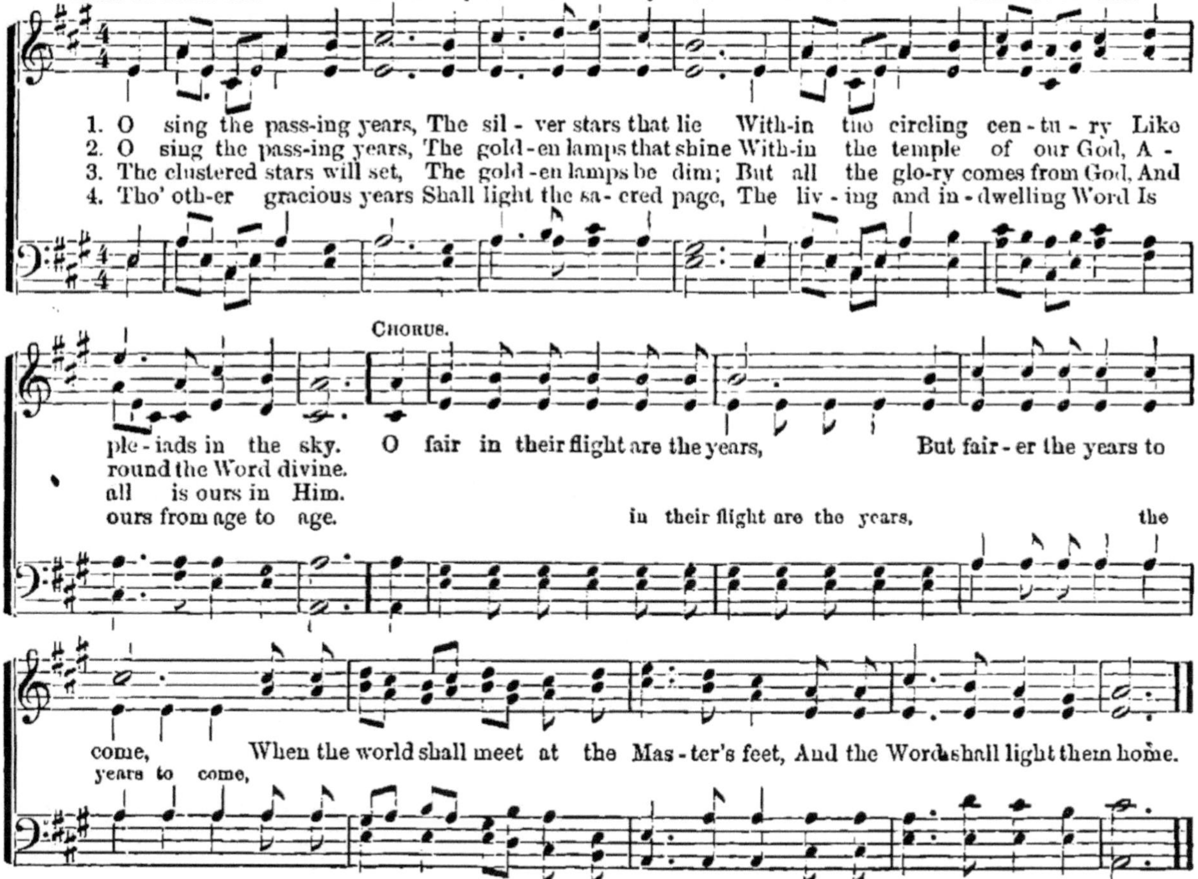
1. O sing the pass-ing years, The sil - ver stars that lie With-in the circling cen - tu - ry Like
2. O sing the pass-ing years, The gold - en lamps that shine With-in the temple of our God, A -
3. The clustered stars will set, The gold - en lamps be dim; But all the glo-ry comes from God, And
4. Tho' oth-er gracious years Shall light the sa - cred page, The liv - ing and in - dwelling Word Is
CHORUS.
ple - iads in the sky. O fair in their flight are the years, But fair - er the years to
round the Word divine.
all is ours in Him.
ours from age to age.
in their flight are the years, the
come, When the world shall meet at the Mas - ter's feet, And the Word shall light them home.
years to come,

All will be Well.

63

Say ye to the righteous that it shall be well with him.—Is. 3 : 10.

MRS. MARY BOWLY PETERS. R. LOWRY.

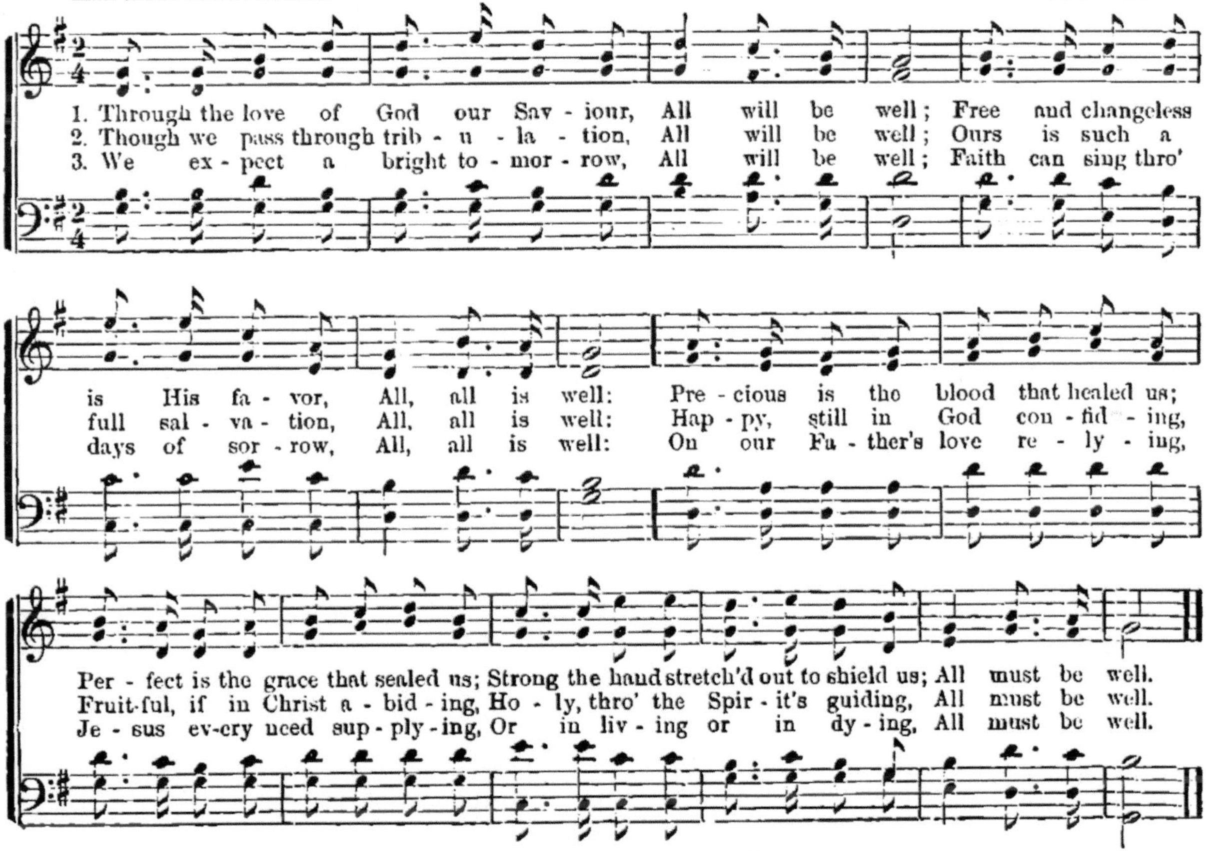
1. Through the love of God our Sav - iour, All will be well; Free and changeless
2. Though we pass through trib - u - la - tion, All will be well; Ours is such a
3. We ex - pect a bright to - mor - row, All will be well; Faith can sing thro'
is His fa - vor, All, all is well: Pre - cious is the blood that healed us;
full sal - va - tion, All, all is well: Hap - py, still in God con - fid - ing,
days of sor - row, All, all is well: On our Fa - ther's love re - ly - ing,
Per - fect is the grace that sealed us; Strong the hand stretch'd out to shield us; All must be well.
Fruit-ful, if in Christ a - bid - ing, Ho - ly, thro' the Spir - it's guiding, All must be well.
Je - sus ev-ery need sup - ply - ing, Or in liv - ing or in dy - ing, All must be well.

64 This I Know.

Fanny J. Crosby. *I know whom I have believed.*—2 Tim. 1: 12. W. H. Doane.

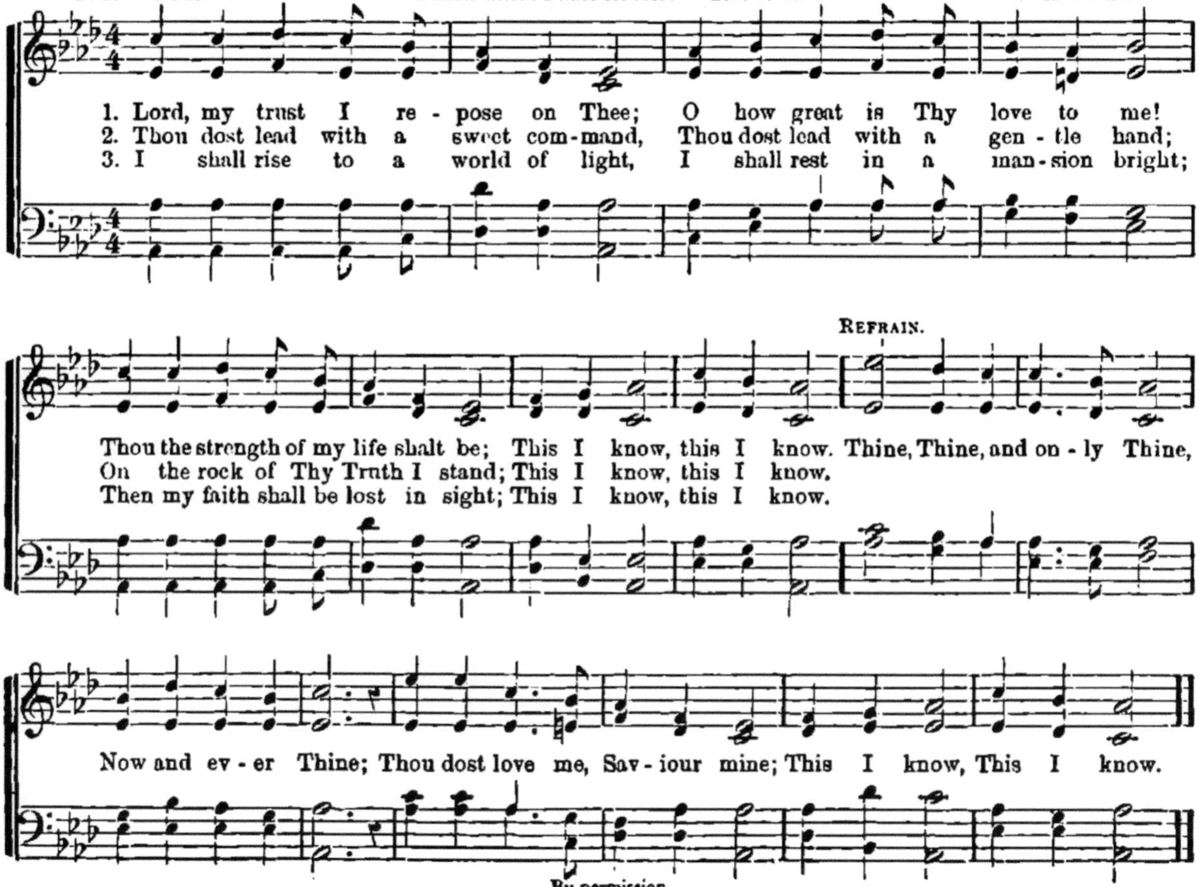
1. Lord, my trust I re - pose on Thee; O how great is Thy love to me!
2. Thou dost lead with a sweet com-mand, Thou dost lead with a gen - tle hand;
3. I shall rise to a world of light, I shall rest in a man - sion bright;
Thou the strength of my life shalt be; This I know, this I know.
On the rock of Thy Truth I stand; This I know, this I know.
Then my faith shall be lost in sight; This I know, this I know.
Refrain.
Thine, Thine, and on - ly Thine,
Now and ev - er Thine; Thou dost love me, Sav - iour mine; This I know, This I know.

By permission.

Gathering Home to the Silent Shore.

Rev. W. O. Cushing. *Therefore be ye also ready.*—Matt. 24: 44. Hubert P. Main.

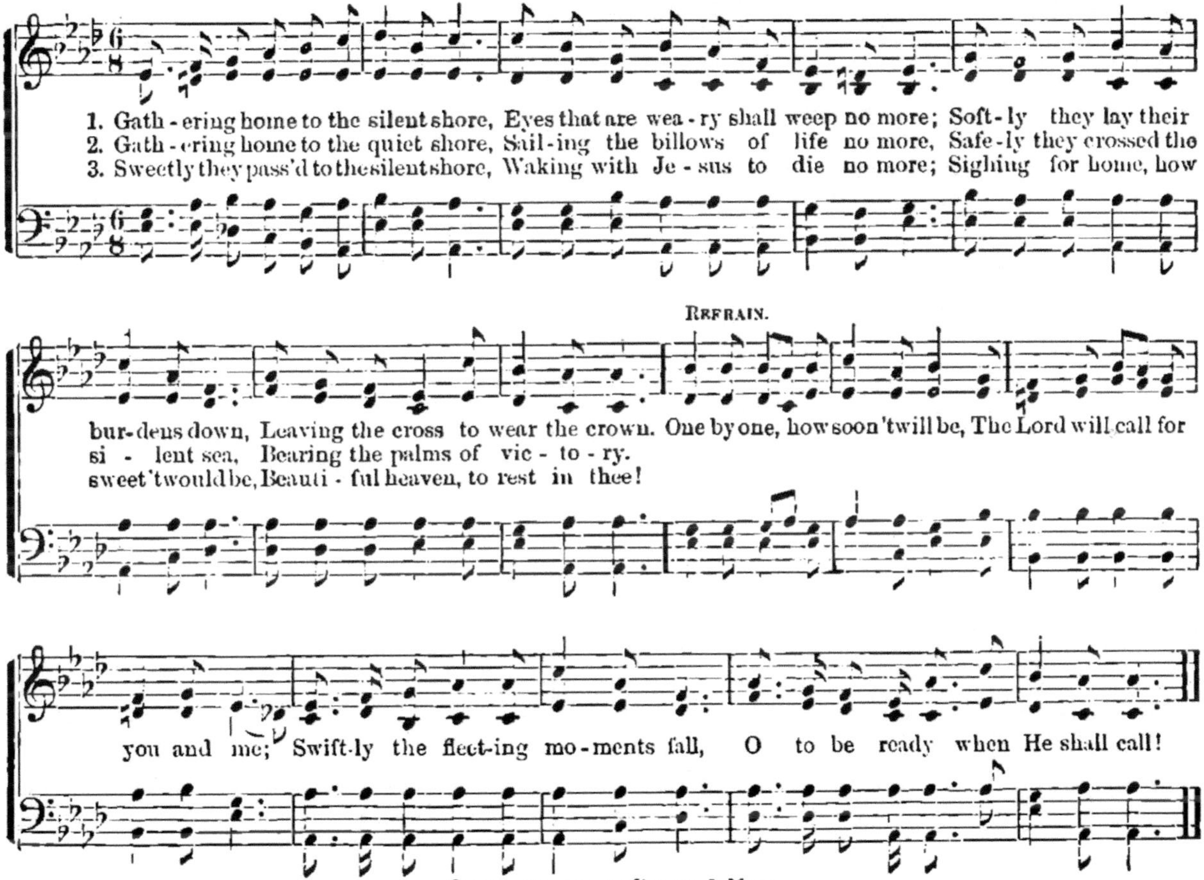
1. Gath-ering home to the silent shore, Eyes that are wea-ry shall weep no more; Soft-ly they lay their
2. Gath-ering home to the quiet shore, Sail-ing the billows of life no more, Safe-ly they crossed the
3. Sweetly they pass'd to the silent shore, Waking with Je-sus to die no more; Sighing for home, how
bur-dens down, Leaving the cross to wear the crown.
si - lent sea, Bearing the palms of vic - to - ry.
sweet 'twould be, Beauti - ful heaven, to rest in thee!
Refrain.
One by one, how soon 'twill be, The Lord will call for
you and me; Swift-ly the fleet-ing mo-ments fall, O to be ready when He shall call!

The Door was Shut.

Arthur J. Hodge. *Then shall the kingdom of heaven be likened unto ten virgins.*—Matt. 25: 1. R. Lowry.

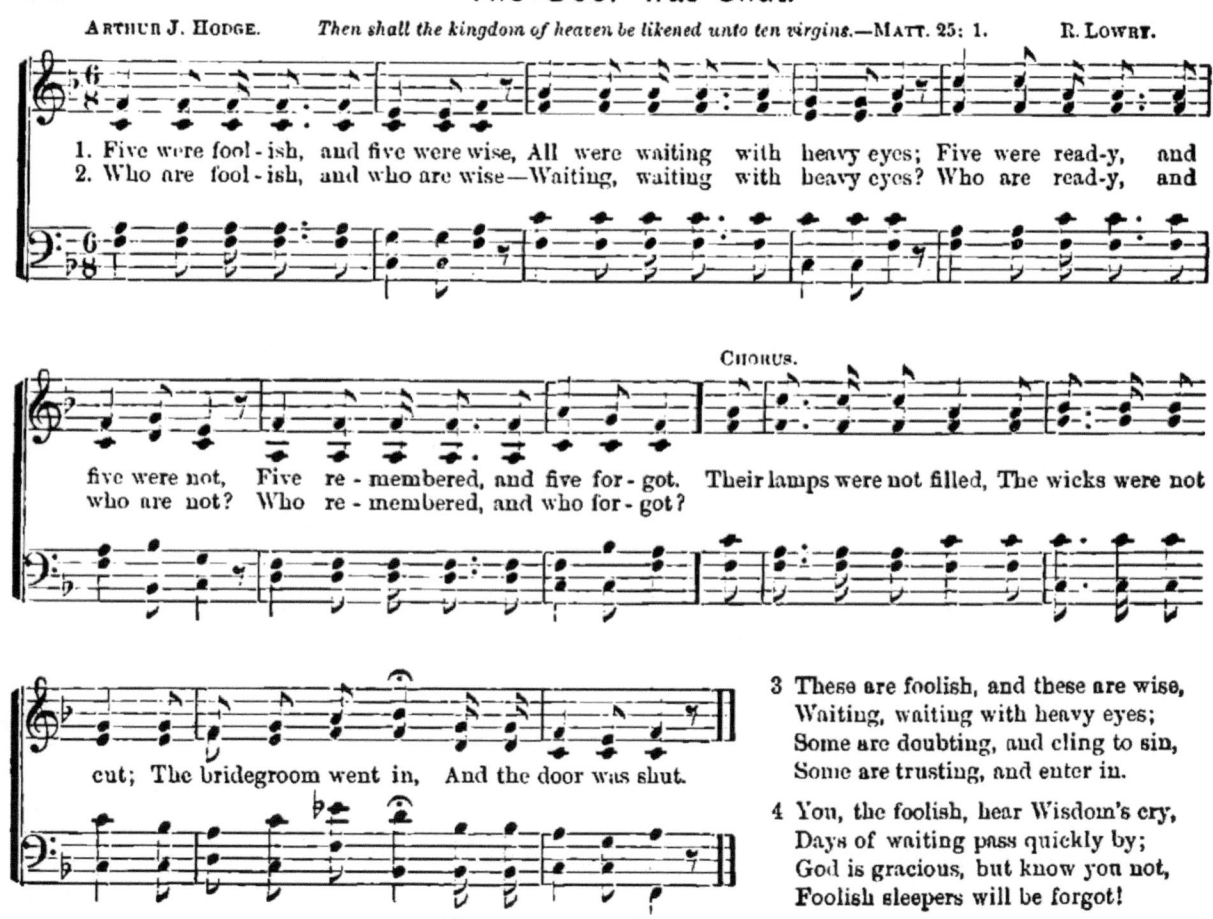

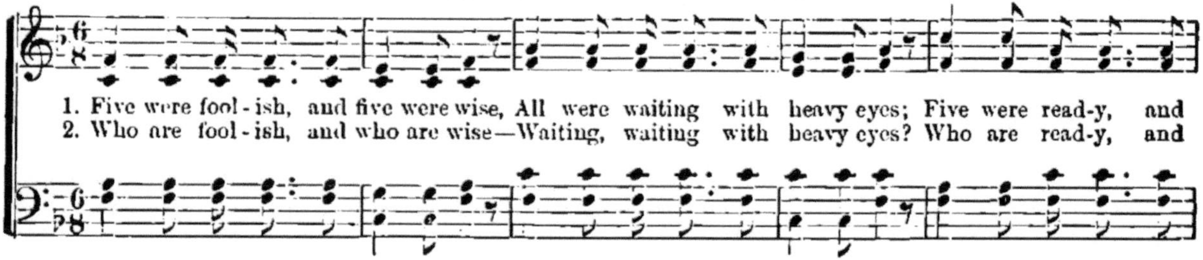
1. Five were fool - ish, and five were wise, All were waiting with heavy eyes; Five were read-y, and
2. Who are fool - ish, and who are wise—Waiting, waiting with heavy eyes? Who are read-y, and

Chorus.
five were not, Five re - membered, and five for - got. Their lamps were not filled, The wicks were not
who are not? Who re - membered, and who for - got?

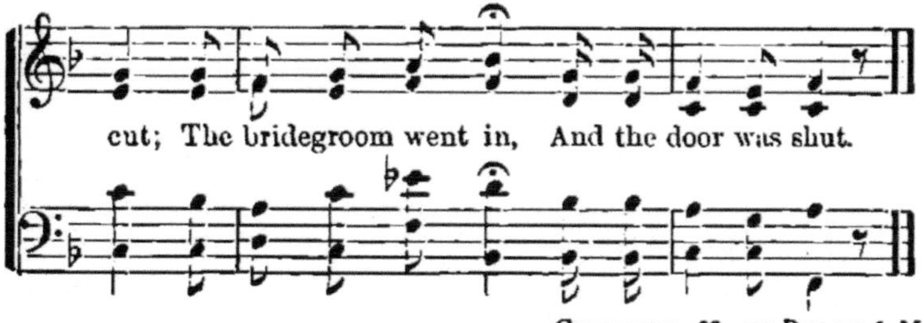
cut; The bridegroom went in, And the door was shut.

3 These are foolish, and these are wise,
Waiting, waiting with heavy eyes;
Some are doubting, and cling to sin,
Some are trusting, and enter in.

4 You, the foolish, hear Wisdom's cry,
Days of waiting pass quickly by;
God is gracious, but know you not,
Foolish sleepers will be forgot!

MARTYN.

1 Jesus, lover of my soul,
Let me to Thy bosom fly,
While the raging billows roll,
While the tempest still is high;
Hide me, O my Saviour, hide,
Till the storm of life is past,
Safe into the haven guide;
O receive my soul at last.

2 Other refuge have I none;
Hangs my helpless soul on Thee;
Leave, O leave me not alone;
Still support and comfort me;
All my trust on Thee is stay'd;
All my help from Thee I bring;
Cover my defenceless head
With the shadow of Thy wing.

Rev. Charles Wesley.

CORONATION.

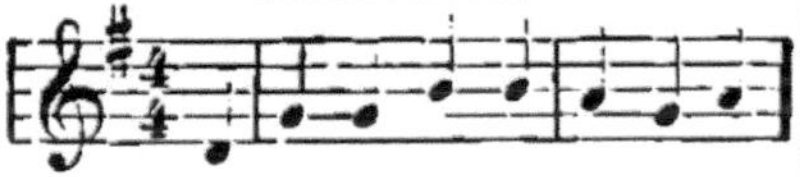

1 All hail the power of Jesus' name!
Let angels prostrate fall;
Bring forth the royal diadem,
And crown Him Lord of all.

2 Ye chosen seed of Israel's race,
Ye ransomed from the fall,
Hail Him who saves you by His grace,
And crown Him Lord of all.

3 Sinners, whose love can ne'er forget
The wormwood and the gall,
Go, spread your trophies at His feet,
And crown Him Lord of all.

4 Let every kindred, every tribe,
On this terrestrial ball,
To Him all majesty ascribe,
And crown Him Lord of all.

Rev. Edward Perronet.

TOPLADY.

1 Rock of Ages, cleft for me,
Let me hide myself in Thee;
Let the water and the blood,
From Thy wounded side which flow'd,
Be of sin the double cure—
Save from wrath and make me pure.

2 Could my tears forever flow,
Could my zeal no languour know,
These for sin could not atone;
Thou must save, and Thou alone;
In my hand no price I bring;
Simply to Thy cross I cling.

3 While I draw this fleeting breath,
When my eyes shall close in death,
When I rise to worlds unknown,
And behold Thee on Thy throne,—
Rock of Ages, cleft for me,
Let me hide myself in Thee.

Rev. A. M. Toplady.

JESUS LOVES ME.

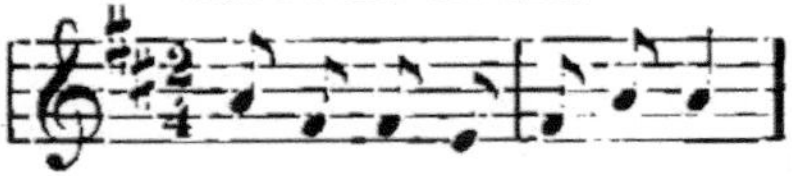

1 Jesus loves me! this I know,
For the Bible tells me so;
Little ones to Him belong,
They are weak, but He is strong.

CHO.—Yes, Jesus loves me,
Yes, Jesus loves me,
Yes, Jesus loves me,
The Bible tells me so.

2 Jesus loves me! He who died,
Heaven's gate to open wide,
He will wash away my sin,
Let His little child come in.
CHO.—Yes, Jesus loves me, &c.

3 Jesus loves me! He will stay
Close beside me all the way;
If I love Him, when I die
He will take me home on high.
CHO.—Yes, Jesus loves me, &c.

Miss Anna Warner.

OLIVET.

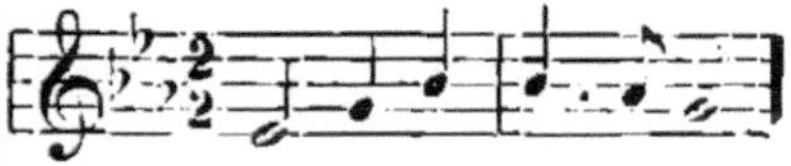

1 My faith looks up to Thee,
Thou Lamb of Calvary,
Saviour divine!
Now hear me while I pray,
Take all my guilt away,
O let me from this day
Be wholly Thine.

2 May Thy rich grace impart
Strength to my fainting heart,
My zeal inspire;
As Thou hast died for me,
O may my love to Thee
Pure, warm, and changeless be,
A living fire.

Ray Palmer, D. D.

68 Waiting for the Crown.

Rev. Wm. O. Cushing. *I will give thee a crown of life.*—Rev. 2: 10. James A. Smith.

1. The Christian, faint and wea - ry, Still journeys bravely on; His brow with home-light beaming, He is
2. The war will soon be o - ver, The wea - ry strife be done; O Christian, do not fal - ter, For the
3. O Christian, faint no long-er; Gird up thy loins with prayer; Since Je - sus bore thy sorrows, He will
Refrain.
waiting for the crown.
victory's al - most won.
car - ry all thy care.
Waiting for the crown, Christian, Waiting for the crown; Trusting in the
name of Jesus, Keep on praying, keep on praying, keep on praying,
Waiting for the crown: Waiting for the crown.

They have Triumphed at Last.

Rev. W. O. Cushing. *He that overcometh shall inherit all things.*—Rev. 3: 5. R. Lowry.

1. They have triumphed at last, They are safe on the shore, For the warfare is end-ed, And they hunger no more.
2. 'Tis a song of the blest, Rolling o'er the bright plain; 'Tis the song of Redemption, Of the Lamb that was slain.
3. They are safe home at last, From the wide rolling sea; 'Tis the song of the ransomed, 'Tis the shout of the free.
Chorus.
Hal - le - lu-jah! A-men! We will praise Him again; They have triumphed. O the glo - ry! Hal - le - lu-jah! A -
men! They have triumphed in Jesus, And the warfare is o'er; O glory, hallelujah! We'll crown Him once more.

70

Follow Close.

Fanny J. Crosby. *I will follow thee.* —Luke 9: 57. W. H. Doane.

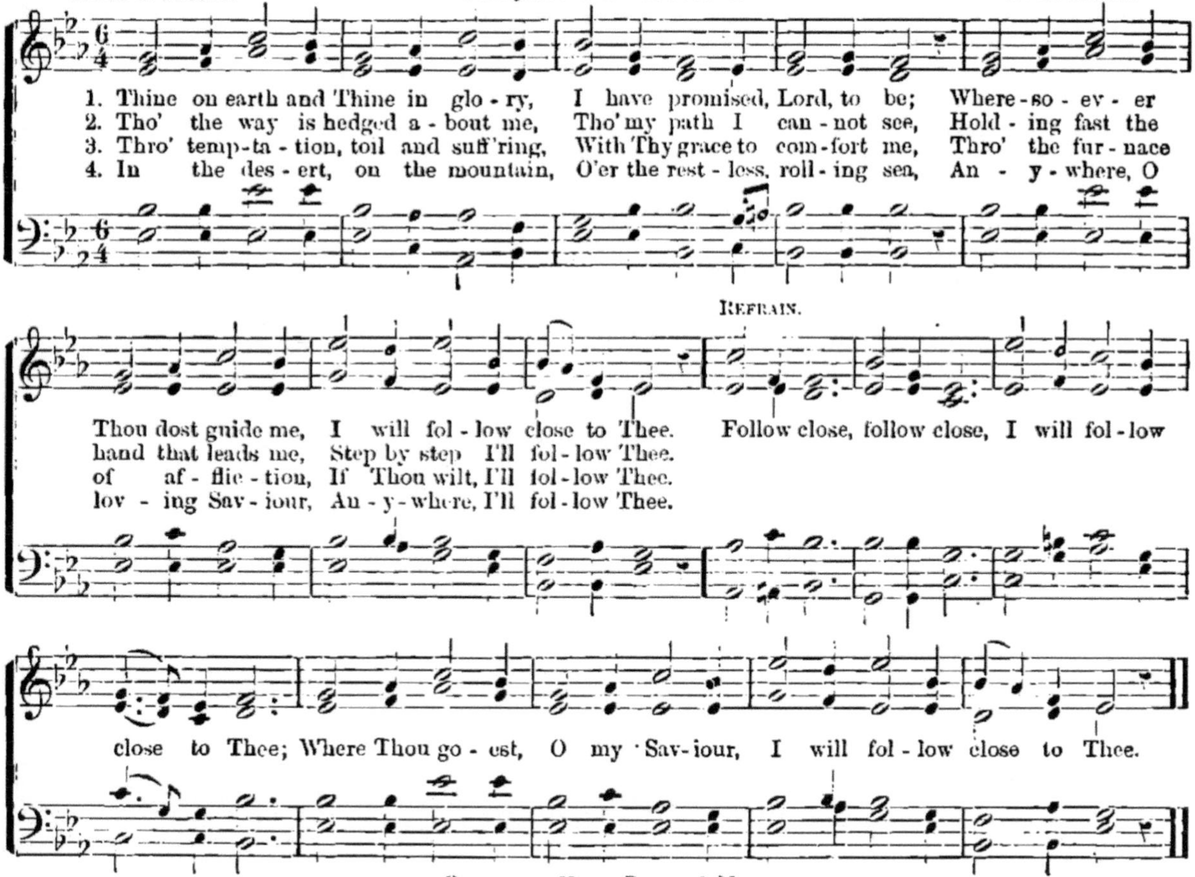
1. Thine on earth and Thine in glo - ry, I have promised, Lord, to be; Where-so - ev - er Thou dost guide me, I will fol - low close to Thee.
2. Tho' the way is hedged a - bout me, Tho' my path I can - not see, Hold - ing fast the hand that leads me, Step by step I'll fol - low Thee.
3. Thro' temp-ta - tion, toil and suff'ring, With Thy grace to com - fort me, Thro' the fur - nace of af - flic - tion, If Thou wilt, I'll fol - low Thee.
4. In the des - ert, on the mountain, O'er the rest - less, roll - ing sea, An - y - where, O lov - ing Sav - iour, An - y - where, I'll fol - low Thee.
Refrain.
Follow close, follow close, I will fol - low close to Thee; Where Thou go - est, O my Sav - iour, I will fol - low close to Thee.

A Few more Years shall Roll.

HORATIUS BONAR, D. D. *That great day of God Almighty.*—REV. 16: 14. EDWARD ROBERTS.

1. A few more years shall roll, A few more seasons come, And we shall be with those that rest, A -
2. A few more struggles here, A few more partings o'er, A few more toils, a few more tears, And
3. 'Tis but a lit - tle while, And He shall come a - gain, Who died that we might live, who lives That
CHORUS.
sleep within the tomb. Then, O my Lord, prepare My soul for that great day; O wash me in Thy
we shall weep no more.
we with Him may reign.
precious blood, And take my sins a - way; O wash me in Thy precious blood, And wash my sins a-way.

72 We've been Singing.

Mrs. Ellen Douglass. *I will sing of mercy.*—Ps. 101: 1. W. H. Doane.

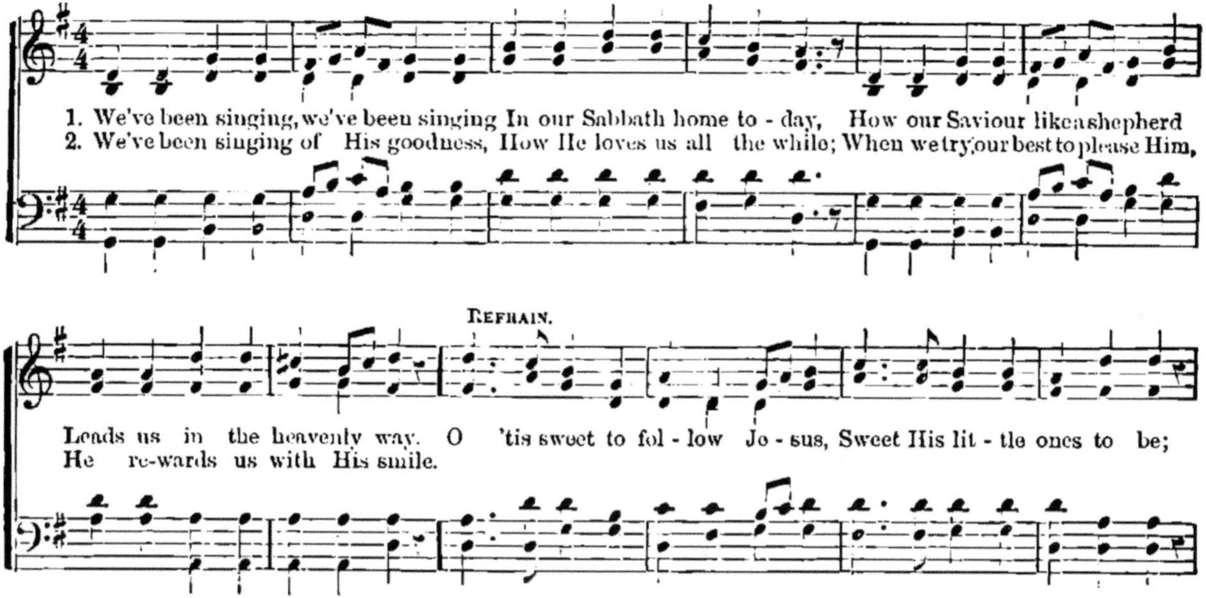
1. We've been singing, we've been singing In our Sabbath home to - day, How our Saviour like a shepherd
2. We've been singing of His goodness, How He loves us all the while; When we try, our best to please Him,
Leads us in the heavenly way.
He re-wards us with His smile.
Refrain.
O 'tis sweet to fol - low Je - sus, Sweet His lit - tle ones to be;

He is call-ing us so gent-ly, Children, give your hearts to me.

3 We've been singing of His mercy
That will save us, every one,
If we come to God the Father
Thro' our Saviour, Christ the Son.

4 Now our happy song is over,
Once again we meet to part;
But we pray that God will bless us,
And abide in every heart.

Make Haste and Come Down.

Mrs. Mary A. W. Cooke. *To-day I must abide at thy house.*—Luke 19: 5. R. Lowry.

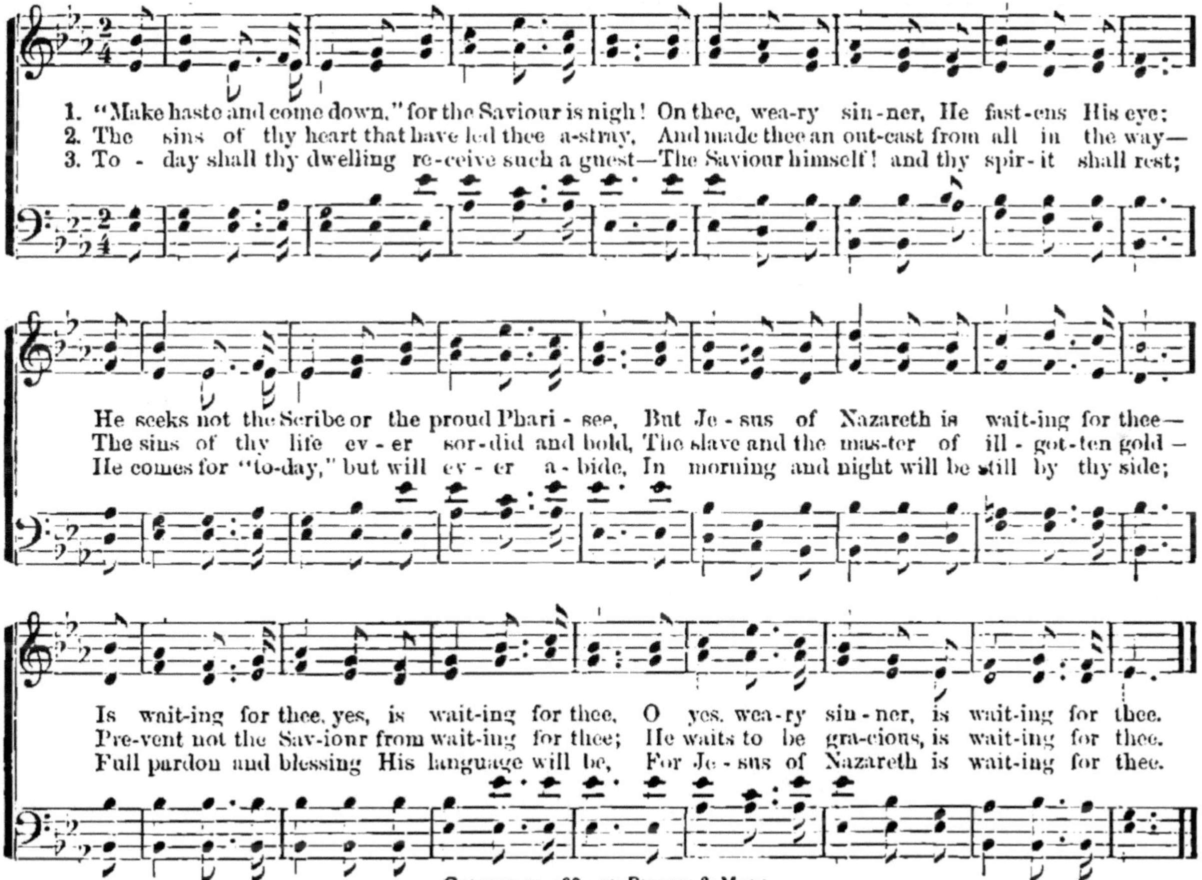
1. "Make haste and come down," for the Saviour is nigh! On thee, wea-ry sin-ner, He fast-ens His eye;
2. The sins of thy heart that have led thee a-stray, And made thee an out-cast from all in the way—
3. To-day shall thy dwelling re-ceive such a guest—The Saviour himself! and thy spir-it shall rest;
He seeks not the Scribe or the proud Phari-see, But Je-sus of Nazareth is wait-ing for thee—
The sins of thy life ev-er sor-did and bold, The slave and the mas-ter of ill-got-ten gold—
He comes for "to-day," but will ev-er a-bide, In morning and night will be still by thy side;
Is wait-ing for thee, yes, is wait-ing for thee, O yes, wea-ry sin-ner, is wait-ing for thee.
Pre-vent not the Sav-iour from wait-ing for thee; He waits to be gra-cious, is wait-ing for thee.
Full pardon and blessing His language will be, For Je-sus of Nazareth is wait-ing for thee.

74 Soldiers of Christ are We.

*** Boston, 1854. *They shall march with an army.*—Jer. 46: 22. W. H. Doane.

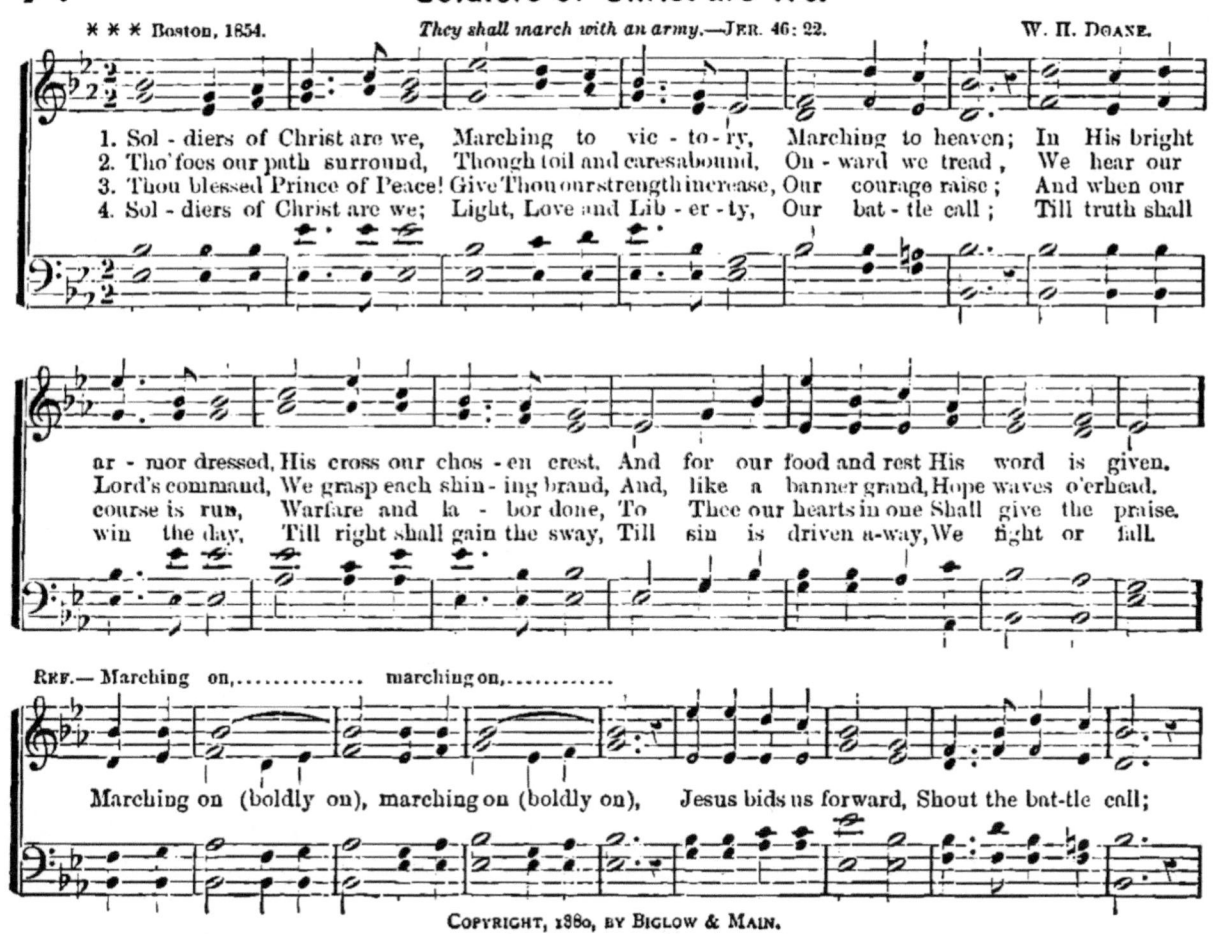

1. Sol - diers of Christ are we, Marching to vic - to - ry, Marching to heaven; In His bright ar - mor dressed, His cross our chos - en crest, And for our food and rest His word is given.
2. Tho' foes our path surround, Though toil and cares abound, On - ward we tread, We hear our Lord's command, We grasp each shin - ing brand, And, like a banner grand, Hope waves o'erhead.
3. Thou blessed Prince of Peace! Give Thou our strength increase, Our courage raise; And when our course is run, Warfare and la - bor done, To Thee our hearts in one Shall give the praise.
4. Sol - diers of Christ are we; Light, Love and Lib - er - ty, Our bat - tle call; Till truth shall win the day, Till right shall gain the sway, Till sin is driven a-way, We fight or fall.

Ref.— Marching on,............ marching on,............

Marching on (boldly on), marching on (boldly on), Jesus bids us forward, Shout the bat-tle call;

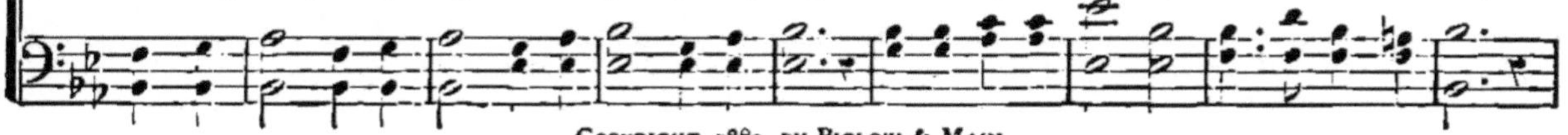

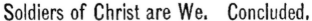

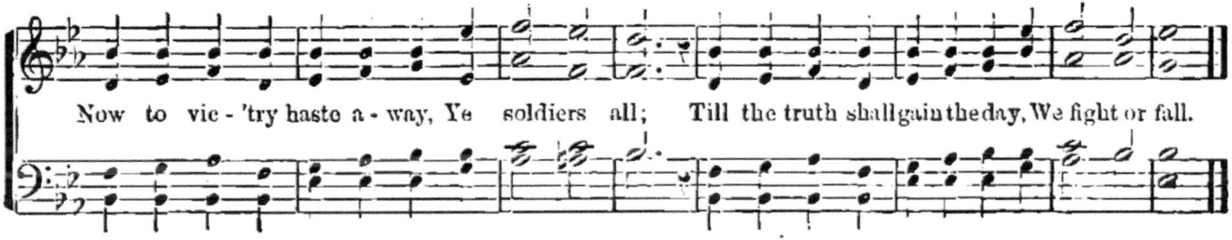
Now to vic - 'try haste a - way, Ye soldiers all; Till the truth shall gain the day, We fight or fall.

Dear Saviour, take us Home.

MRS. LAURA ELMER. *Having a desire to depart.*—PHIL. 1: 23. R. LOWRY.

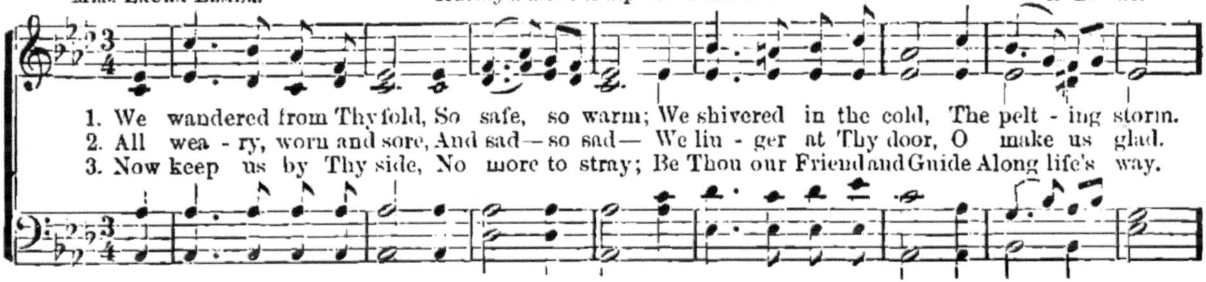
1. We wandered from Thy fold, So safe, so warm; We shivered in the cold, The pelt - ing storm.
2. All wea - ry, worn and sore, And sad — so sad — We lin - ger at Thy door, O make us glad.
3. Now keep us by Thy side, No more to stray; Be Thou our Friend and Guide Along life's way.

CHORUS.

O take us, take us home.
Dear Saviour, take us home;
Too long, too long we've wandered,
Dear Saviour, take us home.

76 Will you Stand?

FANNY J. CROSBY. *Stand fast by the faith.*—1 COR. 16: 13. W. H. DOANE.

1. O re - member there's a work to be done; Are you read - y for the race? will you
2. Are you read-y for the cross? can you say You are read - y for the toils of the
3. Are you giv - ing up the ways of the world? Are you lay - ing ev - ery weight now a -
to be done;
run? Are you striving for the crown to be won, With a per - se - vering faith and love?
way? Are you trusting in the Lord? do you pray With a per - se - vering faith and love?
side? Are you clinging to the arm of your guide With a per - se - vering faith and love?
will you run?
to be won,
REFRAIN.
Will you stand for truth, and bat - tle for the right? Will you firm - ly stand and keep your armor bright?

Then re - joice with vig-or new, There's a crown of life for you, In the mansion of glo - ry a - bove.

I am Resting in Hope.

GRACE J. FRANCES. *My flesh shall rest in hope.*—ACTS 2: 26. HUBERT P. MAIN.

1. I am resting in hope, I am looking a way To the close of the night And the dawn of the day;
2. I am resting in hope Of the friends I shall see. For I know on the shore They are watching for me;
3. I am resting in hope Of a crown and a palm, Of a robe that is wash'd In the blood of the Lamb;
When my soul from its casket Of earth shall remove, Where the Lord has a mansion for me a - bove.
By the riv - er of crystal They'll greet me in love, Where the Lord has a mansion for me a - bove.
O the joy that a-waits me, The rapture and love, Where the Lord has a mansion for me a - bove.

Long Ago.

The Son of man is come to seek and to save that which was lost.—LUKE 19: 10.

JOSEPHINE POLLARD. R. LOWRY.

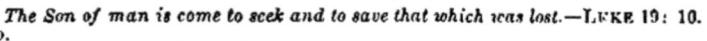

1. Long a - go my Sav-iour sought me, Long a - go, long a - go; With His pre-cious life He bought me, Long a - go, long a - go.
2. Such a lov - ing Friend I need-ed, Long a - go, long a - go; Yet His of - fer was un - heed - ed, Long a - go, long a - go.
3. Fool-ish was I not to hear Him, Long a - go, long a - go; Fool-ish not to ven-ture near Him, Long a - go, long a - go.
4. By His death was I for - giv - en, Long a - go, long a - go; And for me He purchased heav - en, Long a - go, long a - go.
CHORUS.
Love and grat - i - tude I owe Un - to Je - sus, for He bought me, Un - to Je - sus, for He sought me, Long a - go, long a - go.

HAMBURG.

1 Just as I am, without one plea.
But that Thy blood was shed for me,
And that Thou bidst me come to Thee,
O Lamb of God! I come, I come.

2 Just as I am, and waiting not
To rid my soul of one dark blot,
To Thee, whose blood can cleanse each spot,
O Lamb of God! I come, I come.

3 Just as I am, though tossed about
With many a conflict, many a doubt,
With fears within, and foes without,
O Lamb of God, I come, I come.

4 Just as I am, poor, wretched, blind,
Sight, riches, healing of the mind,
Yea, all I need, in Thee to find,
O Lamb of God! I come, I come.

Charlotte Elliott.

Just as thou art.

1 Just as thou art, without one trace
Of love, or joy, or inward grace,
Or meetness for that heavenly place,
O guilty sinner, come, O come.

2 Thy sins I bore on Calvary's tree;
The stripes thy due, were laid on me,
That peace and pardon might be free,
O wretched sinner, come, O come.

3 Come, leave thy burden at the cross;
Count all thy gains but empty dross;
My grace repays all earthly loss—
O needy sinner, come, O come.

4 "The Spirit and the Bride say, Come;"
Rejoicing saints re-echo, Come;
Who faints, who thirsts, who will, may come;
Thy Saviour bids thee come, O come.

Rev. R. S. Cook.

THE SOLID ROCK.

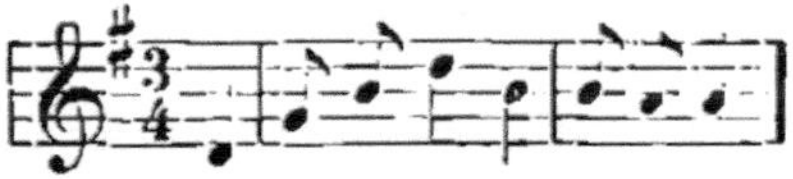

1 My hope is built on nothing less
Than Jesus' blood and righteousness;
I dare not trust the sweetest frame,
But wholly lean on Jesus' name:
On Christ, the solid rock, I stand;
All other ground is sinking sand.

2 When darkness seems to veil His face,
I rest on His unchanging grace;
In every high and stormy gale,
My anchor holds within the vail:
On Christ, the solid rock, I stand;
All other ground is sinking sand.

3 His oath, His covenant, and blood,
Support me in the whelming flood;
When all around my soul gives way,
He then is all my hope and stay:
On Christ, the solid rock, I stand,
All other ground is sinking sand.

Rev. Edward Mote.

SWEET HOUR OF PRAYER.

1 Sweet hour of prayer! sweet hour of prayer!
That calls me from a world of care,
And bids me at my Father's throne
Make all my wants and wishes known;
In seasons of distress and grief,
My soul has often found relief,
And oft escaped the tempter's snare,
By thy return, sweet hour of prayer.

2 Sweet hour of prayer! sweet hour of prayer!
Thy wings shall my petition bear
To Him whose truth and faithfulness
Engage the waiting soul to bless;
And since He bids me seek His face,
Believe His word and trust His grace,
I'll cast on Him my every care,
And wait for thee, sweet hour of prayer.

Rev. W. W. Walford.

DRAW ME NEARER.

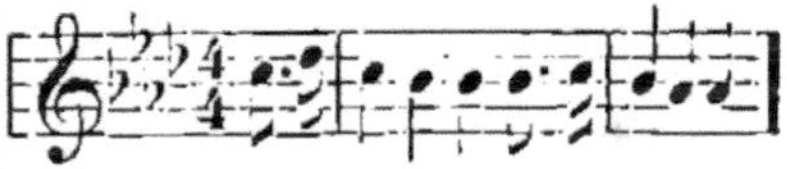

1 I am Thine, O Lord, I have heard Thy voice,
And it told Thy love to me;
But I long to rise in the arms of faith,
And be closer drawn to Thee.

REF.—
Draw me nearer, nearer, blessed Lord,
To the cross where Thou hast died;
Draw me nearer, nearer, nearer, blessed Lord,
To Thy precious, bleeding side.

2 There are depths of love that I cannot know
Till I cross the narrow sea;
There are heights of joy that I may not reach
Till I rest in peace with Thee.

Fanny J. Crosby.

Over and Over Again.

FANNY J. CROSBY. *We love him, because he first loved us.*—JOHN 4: 19. W. H. DOANE.

1. O - ver and o - ver a - gain The sto - ry of Je - sus I'll tell; It fills me with rapture and
2. O - ver and o - ver a - gain, When tempted and burdened with grief, A promise from Jesus has
3. O - ver and o - ver a - gain His goodness and mer - cy I prove; He makes me to sit at His
ho - ly delight, No music can charm me so well; Dear to my soul and treasur'd each word, Nothing such
come to my heart And brought me a happy re - lief; Kind - ly His hand has prosper'd my way, Pleasant thus
banquet on earth, And covers me o - ver with love; This be my boast wherev - er I go, This be my
joy and comfort can give; O - ver a - gain, yes, o - ver a - gain, I'll tell it as long as I live.
far life's journey has been; Blessings I share in answer to prayer, Yes, o - ver and o - ver a - gain.
work in pleasure or pain, Telling of Him who comforts my soul And cheers me again and a - gain.

Hide Thou Me.

FANNY J. CROSBY. *Thou art my hiding place.—Ps. 32: 7.* R. LOWRY.

1. In Thy cleft, O Rock of A - ges, Hide Thou me; When the fit - ful tem - pest
2. From the snare of sin - ful pleasure, Hide Thou me; Thou, my soul's e - ter - nal
3. In the lone - ly night of sor - row, Hide Thou me; Till in glo - ry dawns the
rag - es, Hide Thou me; Where no mor - tal arm can sev - er From my
treas - ure, Hide Thou me; When the world its power is wield - ing, And my
mor - row, Hide Thou me; In the sight of Jor - dan's bil - low, Let Thy
heart Thy love for - ev - er, Hide me, O Thou Rock of A - ges, Safe in Thee.
heart is al - most yield - ing. Hide me, O Thou Rock of A - ges, Safe in Thee.
bo - som be my pil - low; Hide me, O Thou Rock of A - ges, Safe in Thee.

82 Scatter the Seed.

Ella Dale. *Blessed are ye that sow.*—Isa. 32: 20. W. H. Doane.

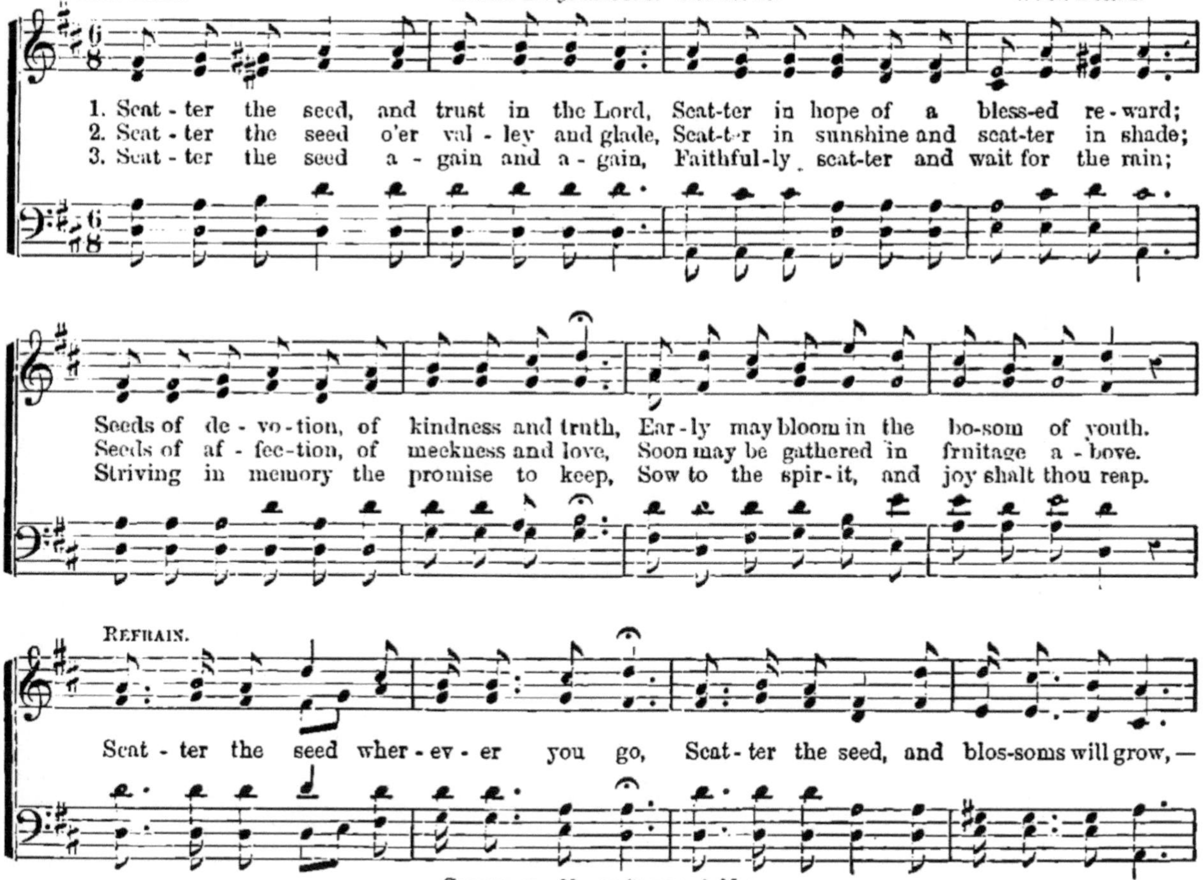
1. Scat - ter the seed, and trust in the Lord, Scat-ter in hope of a bless-ed re - ward;
2. Scat - ter the seed o'er val - ley and glade, Scat-ter in sunshine and scat-ter in shade;
3. Scat - ter the seed a - gain and a - gain, Faithful-ly scat-ter and wait for the rain;
Seeds of de - vo - tion, of kindness and truth, Ear - ly may bloom in the bo-som of youth.
Seeds of af - fec - tion, of meekness and love, Soon may be gathered in fruitage a - bove.
Striving in memory the promise to keep, Sow to the spir - it, and joy shalt thou reap.
Refrain.
Scat - ter the seed wher - ev - er you go, Scat - ter the seed, and blos-soms will grow,—

Blos-soms that soon to fruit will ex-pand; Scat-ter the seed with a boun-ti-ful hand.

Sweet Hallelujahs.

REV. EDWIN PAXTON HOOD. *Let them praise the name of the Lord.*—Ps. 148: 5. WM. F. SHERWIN.

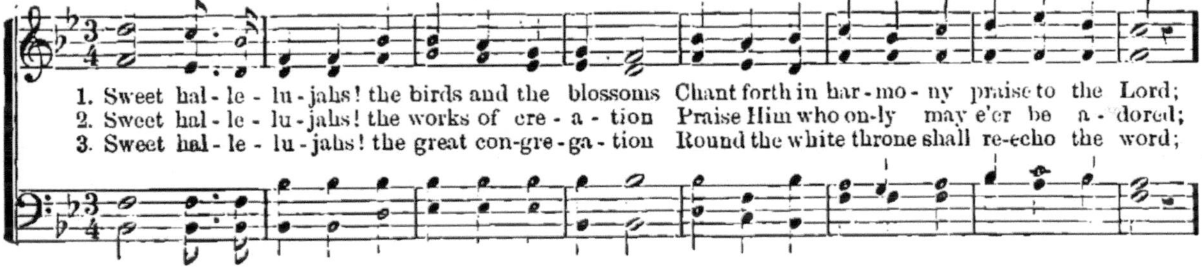
1. Sweet hal-le-lu-jahs! the birds and the blossoms Chant forth in har-mo-ny praise to the Lord;
2. Sweet hal-le-lu-jahs! the works of cre-a-tion Praise Him who on-ly may e'er be a-dored;
3. Sweet hal-le-lu-jahs! the great con-gre-ga-tion Round the white throne shall re-echo the word;

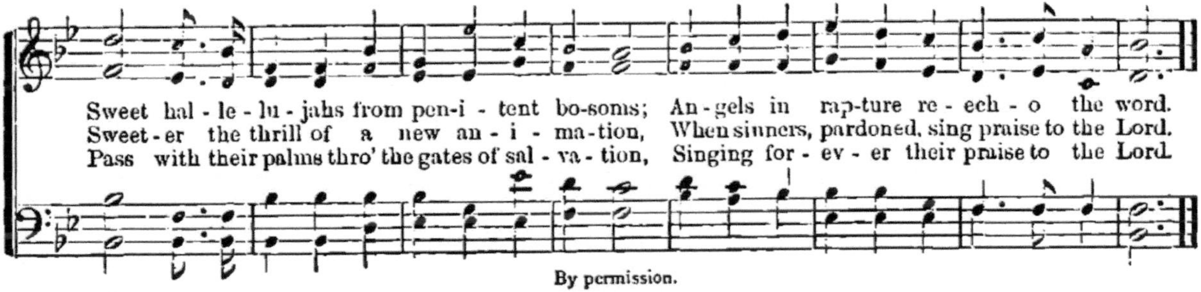
Sweet hal-le-lu-jahs from pen-i-tent bo-soms; An-gels in rap-ture re-ech-o the word.
Sweet-er the thrill of a new an-i-ma-tion, When sinners, pardoned, sing praise to the Lord.
Pass with their palms thro' the gates of sal-va-tion, Singing for-ev-er their praise to the Lord.

By permission.

84 When Jesus Comes.

REV. W. O. CUSHING. *Shall he appear the second time.*—HEB. 9: 28. R. LOWRY.

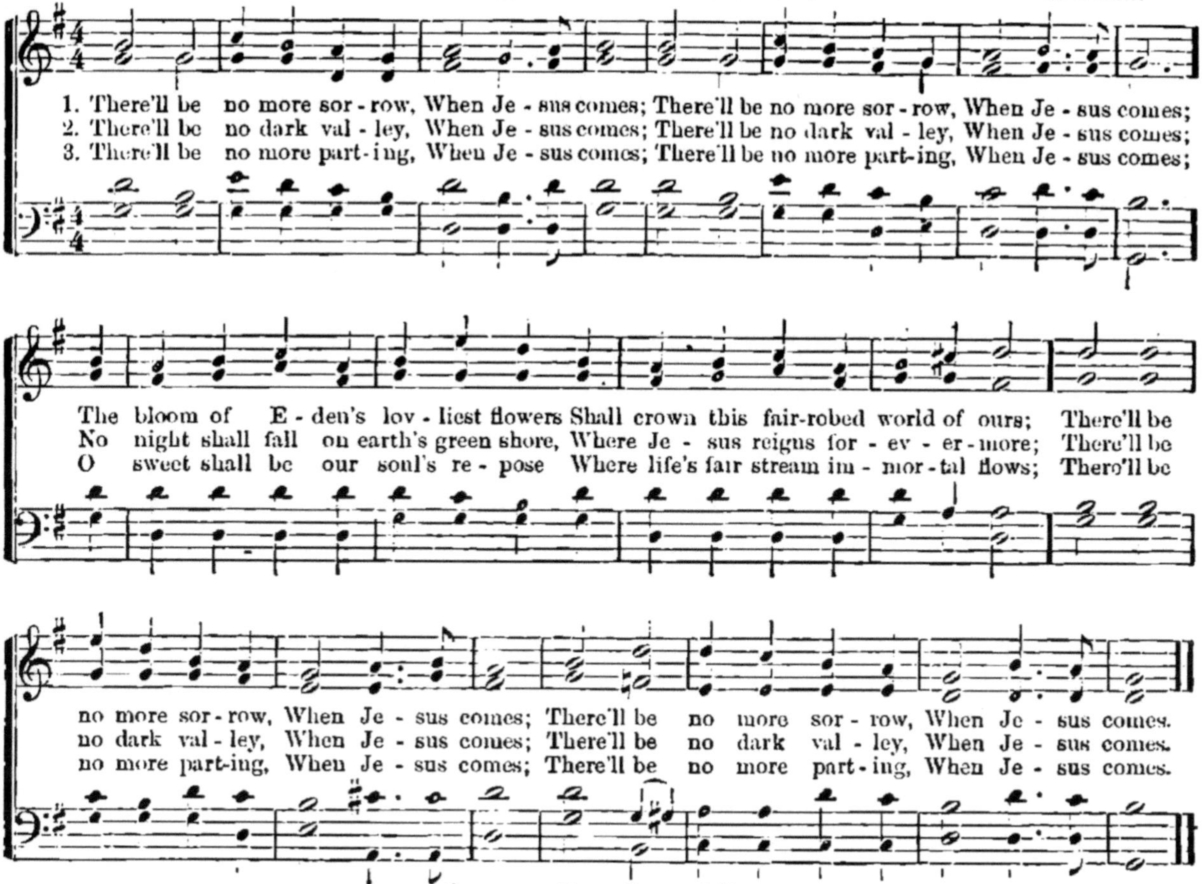
1. There'll be no more sor - row, When Je - sus comes; There'll be no more sor - row, When Je - sus comes;
2. There'll be no dark val - ley, When Je - sus comes; There'll be no dark val - ley, When Je - sus comes;
3. There'll be no more part - ing, When Je - sus comes; There'll be no more part - ing, When Je - sus comes;
The bloom of E - den's lov - liest flowers Shall crown this fair-robed world of ours; There'll be
No night shall fall on earth's green shore, Where Je - sus reigns for - ev - er - more; There'll be
O sweet shall be our soul's re - pose Where life's fair stream im - mor - tal flows; There'll be
no more sor - row, When Je - sus comes; There'll be no more sor - row, When Je - sus comes.
no dark val - ley, When Je - sus comes; There'll be no dark val - ley, When Je - sus comes.
no more part-ing, When Je - sus comes; There'll be no more part - ing, When Je - sus comes.

MRS. ELLEN M. H. GATES. *I have set watchmen upon thy walls.*—ISA. 62: 6. W. H. DOANE.

DUET.
1. Tell us, O ye watchers, Can ye see a sign Of the wondrous glo - ries, Of the com-ing time?
2. Tell us, O ye watchers, Can ye, where ye stand, See the mists roll up - ward From the sea and land?
3. Not in vain, ye watchers, Thro' the cold and damps, With a tireless pa-tience Do ye trim your lamps;
4. Patient, O ye watchers; Do not count the hours That ye keep a look-out From the lone-ly towers;
On the mountains standing, Looking far and near, Can ye see the gleam-ing Of the morning star?
Can ye hear the mu - sic, Faint and far away, That will break a-round us In the lat-ter day?
Oft the weary stran - ger, In the dreary night, Smiles with sudden pleasure When he sees the light.
Sweetest words of blessing Will that servant hear, Whom the Lord finds waking When He shall appear.
CHORUS.
O ye ever faithful watchers, Tho' the night be long and dark, Slumber not, slumber not, Soon the morn will break.

By permission.

86 Work, Sing, and Hope.

Edward A. Barnes. *Do all to the glory of God.*—1 Cor. 10: 31. R. Lowry.

1. To work for Je - sus and His cause,—This is the work for me; That they who sit in
2. To sing of Je - sus and His love,—This is the song for me; The bless-ed ti - dings
3. To hope in Je - sus and His cross,—This is the hope for me; 'Tis found-ed on His
dark-ness now, The Gos - pel light may see.
fill my soul In heaven-ly mel - o - dy.
ho - ly word, And sweet be - yond de - gree.
Chorus.
Work-ing for Je - sus, bless-ed work,—
Sing - ing of Je - sus, bless-ed song,—
Hop - ing in Je - sus, bless-ed hope,—
Sweet will it ev - er be; Work-ing for Je - sus, bless-ed work,—This is the work for me.
Sweet will it ev - er be; Sing - ing of Je - sus, bless-ed song,—This is the song for me.
Sweet will it ev - er be; Hop - ing in Je - sus, bless-ed hope,—This is the hope for me.

Traveling Homeward.

W. H. D. *Gathering together unto him.*—2 Thess. 2: 1. W. H. Doane.

1. Trav'ling homeward, trav'ling homeward, In the Saviour we are strong; He di - rects us on our jour - ney, Fills our hearts with love and song.
2. Trav'ling homeward, trav'ling homeward, Drawing near-er ev - ery day, To a mansion bright with glo - ry That shall never fade a - way.
3. Trav'ling homeward, trav'ling homeward, Tho' our hearts are oft oppressed; Je - sus kindly bears our burdens, Gives the weary spir - it rest.
4. Trav'ling homeward, trav'ling homeward, Our Redeemer's love to share; We shall see Him in His kingdom, We shall dwell for-ev - er there.
Refrain.
Hal - le - lu - jah! Hal - le - lu - jah! Hal - le - lu - jah glad - ly sing; We are go - ing, we are go - ing To the pal - ace of a King.
(sing)
(sing)
(sing)

88 Take Me as I Am.

E. H. H. *Take with you words, and turn to the Lord.*—Hosea 14 : 2. Rev. Samuel Alman.

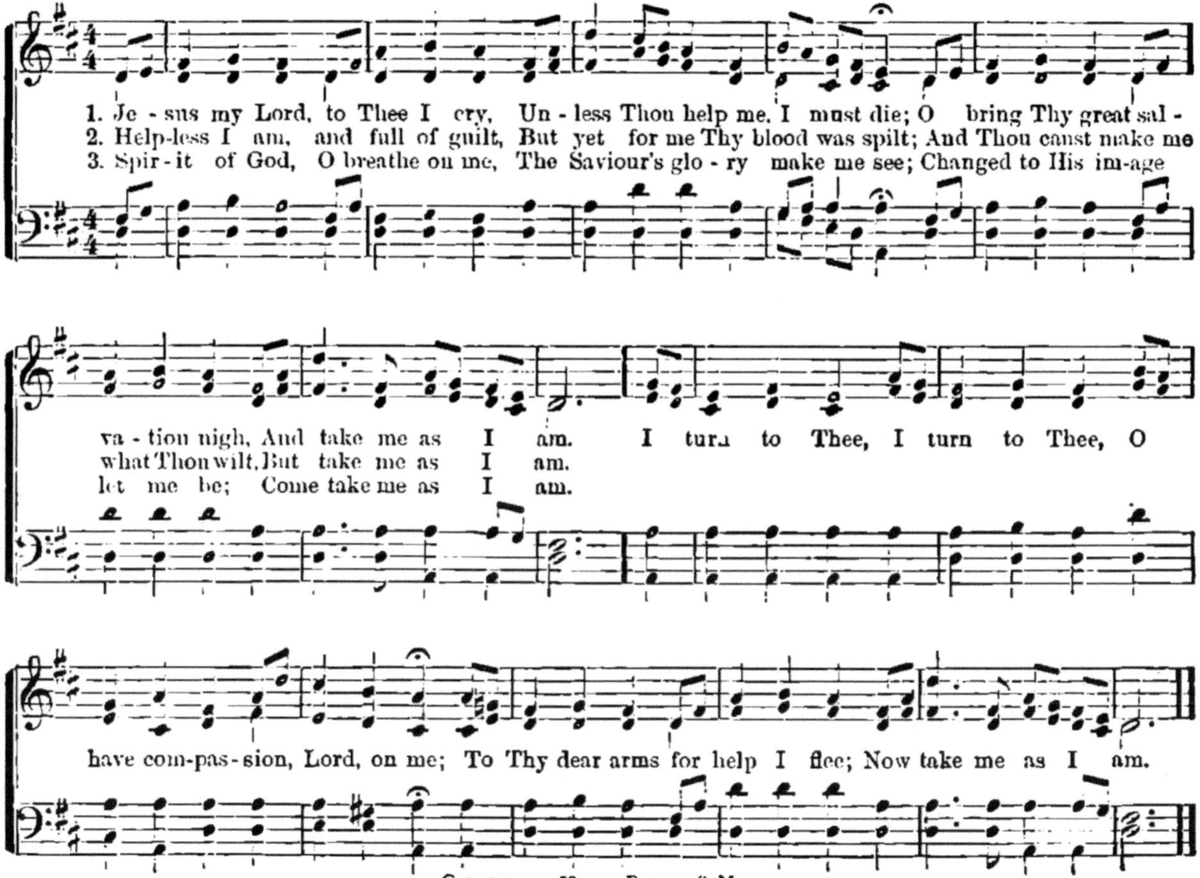
1. Je - sus my Lord, to Thee I cry, Un - less Thou help me, I must die; O bring Thy great sal - va - tion nigh, And take me as I am.
2. Help-less I am, and full of guilt, But yet for me Thy blood was spilt; And Thou canst make me what Thou wilt, But take me as I am.
3. Spir - it of God, O breathe on me, The Saviour's glo - ry make me see; Changed to His im-age let me be; Come take me as I am.
I turn to Thee, I turn to Thee, O have com-pas - sion, Lord, on me; To Thy dear arms for help I flee; Now take me as I am.

No Room for Jesus.

Rev. W. F. Crafts. *There was no room for them in the inn.*—Luke 2: 7. R. Lowry.

1. No room for Je - sus in the inn! The manger was His bed; The King of glory finds on earth No
2. Up - on the cross the Saviour dies That we may be for-given, And af - ter all our life on earth, May
place to lay His head; 'Twas love for us that brought Him, A-mid the woes of men, To share our tears and
find a place in heaven; How great the love of Je - sus, To die for oth - ers' sin! In Him I'll live my
D. S.—'Tis He who lived and
Fine. Chorus. D. S.
toils and fears, And save us from our sin. I ought to love my Saviour, 'Twas He who first loved me;
life be - low, And life e - ter - nal win.
died to save me; Lord, I will love Thee.

Coming, One and All.

Mrs. Kate Smiley.

Come, and let us return unto the Lord.—Hos. 6: 1.

W. H. Doane.

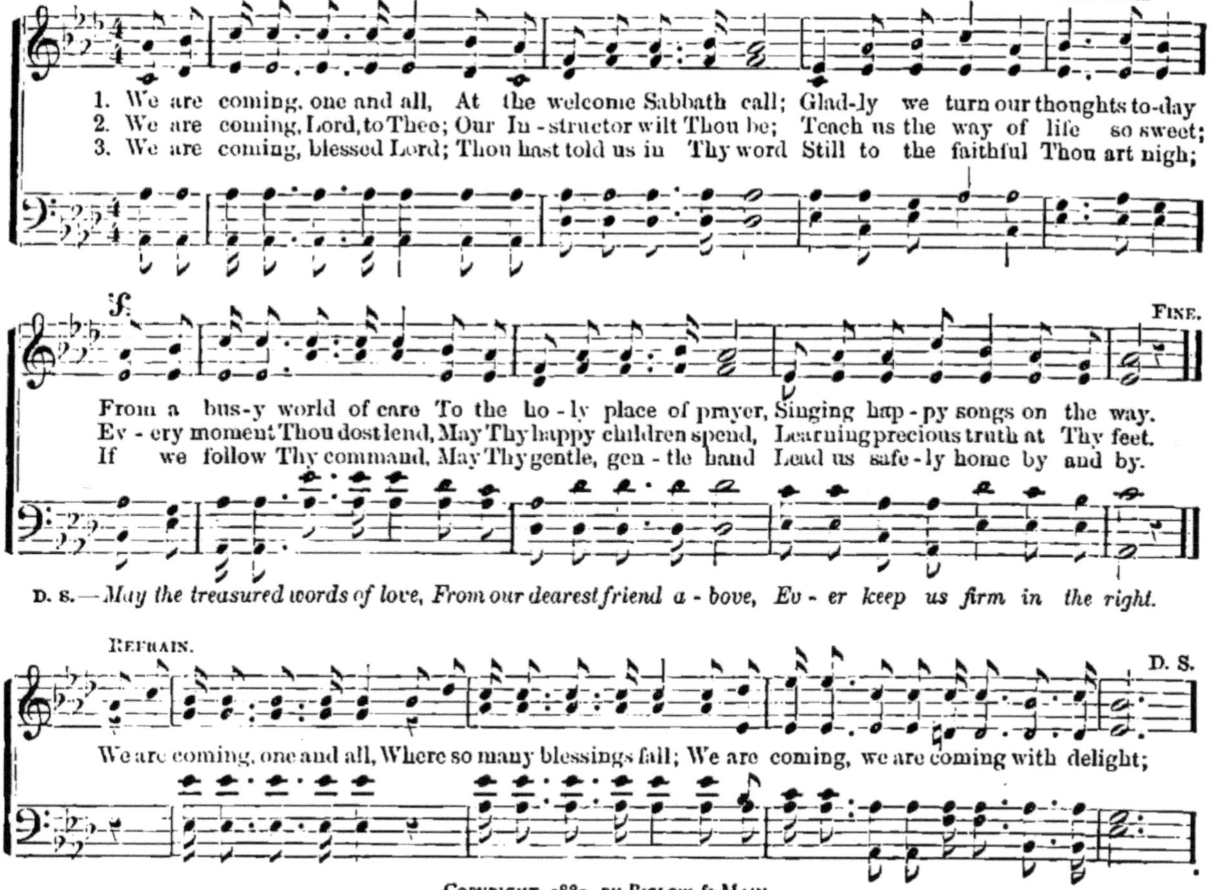
1. We are coming, one and all, At the welcome Sabbath call; Glad-ly we turn our thoughts to-day
2. We are coming, Lord, to Thee; Our In-structor wilt Thou be; Teach us the way of life so sweet;
3. We are coming, blessed Lord; Thou hast told us in Thy word Still to the faithful Thou art nigh;
From a bus-y world of care To the ho-ly place of prayer, Singing hap-py songs on the way.
Ev-ery moment Thou dost lend, May Thy happy children spend, Learning precious truth at Thy feet.
If we follow Thy command, May Thy gentle, gen-tle hand Lead us safe-ly home by and by.
Fine.
D. S.—May the treasured words of love, From our dearest friend a-bove, Ev-er keep us firm in the right.
Refrain.
We are coming, one and all, Where so many blessings fall; We are coming, we are coming with delight;
D. S.

BEAUTIFUL RIVER.

1 Shall we gather at the river,
Where bright angel feet have trod—
With its crystal tide forever
Flowing from the throne of God?
CHO.—
Yes, we'll gather at the river,
The beautiful, the beautiful river—
Gather with the saints at the river
That flows from the throne of God.

2 On the margin of the river,
Washing up its silver spray,
We will walk and worship ever,
All the happy, golden day.

3 On the bosom of the river,
Where the Saviour-King we own,
We shall meet and sorrow never,
'Neath the glory of the throne.

4 Soon we'll reach the shining river,
Soon our pilgrimage will cease;
Soon our happy hearts will quiver
With the melody of peace.
Rev. R. Lowry.

THERE IS A FOUNTAIN.

1 There is a fountain, filled with blood,
Drawn from Immanuel's veins,
And sinners plung'd beneath that flood
Lose all their guilty stains.

2 The dying thief rejoiced to see
That fountain in his day;
And there may I, though vile as he,
Wash all my sins away.

3 Dear dying Lamb, Thy precious blood
Shall never lose its power,
Till all the ransomed Church of God
Are saved to sin no more.

SAVIOUR, MORE THAN LIFE.

1 Saviour, more than life to me,
I am clinging, clinging close to Thee;
Let Thy precious blood applied
Keep me ever, ever near Thy side.
REF.—
Every day, every hour,
Let me feel Thy cleansing power;
May Thy tender love to me
Bind me closer, closer, Lord, to Thee.

2 Let me love Thee more and more,
Till this fleeting, fleeting life is o'er;
Till my soul is lost in love,
In a brighter, brighter world above.
Fanny J. Crosby.

DYING LOVE.

1 Saviour! Thy dying love
Thou gavest me,
Nor should I aught withhold,
Dear Lord, from Thee:
In love my soul would bow,
My heart fulfil its vow,
Some offering bring Thee now,
Something for Thee.

2 O'er the blest mercy-seat,
Pleading for me,
My feeble faith looks up,
Jesus, to Thee!
Help me the cross to bear,
Thy wondrous love declare,
Some song to raise, or prayer,
Something for Thee.
S. D. Phelps, D. D.

WE PRAISE THEE.

1 We praise Thee, O God! for the Son of Thy love,
For Jesus who died, and is now gone above.
CHO.—Hallelujah! Thine the glory;
Hallelujah! Amen;
Hallelujah! Thine the glory; revive us again.

2 We praise Thee, O God! for Thy Spirit of light,
Who has shown us our Saviour, and scattered our night.

3 All glory and praise to the Lamb that was slain,
Who has borne all our sins, and has cleansed every stain.

4 Revive us again; fill each heart with Thy love;
May each soul be rekindled with fire from above.
Rev. W. P. Mackay.

92 Awake, Ye Saints.

Now is our salvation nearer than when we believed.—Rom. 13: 11.

Philip Doddridge, D. D. — R. Lowry.

1. A - wake, ye saints, and lift your eyes, And raise your voices high; A - wake, and praise the sovereign love That shows sal - va - tion nigh.
2. Not ma - ny years their round shall run, Not ma - ny mornings rise, Till all its glo - ries stand re - vealed To our ad - mir - ing eyes.
3. Ye wheels of nature, speed your course, Ye mor - tal powers, de - cay; Fast as ye bring the night of death, Ye bring e - ter - nal day.
Chorus.
We are now looking o'er, At the bright, sunny shore; We are waiting till the Master calls us To rest for - ev - er - more.
We are now looking o'er,
At the bright, sunny shore;

Give me Jesus.

FANNY J. CROSBY. *The love of Christ constraineth us.*—2 COR. 5: 14. JOHN R. SWENEY.

1. Take the world, but give me Je - sus, All its joys are but a name; But His love a - bid - eth
2. Take the world, but give me Je - sus, Sweetest comfort of my soul; With my Sav - iour watching
3. Take the world, but give me Je - sus, Let me see His constant smile; Then throughout my pilgrim
4. Take the world, but give me Je - sus; In His cross my trust shall be, Till, with clearer, brighter
ev - er, Thro' e - ter - nal years the same.
o'er me, I can sing tho' bil - lows roll.
jour - ney, Light will cheer me all the while.
vis - ion, Face to face my Lord I see.
CHORUS.
O the height and depth of mer - cy! O the
length and breadth of love! O the full - ness of re - demption, Pledge of end - less life a - bove!

By permission.

94

We have Found the Messiah.

MRS. KATE S. BURR. *And he brought him to Jesus.*—JOHN 1 : 42. R. LOWRY.

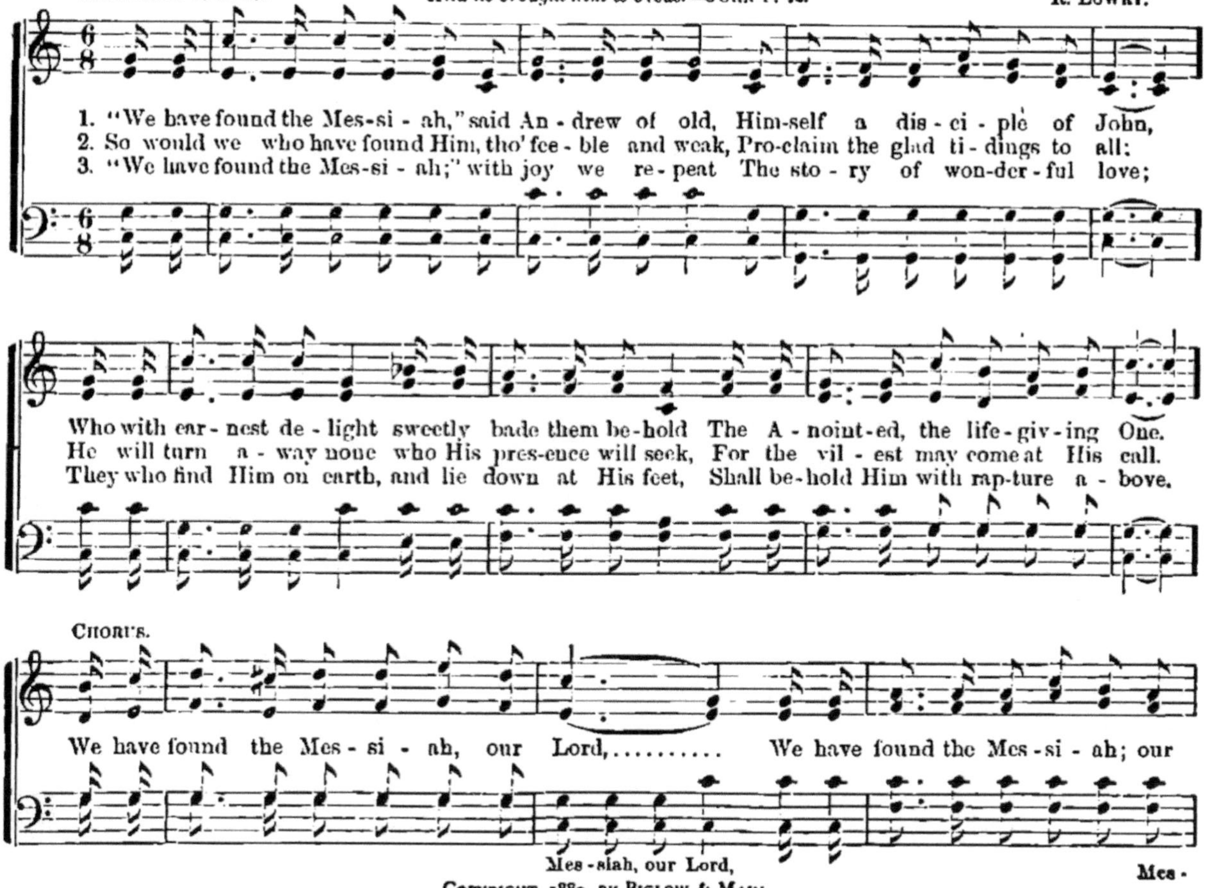
1. "We have found the Mes-si - ah," said An - drew of old, Him-self a dis - ci - ple of John,
2. So would we who have found Him, tho' fee - ble and weak, Pro-claim the glad ti - dings to all:
3. "We have found the Mes-si - ah;" with joy we re - peat The sto - ry of won-der - ful love;
Who with ear - nest de - light sweetly bade them be-hold The A - noint-ed, the life-giv-ing One.
He will turn a - way none who His pres-ence will seek, For the vil - est may come at His call.
They who find Him on earth, and lie down at His feet, Shall be-hold Him with rap-ture a - bove.
CHORUS.
We have found the Mes - si - ah, our Lord, ... We have found the Mes - si - ah; our
Mes - siah, our Lord,
Mes -

Lord;...... O come and be-hold Him, the life-giv-ing Word; Be-hold the Messi-ah, our Lord.
si-ah our Lord;

Praise ye the Father.

MRS. ELIZABETH CHARLES. *Thou art my praise.*—JER. 17: 14. FRIEDRICH F. FLEMMING, M.D.

1. Praise ye the Fa-ther for His lov-ing kind-ness, Ten-der-ly cares He for His err-ing
2. Praise ye the Sav-iour, great is His com-pas-sion, Gra-ciously cares He for His chos-en
3. Praise ye the Spir-it, Com-fort-er of Is-rael, Sent of the Fa-ther and the Son to
chil-dren; Praise Him, ye an-gels, praise Him in the heav-ens, Praise ye Je-ho-vah!
peo-ple; Young men and maid-ens, ye old men and chil-dren, Praise ye the Sav-iour!
bless us; Praise ye the Fa-ther, Son, and Ho-ly Spir-it, Praise ye the Triune God!

By permission.

One True Way.

Harriet McEwen Kimball. *Narrow is the way which leadeth unto life.*—Matt. 7: 14. R. Lowry.

1. There is but one true way; No oth - er choice be mine! Lord, ev - ery path must
2. Here Christ's a - pos - tles trod, His mar - tyrs won their crown; Here ev - ery saint for
3. The Lord's own bless-ed feet This nar - row path-way wore, And pangs no an - guish
4. Be - cause the way is His, And vic - to - ry is sure, And faith is more than
lead a - stray Save on - ly Thine.
love of God The world laid down.
can re - peat For us He bore.
pres - ent bliss, I can en - dure.
Refrain.
There is but one true way, There is but one true
but one true way,
but
way; And ev - ery path must lead a - stray Save on - ly Thine.
one true way,

Friend of Sinners.

REV. H. L. MOREHOUSE. *Cleanse me from my sin.*—Ps: 51: 2. W. H. DOANE.

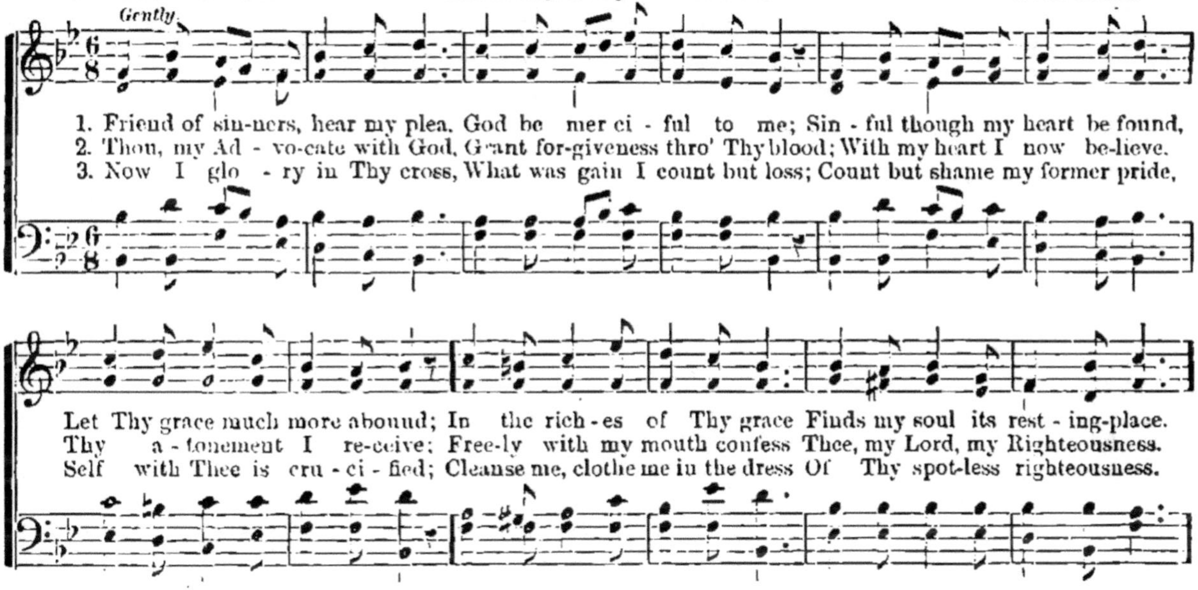
Gently.
1. Friend of sin-ners, hear my plea, God be mer-ci-ful to me; Sin-ful though my heart be found,
2. Thou, my Ad-vo-cate with God, Grant for-giveness thro' Thy blood; With my heart I now be-lieve,
3. Now I glo-ry in Thy cross, What was gain I count but loss; Count but shame my former pride,
Let Thy grace much more abound; In the rich-es of Thy grace Finds my soul its rest-ing-place.
Thy a-tonement I re-ceive; Free-ly with my mouth confess Thee, my Lord, my Righteousness.
Self with Thee is cru-ci-fied; Cleanse me, clothe me in the dress Of Thy spot-less righteousness.

REFRAIN.
Cleanse and clothe this heart of mine With Thy righteousness divine.

4.

Trusting Thee, O Christ, my King,
Shall my soul Thy praises sing;
Saved by Thee, Thou Holy One,
Not by works which I have done;
Heart and tongue confess again,
Thine the glory, Lord, Amen.

By permission.

98 Freely it Flows.

Wm. Stevenson. *—the fountain of the water of life freely.*—Rev. 21 : 6. R. Lowry.

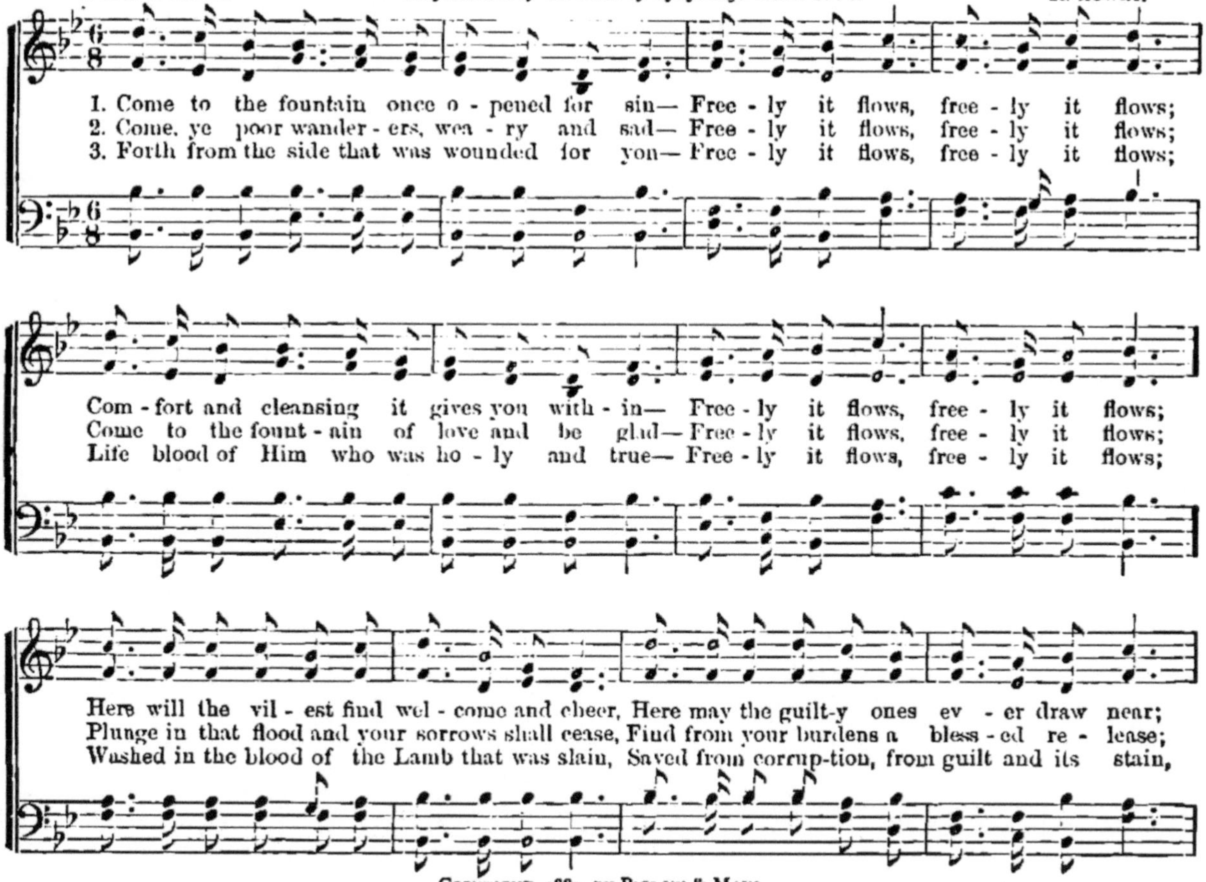
1. Come to the fountain once o - pened for sin— Free - ly it flows, free - ly it flows;
2. Come, ye poor wander - ers, wea - ry and sad— Free - ly it flows, free - ly it flows;
3. Forth from the side that was wounded for you— Free - ly it flows, free - ly it flows;
Com - fort and cleansing it gives you with - in— Free - ly it flows, free - ly it flows;
Come to the fount - ain of love and be glad— Free - ly it flows, free - ly it flows;
Life blood of Him who was ho - ly and true— Free - ly it flows, free - ly it flows;
Here will the vil - est find wel - come and cheer, Here may the guilt-y ones ev - er draw near;
Plunge in that flood and your sorrows shall cease, Find from your burdens a bless - ed re - lease;
Washed in the blood of the Lamb that was slain, Saved from corrup-tion, from guilt and its stain,

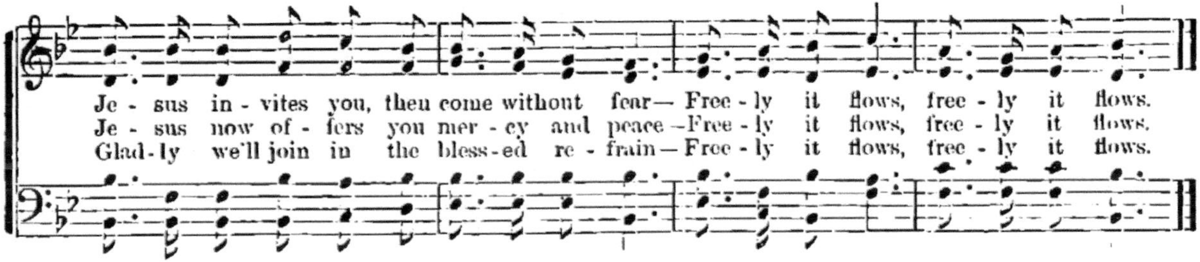
Je - sus in - vites you, then come without fear— Free - ly it flows, free - ly it flows.
Je - sus now of - fers you mer - cy and peace —Free - ly it flows, free - ly it flows.
Glad - ly we'll join in the bless - ed re - frain— Free - ly it flows, free - ly it flows.

The Name I Love.

REV. FREDERICK WHITFIELD. *I will praise thy name forever and ever.*—Ps. 145: 2. W. H. DOANE.

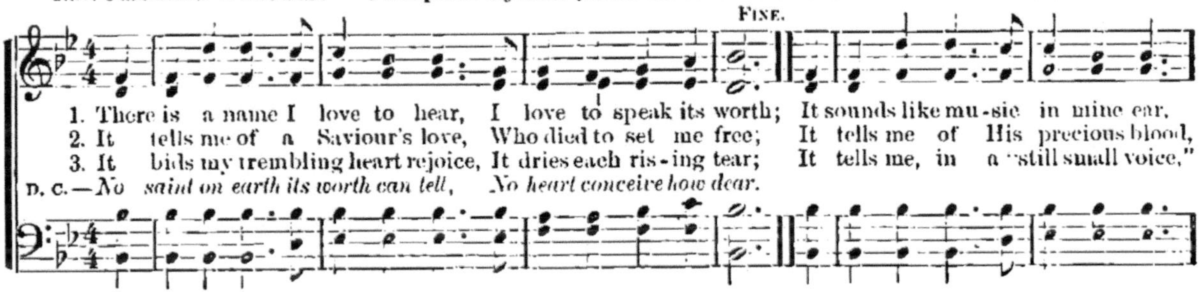
FINE.
1. There is a name I love to hear, I love to speak its worth; It sounds like mu - sic in mine ear,
2. It tells me of a Saviour's love, Who died to set me free; It tells me of His precious blood,
3. It bids my trembling heart rejoice, It dries each ris - ing tear; It tells me, in a "still small voice,"
D. C.—*No saint on earth its worth can tell, No heart conceive how dear.*

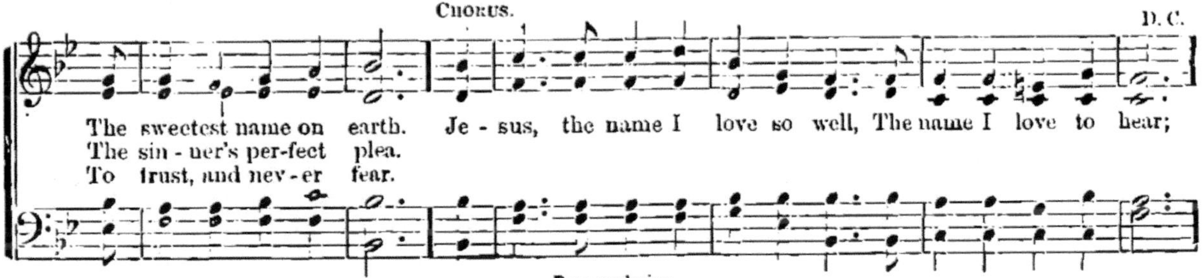
CHORUS.
D. C.
The sweetest name on earth. Je - sus, the name I love so well, The name I love to hear;
The sin - ner's per-fect plea.
To trust, and nev - er fear.

By permission.

100 Not My Own.

Wm. Stevenson. *Ye are not your own.*—1 Cor. 6: 19. R. Lowry.

1. Not my own! not my own! Purchased by a Sav-iour's blood; He hath suffered to a -
2. Not my own! not my own! Sav - iour, Thine this mor - tal frame; All its powers, for Thee a -
3. Not my own! not my own! Sav - iour, Thine this ransomed soul; In - to Thy blest im - age
4. Not my own! not my own! Bod - y, soul, resigned to Thee; Mine no more, but Thine a -
Refrain.
tone, He hath rec - on - ciled to God. Not my own! not my own! Purchased
lone, All shall glo - ri - fy Thy name.
grown, Thou pos - sess and use the whole.
lone, Thine to all e - ter - ni - ty.
by a price di - vine; Not my own! not my own! Keep me, Lord, for - ev - er Thine.

Send the Bible.

* * * *Come over into Macedonia, and help us.*—Acts. 16: 9. W. H. Doane.

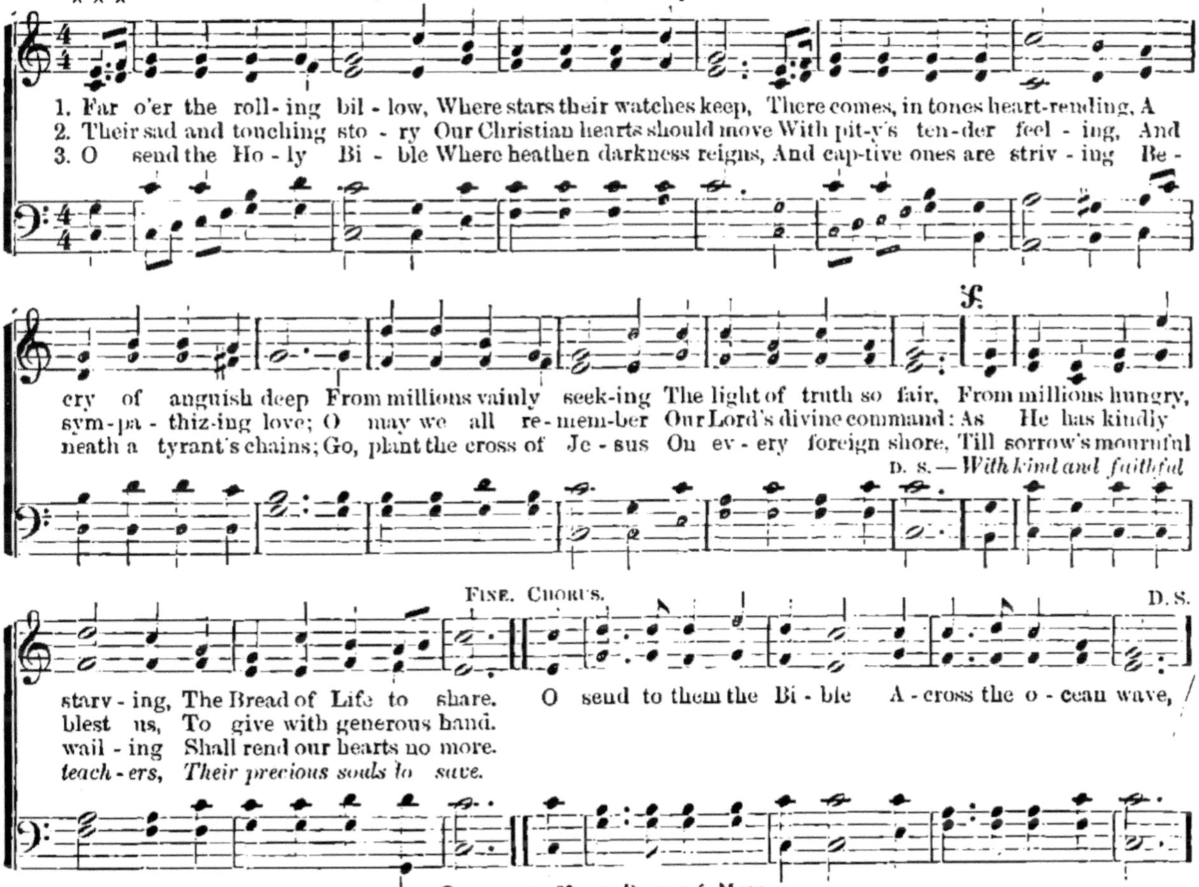
1. Far o'er the roll-ing bil-low, Where stars their watches keep, There comes, in tones heart-rending, A
2. Their sad and touching sto-ry Our Christian hearts should move With pit-y's ten-der feel-ing, And
3. O send the Ho-ly Bi-ble Where heathen darkness reigns, And cap-tive ones are striv-ing Be-
cry of anguish deep From millions vainly seek-ing The light of truth so fair, From millions hungry,
sym-pa-thiz-ing love; O may we all re-mem-ber Our Lord's divine command: As He has kindly
neath a tyrant's chains; Go, plant the cross of Je-sus On ev-ery foreign shore, Till sorrow's mournful
D. S.—With kind and faithful
starv-ing, The Bread of Life to share.
blest us, To give with generous hand.
wail-ing Shall rend our hearts no more.
teach-ers, Their precious souls to save.
Fine. Chorus.
O send to them the Bi-ble A-cross the o-cean wave,
D. S.

Go Forward.

GRACE J. FRANCES. *Thou hast given a banner to them that fear thee.*—Ps. 60: 4. HUBERT P. MAIN.

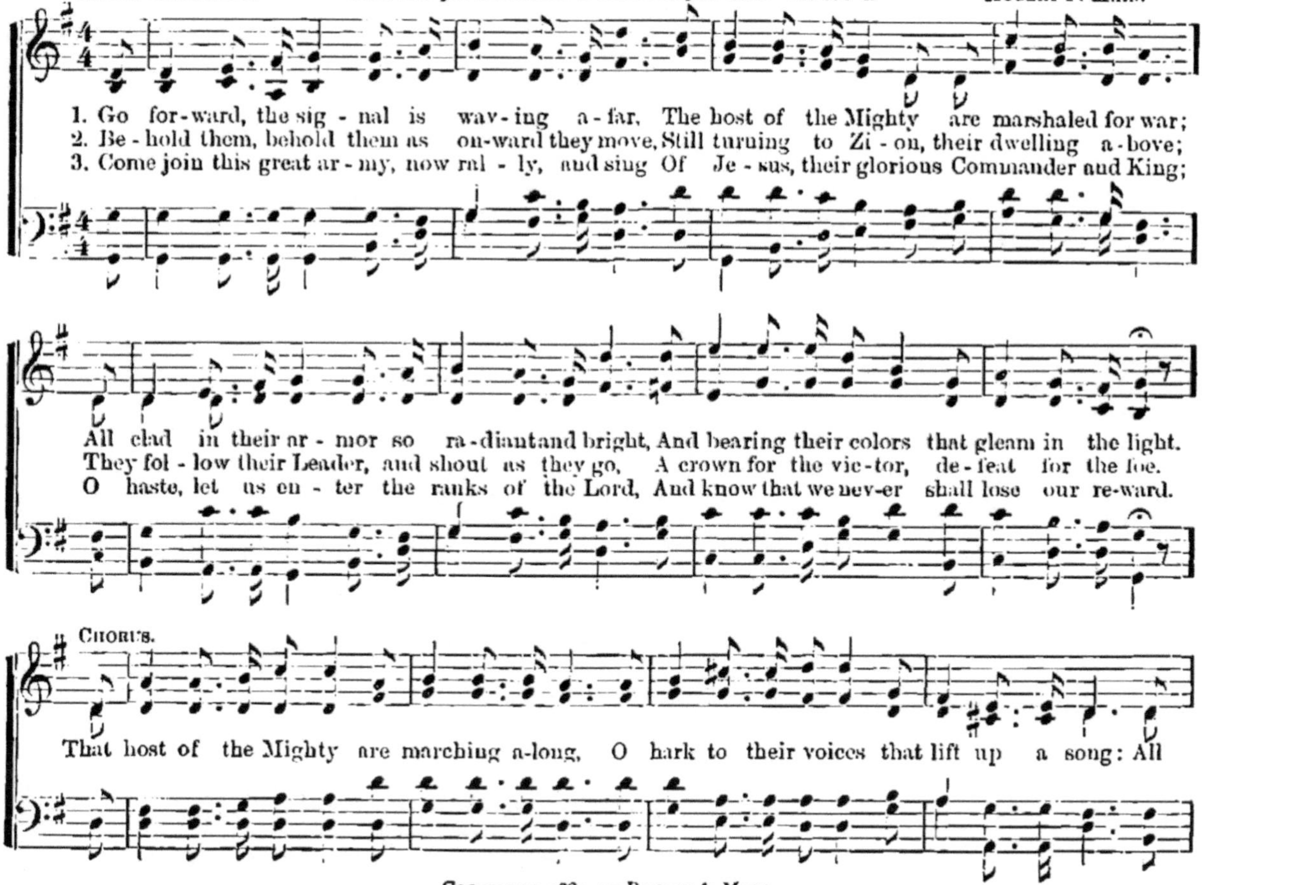
1. Go for-ward, the sig - nal is wav-ing a-far, The host of the Mighty are marshaled for war;
2. Be - hold them, behold them as on-ward they move, Still turning to Zi - on, their dwelling a-bove;
3. Come join this great ar - my, now ral - ly, and sing Of Je - sus, their glorious Commander and King;
All clad in their ar - mor so ra-diant and bright, And bearing their colors that gleam in the light.
They fol - low their Leader, and shout as they go, A crown for the vic-tor, de-feat for the foe.
O haste, let us en - ter the ranks of the Lord, And know that we nev-er shall lose our re-ward.
CHORUS.
That host of the Mighty are marching a-long, O hark to their voices that lift up a song: All

Go Forward. Concluded.

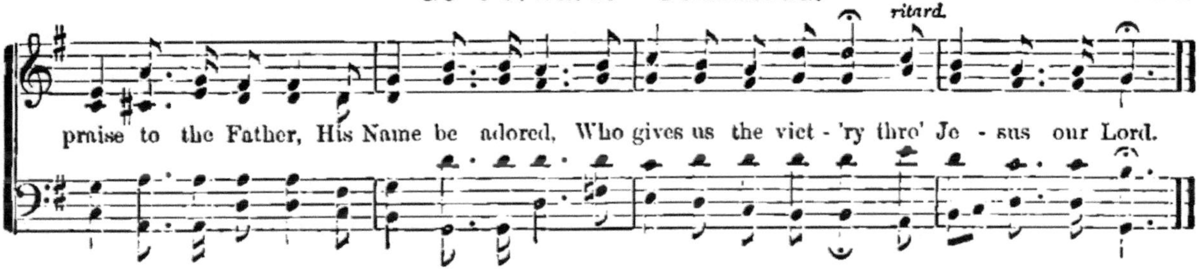
ritard.
praise to the Father, His Name be adored, Who gives us the vict - 'ry thro' Je - sus our Lord.

Chant for Opening Sunday School.

W. H. D. *Our Father which art in heaven.*—Matt. 6: 9. W. H. Doane.

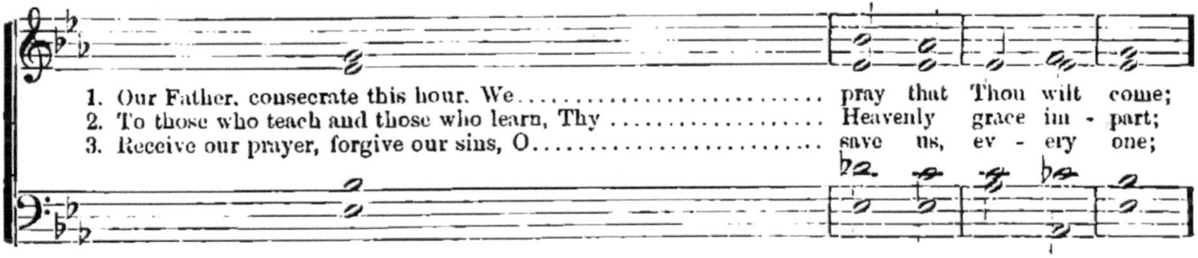
1. Our Father, consecrate this hour. We........................... pray that Thou wilt come;
2. To those who teach and those who learn, Thy .... Heavenly grace im - part;
3. Receive our prayer, forgive our sins, O............................ save us, ev - ery one;

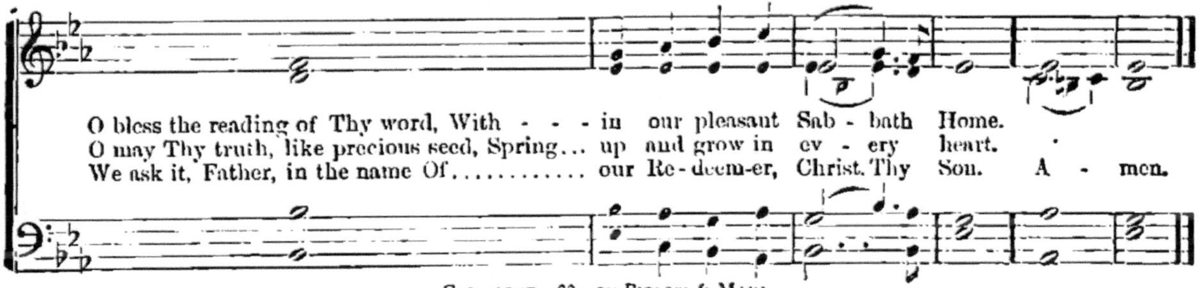
O bless the reading of Thy word, With - - - in our pleasant Sab - bath Home.
O may Thy truth, like precious seed, Spring... up and grow in ev - ery heart.
We ask it, Father, in the name Of........... our Re-deem-er, Christ.Thy Son. A - men.

104 Harvest Home.

Mrs. Annie S. Hawks. *According to the joy in harvest.*—Isa. 9: 3. R. Lowry.

1. Har - vest Home! O hear the chim - ing Of the sweet - toned mem - ory bells,
2. Har - vest Home! the gold - en Pres - ent Tells of har - vests yet to come,
3. Lo! the hearth - stone bright - ly glow - ing, Board with boun - teous cheer o'er - spread;
Till with child - hood's scenes of pleas - ure Ev - ery heart with glad - ness swells;
While we lov - ing - ly and kind - ly Bid the reap - ers wel - come home;
May our hun - gry souls be nour - ished With the ev - er liv - ing Bread;
Think we now of rip - ened har - vests, Au - tumn rich with gar - nered store;
Some in fer - tile fields have gath - ered Some, per - chance, have gath - ered leaves;
Har - vest Home! the songs of glo - ry Ech - o from the oth - er shore,

Reap - ers too with heads now sil - vered, Some whose hands will work no more.
Ma - ny who went forth with weep - ing Bring with joy the smil - ing sheaves.
Where the reap - ers all are shout - ing "Har - vest Home!" for - ev - er - more.
Refrain.
Har - vest Home! sing Har - vest Home! Wake with joy the star - ry dome;
Rest, ye reap - ers, by the way, Sow a - gain at dawn of day.

106

He Saves Me.

C. L. Clifford. *According to his mercy he saved us.*—Tit. 3: 5. W. H. Doane.

1. He saves me, each moment He saves me, I know He a - bides in my soul; I rest me be - neath His pro - tec - tion, And smile tho' the bil - lows may roll.
2. He saves me, each moment He saves me, All glo - ry to Je - sus my Lord; He lifts me a - bove my temp - ta - tion, He anch - ors my soul on His word.
3. He saves me, each moment He saves me, Un - worthy and weak as I am; In this will I boast and be thank - ful, I'm saved thro' the blood of the Lamb.
Refrain.
He saves me, He saves me, O praise to His in - fi - nite mer - cy; He saves me, He saves me, He saves me for - ev - er - more.

OLD, OLD STORY.

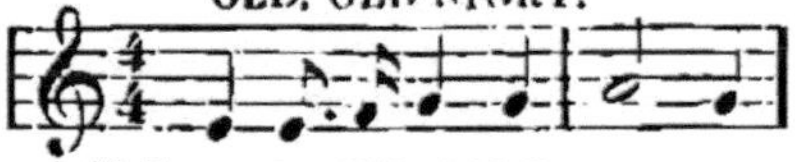

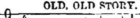

1 Tell me the Old, Old Story
Of unseen things above,
Of Jesus and His glory,
Of Jesus and His love;
Tell me the Story simply,
As to a little child,
For I am weak and weary,
And helpless and defiled.
Cho.—Tell me the Old, Old Story,
Tell me the Old, Old Story,
Tell me the Old, Old Story
Of Jesus and His love.

2 Tell me the same Old Story,
When you have cause to fear
That this world's empty glory
Is costing me too dear;
Yes, and when that world's glory
Is dawning on my soul,
Tell me the Old, Old Story:
"Christ Jesus makes thee whole."

Kate Hankey.

I LOVE TO TELL THE STORY.

1 I love to tell the Story
Of unseen things above,
Of Jesus and His glory,
Of Jesus and His love;
I love to tell the Story,
Because I know it's true;
It satisfies my longings
As nothing else would do.
Cho.—I love to tell the story,
'Twill be my theme in glory,
To tell the Old, Old Story,
Of Jesus and His love.

2 I love to tell the Story!
For those who know it best
Seem hungering and thirsting
To hear it like the rest:
And when, in scenes of glory,
I sing the New, New Song,
'Twill be the Old, Old Story
That I have loved so long.

Kate Hankey.

CROSS AND CROWN.

1 Must Jesus bear the cross alone,
And all the world go free?
No, there's a cross for every one,
And there's a cross for me.

2 How happy are the saints above,
Who once went sorrowing here:
But now they taste unmingled love,
And joy without a tear.

3 The consecrated cross I'll bear,
Till death shall set me free:
And then go home my crown to wear,
For there's a crown for me.

Rev. Thomas Shepherd.

HORTON.

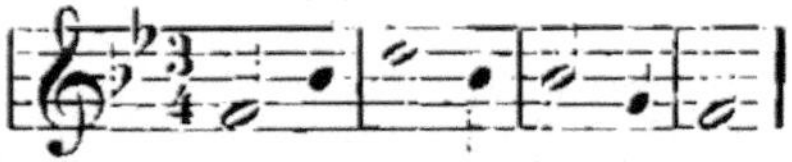

1 Come, saith Jesus' sacred voice,
Come and make my paths your choice;
I will guide you to your home;
Weary pilgrim, hither come.

2 Hither come, for here is found
Balm for every bleeding wound,
Peace which ever shall endure,
Rest eternal, sacred, sure.

Mrs. A. L. Barbauld.

SHINING SHORE.

1 My days are swiftly gliding by,
And I, a pilgrim stranger,
Would not detain them as they fly,—
Those hours of toil and danger.
Cho.—
For now we stand on Jordan's strand,
Our friends are passing over;
And just before, the shining shore
We may almost discover.

2 Should coming days be dark and cold,
We will not yield to sorrow,
For hope will sing, with courage bold,
"There's glory on the morrow."

3 Let sorrow's rudest tempest blow,
Each chord on earth to sever,
Our King says, Come, and there's our
Forever! O forever! [home,

Rev. David Nelson.

The New Year.

1 We meet you here, our brethren dear,
With ne'er a shade of sorrow;
The old year gone, the new comes on
With many a glad to-morrow.
Cho.—
But when we stand on Canaan's land,
And glory shines before us,
To God we'll bring, and ever sing,
Our hallelujah chorus.

2 We meet you here, old dying year,
Thy solemn voice comes o'er us;
But from thy dust we humbly trust
A better year's before us.

Rev. R. Lowry.

108 Praise ye Jehovah.

R. L. *Let everything that hath breath praise the LORD.*—Ps. 150: 6. R. Lowry.

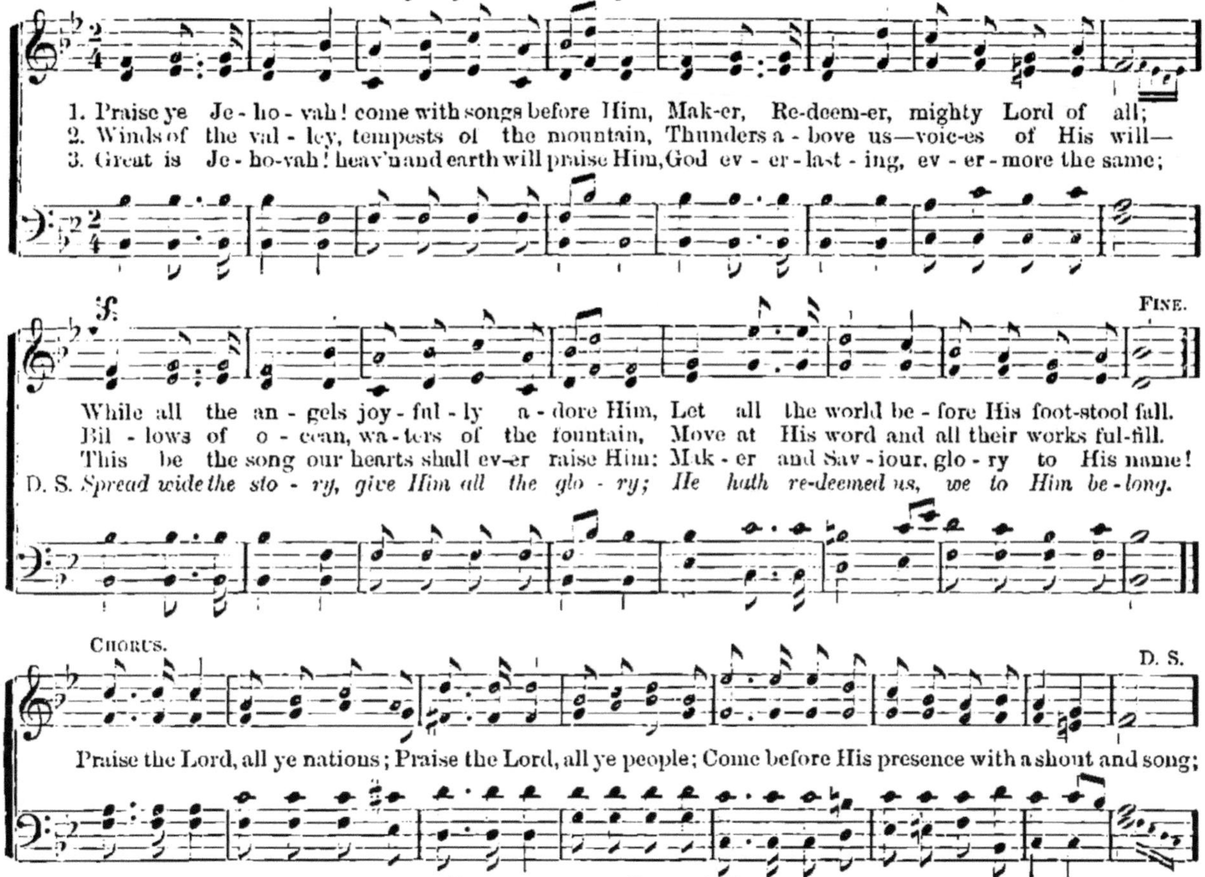
1. Praise ye Je - ho - vah! come with songs before Him, Mak-er, Re-deem-er, mighty Lord of all;
2. Winds of the val - ley, tempests of the mountain, Thunders a - bove us—voic-es of His will—
3. Great is Je - ho-vah! heav'n and earth will praise Him, God ev - er - last - ing, ev - er - more the same;
While all the an - gels joy - ful - ly a - dore Him, Let all the world be - fore His foot-stool fall.
Bil - lows of o - cean, wa - ters of the fountain, Move at His word and all their works ful-fill.
This be the song our hearts shall ev-er raise Him: Mak - er and Sav - iour, glo - ry to His name!
D. S. *Spread wide the sto - ry, give Him all the glo - ry; He hath re-deemed us, we to Him be - long.*
Fine.
Chorus.
Praise the Lord, all ye nations; Praise the Lord, all ye people; Come before His presence with a shout and song;
D. S.

Beyond the Smiling and the Weeping.

HORATIUS BONAR, D.D. *There remaineth a rest therefore to the people of God.*—HEB. 4: 9. WM. B. BRADBURY.

1. Be - yond the smiling and the weeping, I shall be soon; Be - yond the waking and the sleeping, Be - yond the sowing and the reaping, I shall be soon. Love, rest, and home! Sweet, sweet home! O how sweet it will be there to meet The dear ones all at home; O how sweet it will be there to meet The dear ones all at home.
2. Be - yond the parting and the meeting, I shall be soon; Be - yond the farewell and the greeting, Be - yond the pulse's fe-ver beating, I shall be soon. Love, rest, &c.
3. Be - yond the frost-chain and the fever, I shall be soon; Be - yond the rock-waste and the river, Be - yond the ev - er and the never, I shall be soon. Love, rest, &c.

By permission.

110 Is there Room for Me?

C. L. Clifford. *Is there room?*—Gen. 21: 23. W. H. Doane.

1. Sav - iour, at Thy bless - ed feet, Is there room, room for me? Where so ma - ny
2. I would come and seek Thy face; Is there room, room for me? Tell me, in Thy
3. In the ma - ny man - sions fair, Is there room, room for me? Shall I hear Thy
love to meet, Is there room for me? I would tell Thee what I need,
fold of grace Is there room for me? Wilt Thou change this heart of mine—
wel - come there? Is there room for me? May I join the hap - py throng?
I would now Thy promise plead; Je - sus, at Thy blessed feet, Is there room for me?
Make me now a child of Thine? Saviour, at Thy blessed feet, Is there room for me?
May I learn the glad new song? Je - sus, at Thy blessed feet, Is there room for me?

Nearer, Dear Jesus.

M. H. W. *Jesus himself drew near.*—Luke 24: 15. R. Lowry.

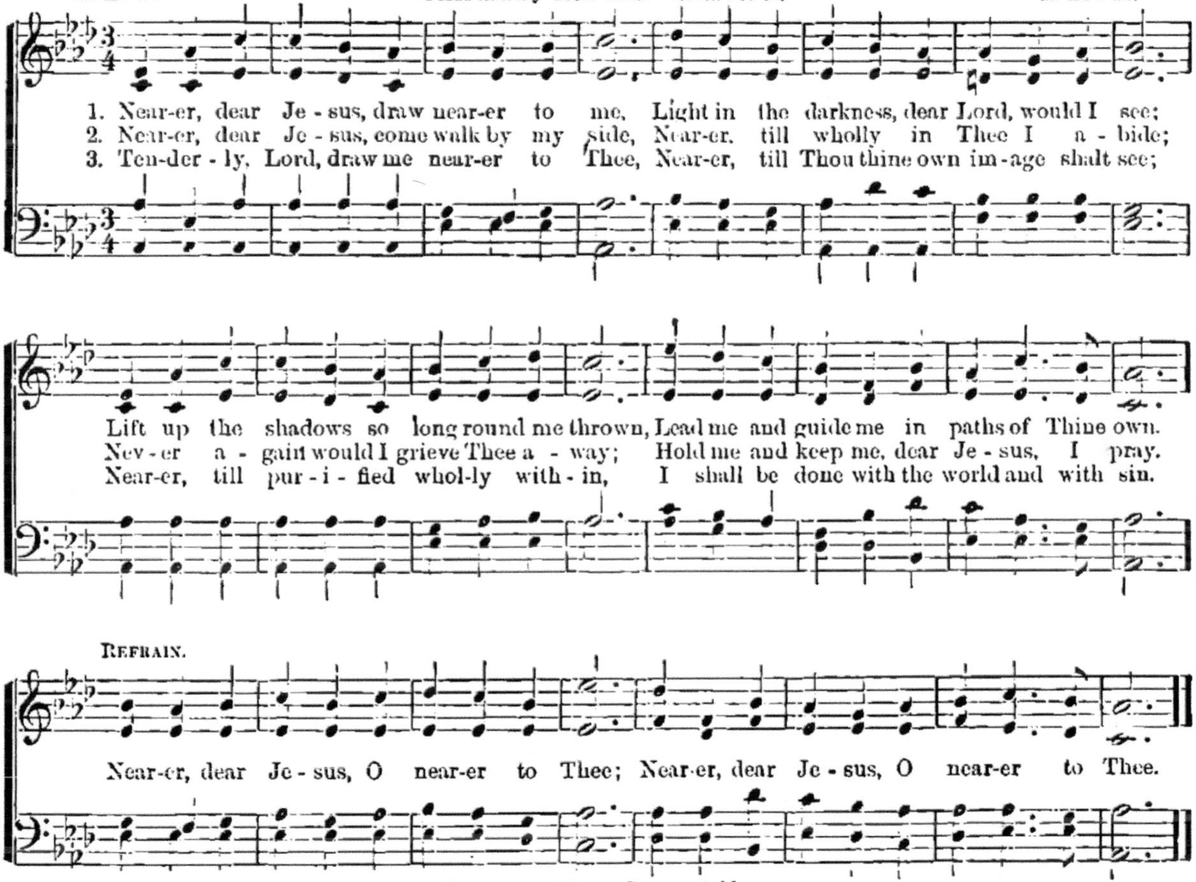
1. Near-er, dear Je - sus, draw near-er to me, Light in the darkness, dear Lord, would I see;
2. Near-er, dear Je - sus, come walk by my side, Near-er, till wholly in Thee I a - bide;
3. Ten-der - ly, Lord, draw me near-er to Thee, Near-er, till Thou thine own im-age shalt see;
Lift up the shadows so long round me thrown, Lead me and guide me in paths of Thine own.
Nev - er a - gain would I grieve Thee a - way; Hold me and keep me, dear Je - sus, I pray.
Near-er, till pur - i - fied whol-ly with - in, I shall be done with the world and with sin.
Refrain.
Near-er, dear Je - sus, O near-er to Thee; Near-er, dear Je - sus, O near-er to Thee.

Hold Thou my Hand.

GRACE J. FRANCES. *I the Lord have called thee * * * and will hold thine hand.*—ISA 42: 6. HUBERT P. MAIN.

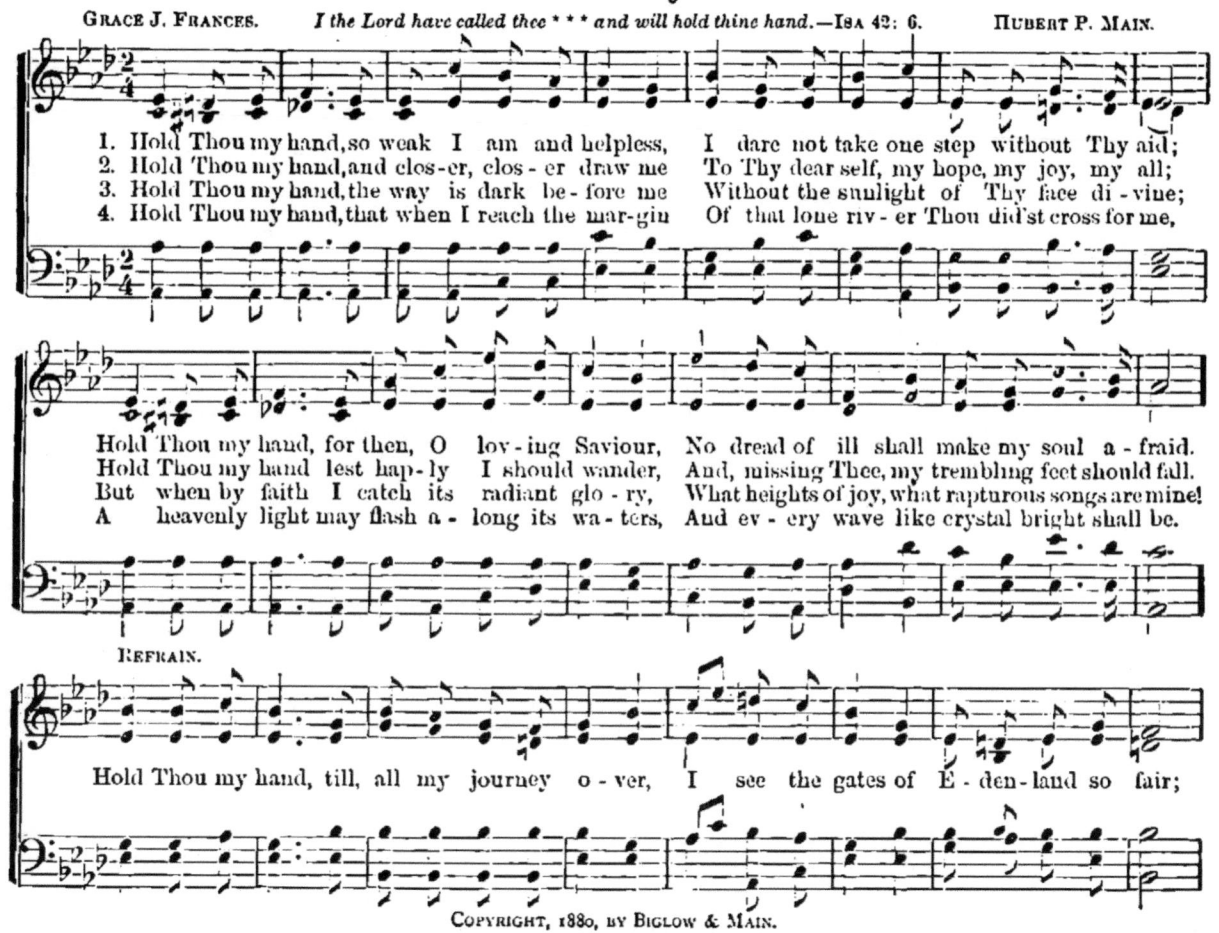

1. Hold Thou my hand, so weak I am and helpless, I dare not take one step without Thy aid;
2. Hold Thou my hand, and clos-er, clos-er draw me To Thy dear self, my hope, my joy, my all;
3. Hold Thou my hand, the way is dark be-fore me Without the sunlight of Thy face di-vine;
4. Hold Thou my hand, that when I reach the mar-gin Of that lone riv-er Thou didst cross for me,

Hold Thou my hand, for then, O lov-ing Saviour, No dread of ill shall make my soul a-fraid.
Hold Thou my hand lest hap-ly I should wander, And, missing Thee, my trembling feet should fall.
But when by faith I catch its radiant glo-ry, What heights of joy, what rapturous songs are mine!
A heavenly light may flash a-long its wa-ters, And ev-ery wave like crystal bright shall be.

REFRAIN.

Hold Thou my hand, till, all my journey o-ver, I see the gates of E-den-land so fair;

Hold Thou my Hand. Concluded.

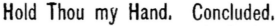

Hold Thou my hand, O do not, do not leave me, Hold Thou my hand till I am safe-ly there.

Breast the Wave, Christian.

JOSEPH STAMMERS. *Let us hold fast the profession of our faith without wavering.*—HEB. 10: 23. R. LOWRY.

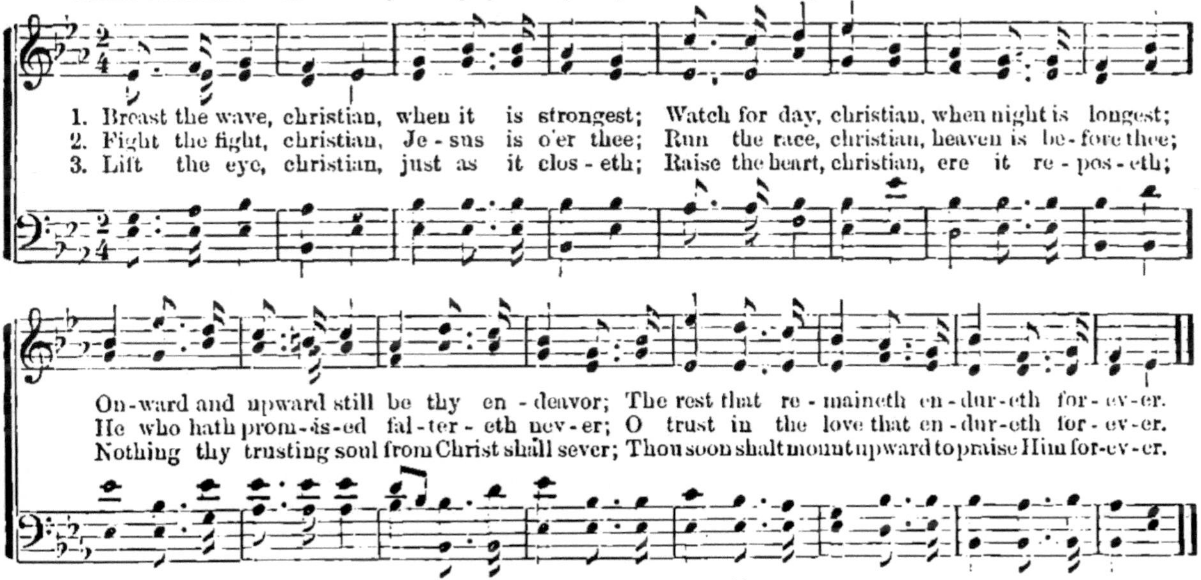
1. Breast the wave, christian, when it is strongest; Watch for day, christian, when night is longest;
2. Fight the fight, christian, Je-sus is o'er thee; Run the race, christian, heaven is be-fore thee;
3. Lift the eye, christian, just as it clos-eth; Raise the heart, christian, ere it re-pos-eth;
On-ward and upward still be thy en-deavor; The rest that re-maineth en-dur-eth for-ev-er.
He who hath prom-is-ed fal-ter-eth nev-er; O trust in the love that en-dur-eth for-ev-er.
Nothing thy trusting soul from Christ shall sever; Thou soon shalt mount upward to praise Him for-ev-er.

114 O Revive Us, Blessed Saviour.

D. H. W. *Wilt thou not revive us again?*—Psa. 85: 6. W. H. Doane.

1. O re - vive us, bless-ed Sav - iour, Fill each heart with Thy love; Come in mer-cy, we en - treat Thee, Come in power from a - bove.
2. O re - vive us, bless-ed Sav - iour, Bind our hearts with Thy chain; Ho - ly Spir-it, we en - treat Thee, Now re - vive us a - gain.
3. O re - vive us, bless-ed Sav - iour, Seal our hearts, we im - plore; Let Thy blessing rest up - on us, O re - vive us once more.
4. O re - vive us, bless-ed Sav - iour, Keep our hearts in Thy love; O pre - pare us for Thy man - sion In Thy king-dom a - bove.
Refrain.
O re - vive us, O re - vive us, Bless our waiting souls, we pray Thee; Hal - le - lu - jah! hal - le - lu - jah! Thine the praise ev - er - more.

Lo! the Fields are White to Harvest.

JOSEPHINE POLLARD. *The harvest truly is plenteous.*—MATT. 9: 37. WM. B. BRADBURY.

1. Lo! the fields are white to har - vest; Who will thrust the sick-le in? Who will reap the golden
2. There are ma - ny, ma - ny chil - dren, Growing up to sin and shame; And their lit - tle lips are
3. Lo! the Mas - ter looks im - plor - ing; Lo! the myr - iad heathen stand, Wait-ing for the gos-pel
glo - ry Sa - tan ev - er strives to win? Prone to e - vil, men will fol - low Paths their
nev - er Taught to speak a Saviour's name; Tho' the sun is shin-ing o'er them, Bath-ing
mes-sage To a - rouse the slumb'ring land; Who will bear the bless-ed ti - dings—Spread the
fa - thers long have known; In their blindness, still they wor-ship Gods of clay, and wood, and stone.
all in glo-rious light, Yet their hearts are full of shadows Dark-er than the dark-est night.
knowledge far and wide—Telling hea - then, wretched heathen, 'Twas for them a Sav-iour died?

By permission.

116 I will Praise my God.

Rev. W. O. Cushing. *I will praise thy name for ever and ever.*—Ps. 145: 2. R. Lowry.

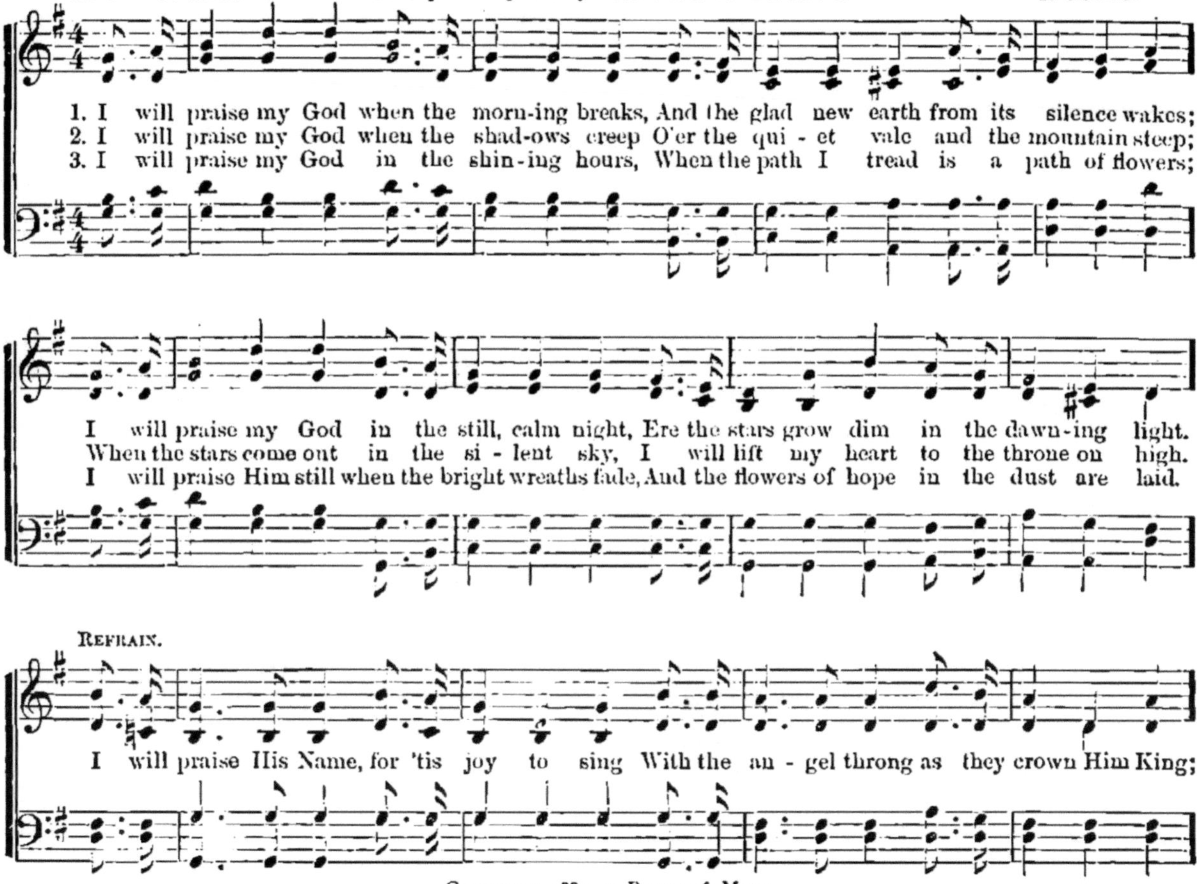
1. I will praise my God when the morn-ing breaks, And the glad new earth from its silence wakes;
2. I will praise my God when the shad-ows creep O'er the qui - et vale and the mountain steep;
3. I will praise my God in the shin-ing hours, When the path I tread is a path of flowers;
I will praise my God in the still, calm night, Ere the stars grow dim in the dawn-ing light.
When the stars come out in the si - lent sky, I will lift my heart to the throne on high.
I will praise Him still when the bright wreaths fade, And the flowers of hope in the dust are laid.
Refrain.
I will praise His Name, for 'tis joy to sing With the an - gel throng as they crown Him King;

I will praise His Name, for 'tis joy to sing With the an - gel throng as they crown Him King.

I Thank Thee, Lord.

MRS. LEAH CARLTON. *Forget not all his benefits.*—Ps. 103: 2. REV. SAMUEL ALMAN.

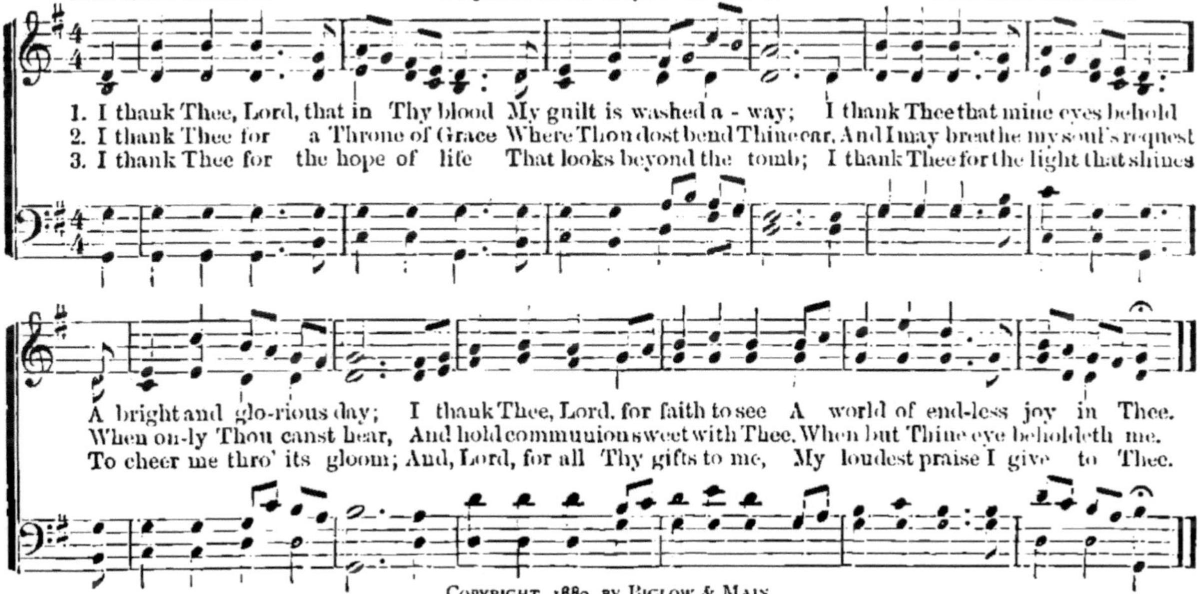
1. I thank Thee, Lord, that in Thy blood My guilt is washed a - way; I thank Thee that mine eyes behold
2. I thank Thee for a Throne of Grace Where Thou dost bend Thine ear, And I may breathe my soul's request
3. I thank Thee for the hope of life That looks beyond the tomb; I thank Thee for the light that shines
A bright and glo-rious day; I thank Thee, Lord, for faith to see A world of end-less joy in Thee.
When on-ly Thou canst hear, And hold communion sweet with Thee, When but Thine eye beholdeth me.
To cheer me thro' its gloom; And, Lord, for all Thy gifts to me, My loudest praise I give to Thee.

118 The Toils of the Way.

B. P. C.

The Lord shall give thee rest.—Isa. 14: 3.

W. H. Doane.

1. My life is a wea - ri - some jour - ney, I'm sick with the dust and the heat;
2. I know there are hills to climb up - ward, And oft I am sigh - ing for rest;
3. O when the last step has been tak - en, And I to the Cit - y draw near,—
The rays of the sun beat up - on me, The bri - ars are wound-ing my feet;
But He who ap - points me my path - way Will lead me as seem - eth Him best;
When beau - ti - ful songs from the an - gels Are waft - ed with joy to my ear,—
But the Cit - y to which I am go - ing Will more than my tri - als re - pay;
Yes, I know in His word He has prom-ised That strength He will give as my day;
O the rap - ture and bliss of that mo - ment Will more than my sor - row re - pay;

All the toils of the road will seem noth-ing, When I get to the end of my way.
All the toils of the road will seem noth-ing, When I get to the end of my way.
All the toils of the road will seem noth-ing, When I get to the end of my way.
Refrain.
All the toils of the way, toils of the way, Je - sus my Saviour will more than re - pay;
All the toils of the road will seem noth-ing, When I get to the end of my way.

Beautiful Heaven, my Home.

Rev. W. O. Cushing. *The hope which is laid up for you in heaven.*—Col. 1 : 5. R. Lowry.

1. Home, home, brightest and fair - est! Hope, hope, sweet - est and best! Thou, thou, home of my Sav - iour, Beau - ti - ful heav - en of rest!
2. Home, home, shall I be - hold thee? Safe, safe, safe from all fear— Bright, bright, o - ver my wak - ing, Will the sweet morning ap - pear?
3. Long, long here I have wandered, Far, far, far from thy rest; Ne'er, ne'er can I for - get thee, Beau - ti - ful home of the blest.
4. Home, home, fade - less, e - ter - nal— Thou, Thou, Je - sus - my King—When, when shall I be - hold thee, When with the glo - ri - fied sing?
Refrain.
Home, home, sweet, sweet home! Beau - ti - ful Heav - en, my home! Home, home, sweet, sweet home! Beauti - ful Heaven, my home!

LENOX.

1 Blow ye the trumpet, blow
The gladly solemn sound;
Let all the nations know,
To earth's remotest bound,
The year of jubilee is come;
Return, ye ransomed sinners, home.

2 Jesus, our great High-priest,
Has full atonement made;
Ye weary spirits, rest;
Ye mourning souls be glad;
The year of jubilee is come;
Return, ye ransomed sinners, home.

3 Exalt the Lamb of God,
The sin-atoning Lamb;
Redemption by His blood
Through all the world proclaim;
The year of jubilee is come;
Return, ye ransomed sinners, home.

Rev. Chas. Wesley.

Faint, yet Pursuing.

1 Soldiers of Christ, arise,
And put your armor on;
Engage your enemies;
Let every fear be gone:
Now take the field, the fight renew,
And never yield; "tho' faint, pursue."

2 Wage war with every foe,
For God is on your side;
Let all the nations know
That you in God confide:
Gird on your sword, the fight renew;
Look to the Lord; "tho' faint, pursue."

3 Ne'er lay your weapons down
Till death shall close the strife—
Till you receive a crown
Of everlasting life:
On God depend, the fight renew;
As Gideon conquered, so shall you.

Rev. Chas. Wesley.

WORK, FOR THE NIGHT.

1 Work, for the night is coming,
Work through the morning hours:
Work while the dew is sparkling,
Work 'mid springing flowers;
Work when the day grows brighter,
Work in the glowing sun;
Work, for the night is coming,
When man's work is done.

2 Work, for the night is coming,
Work through the sunny noon;
Fill brightest hours with labor,
Rest comes sure and soon;
Give every flying minute
Something to keep in store;
Work, for the night is coming,
When man works no more.

3 Work, for the night is coming,
Under the sunset skies;
While their bright tints are glowing,
Work, for the daylight flies;
Work till the last beam fadeth,
Fadeth to shine no more;
Work while the night is darkening,
When man's work is o'er.

Annie L. Walker.

AMERICA.

1 My country 'tis of thee,
Sweet land of liberty,
Of thee I sing;
Land where my fathers died,
Land of the pilgrim's pride,
From every mountain side
Let freedom ring.

2 My native country, thee,
Land of the noble, free,
Thy name I love;
I love thy rocks and rills,
Thy woods and templed hills,
My heart with rapture thrills
Like that above.

3 Our father's God! to Thee,
Author of liberty,
To Thee we sing;
Long may our land be bright
With freedom's holy light;
Protect us by Thy might,
Great God, our King!

S. F. Smith, D. D.

Temperance.

Tune—HOLD THE FORT.

1 Brothers! rally for the conflict,
See the banner wave;
Temperance bands are pressing onward
Fallen men to save.
CHO.—Hear a mighty host of freemen
Songs of triumph raise;
Love hath conquered, chains are broken,
Give to God the praise.

2 Burst the tyrant's bands asunder,
Set the captives free;
Let rejoicing wives and mothers
Shout the jubilee.

3 Led no more by passion captive,
Haunts of vice we shun;
Happy hearts and smiling faces
Tell of victory won.

Wm. Stevenson.

122 All Day I have Gleaned.

Rose Matthews. *Let me glean and gather after the reapers.*—Ruth 2: 7. W. H. Doane.

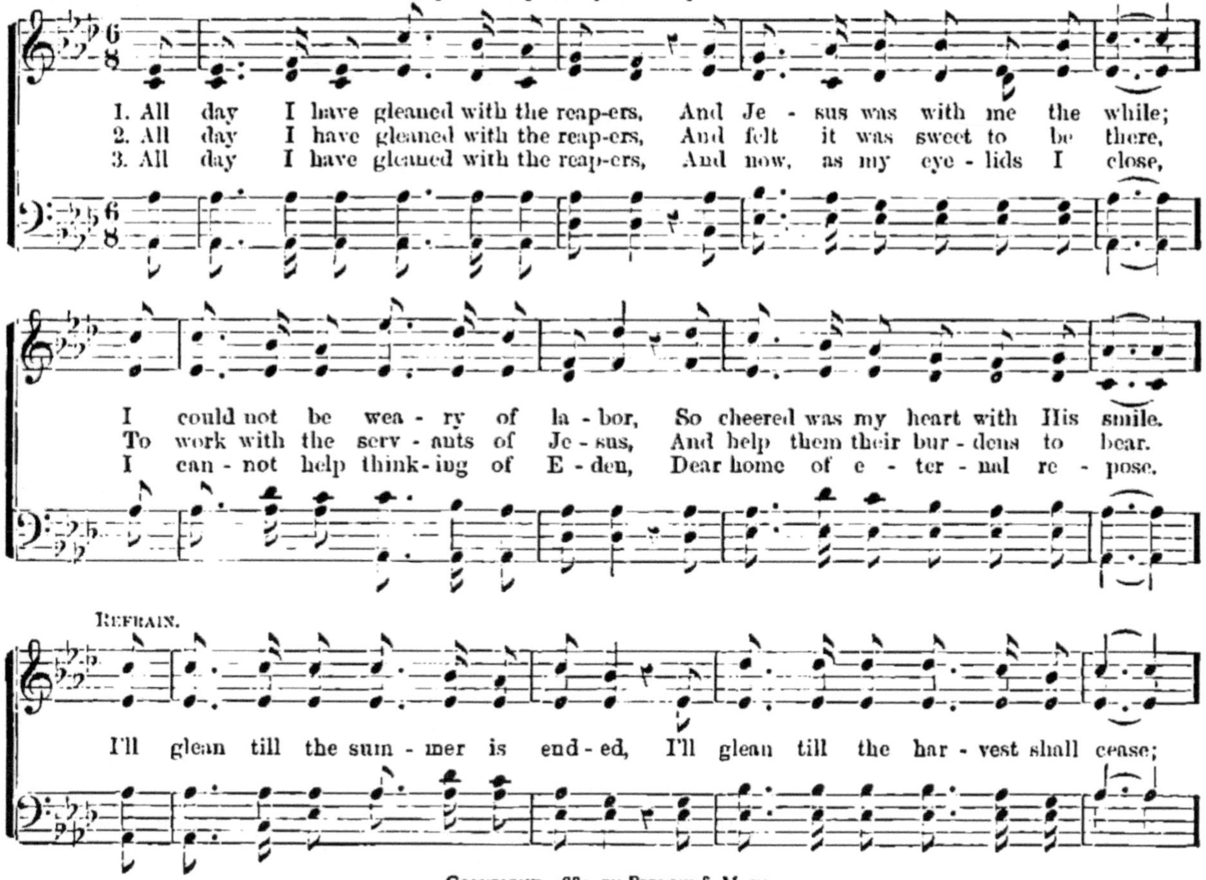
1. All day I have gleaned with the reap-ers, And Je - sus was with me the while;
I could not be wea - ry of la - bor, So cheered was my heart with His smile.
2. All day I have gleaned with the reap-ers, And felt it was sweet to be there,
To work with the serv - ants of Je - sus, And help them their bur - dens to bear.
3. All day I have gleaned with the reap-ers, And now, as my eye - lids I close,
I can - not help think - ing of E - den, Dear home of e - ter - nal re - pose.
Refrain.
I'll glean till the sum - mer is end - ed, I'll glean till the har - vest shall cease;

All Day I have Gleaned. Concluded.

Then, bear - ing the sheaves I have gath-ered, Go home to the Mas - ter in peace.

Tenderly He Leads Us.

FANNY J. CROSBY. *He calleth his own sheep by name, and leadeth them out.*—JOHN 10: 3. W. H. DOANE.

1. Tender - ly He leads us, All our days be - low; Care-ful - ly He shews us, Ev - ery step we go.
2. Thro' the Ho-ly Spir - it, We are taught the way Up-ward to His kingdom, Brighter far than day.
3. They who early seek Him, With an humble mind, Par-don, life and comfort, Ev - er more shall find.

REFRAIN.

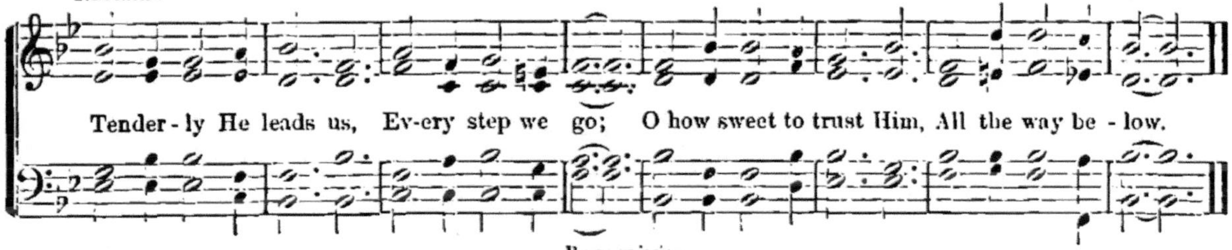
Tender - ly He leads us, Ev-ery step we go; O how sweet to trust Him, All the way be - low.

By permission.

124 What can I give my Saviour?

Mrs. M. A. W. Cooke. *What shall I render to the Lord?*—Ps. 116: 12. R. Lowry.

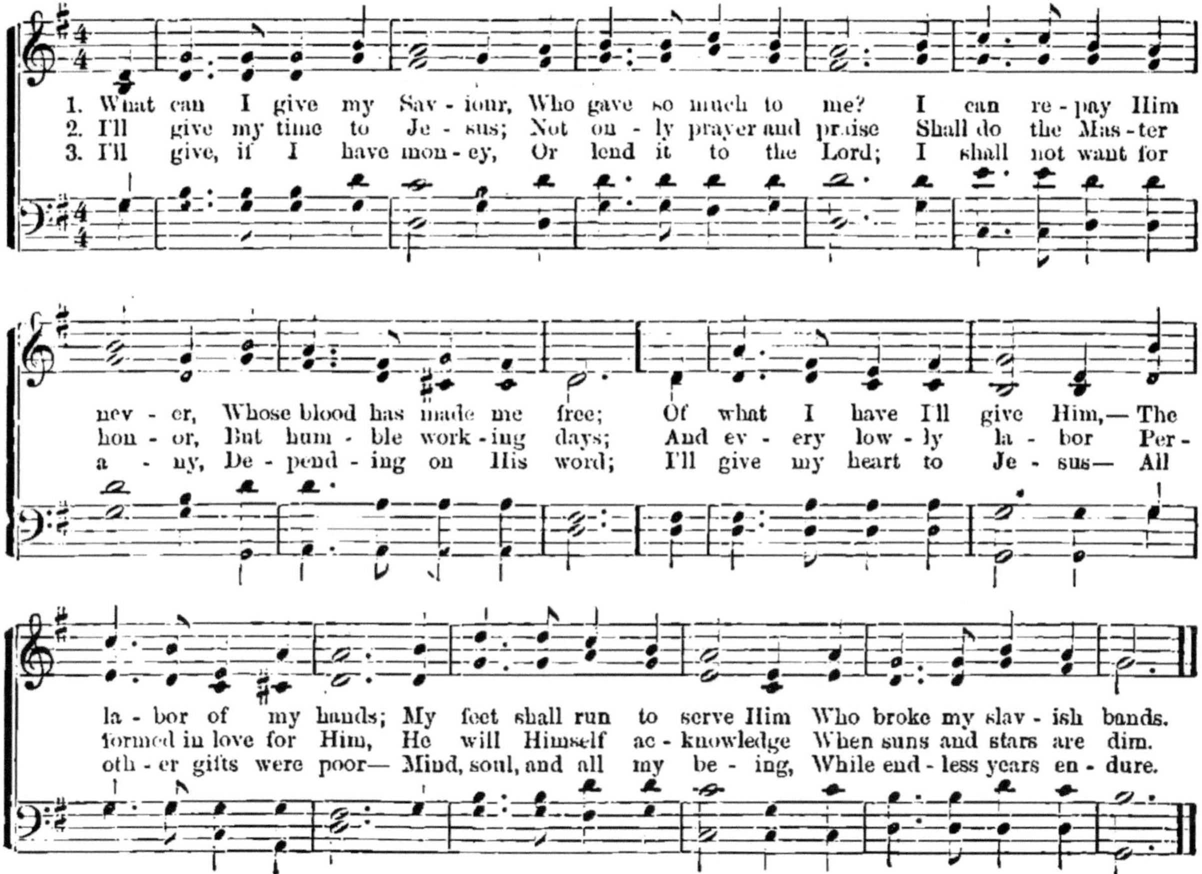
1. What can I give my Sav - iour, Who gave so much to me? I can re - pay Him nev - er, Whose blood has made me free; Of what I have I'll give Him,— The la - bor of my hands; My feet shall run to serve Him Who broke my slav - ish bands.
2. I'll give my time to Je - sus; Not on - ly prayer and praise Shall do the Mas - ter hon - or, But hum - ble work - ing days; And ev - ery low - ly la - bor Per - formed in love for Him, He will Himself ac - knowledge When suns and stars are dim.
3. I'll give, if I have mon - ey, Or lend it to the Lord; I shall not want for a - ny, De - pend - ing on His word; I'll give my heart to Je - sus— All oth - er gifts were poor— Mind, soul, and all my be - ing, While end - less years en - dure.

Fair is the Morning Land.

Rev. W. O. Cushing. *Dwelling in the light which no man can approach unto.*—1 Tim. 6: 16. Hubert P. Main.

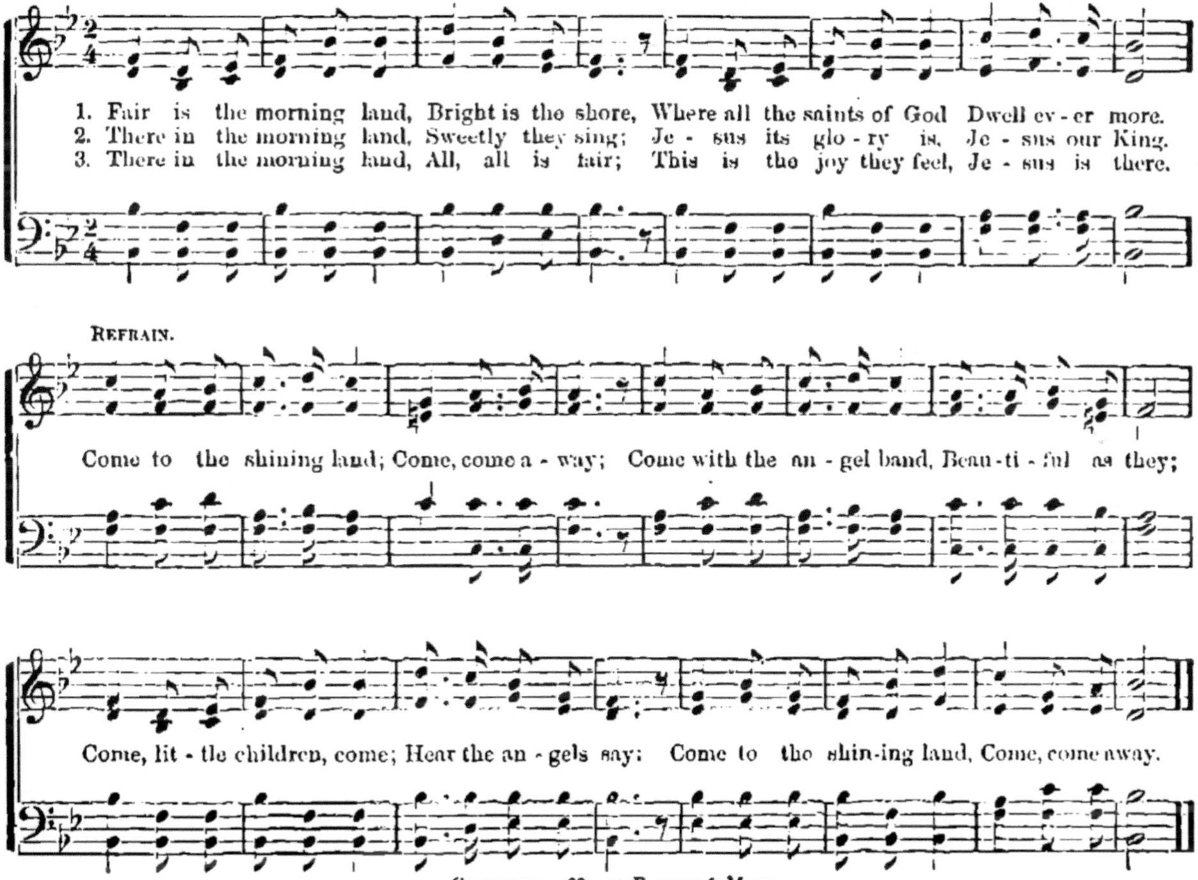
1. Fair is the morning land, Bright is the shore, Where all the saints of God Dwell ev - er more.
2. There in the morning land, Sweetly they sing; Je - sus its glo - ry is, Je - sus our King.
3. There in the morning land, All, all is fair; This is the joy they feel, Je - sus is there.
Refrain.
Come to the shining land; Come, come a - way; Come with the an - gel band, Beau - ti - ful as they;
Come, lit - tle children, come; Hear the an - gels say: Come to the shin-ing land, Come, come away.

Mary's Faith and Love.

Mrs. J. B. Thresher. *She hath wrought a good work upon me.*—Matt. 26: 10. W. H. Doane.

1. I can - not bathe in o - dors sweet My Sav - iour's head with Ma - ry's care; And yet, like Ma - ry, at His feet I sit and learn my du - ty there.
2. O let me bear the Christian's part, And love as Ma - ry loved of yore; O let me in - to some poor heart The balm of con - so - la - tion pour.
3. Henceforth my all I free - ly give To Him whose death my life has won; And by His grace I'll try to live More faith - ful than I yet have done.
Refrain.
Mary's love, so pure, Mary's faith, so di - vine,
Ma - ry's love to her Lord, so pure, so pure, Ma - ry's faith in His truth, so di - vine, di - vine,

Mary's love ev - er deep and strong, Her faith, Her love shall be mine.
Ma - ry's love to her Lord ev - er

Upward where the Stars are Burning.

HORATIUS BONAR, D. D. *Crowned with glory and honor.*—HEB. 2: 9. JOHN BAPTISTE CALKIN, arr.

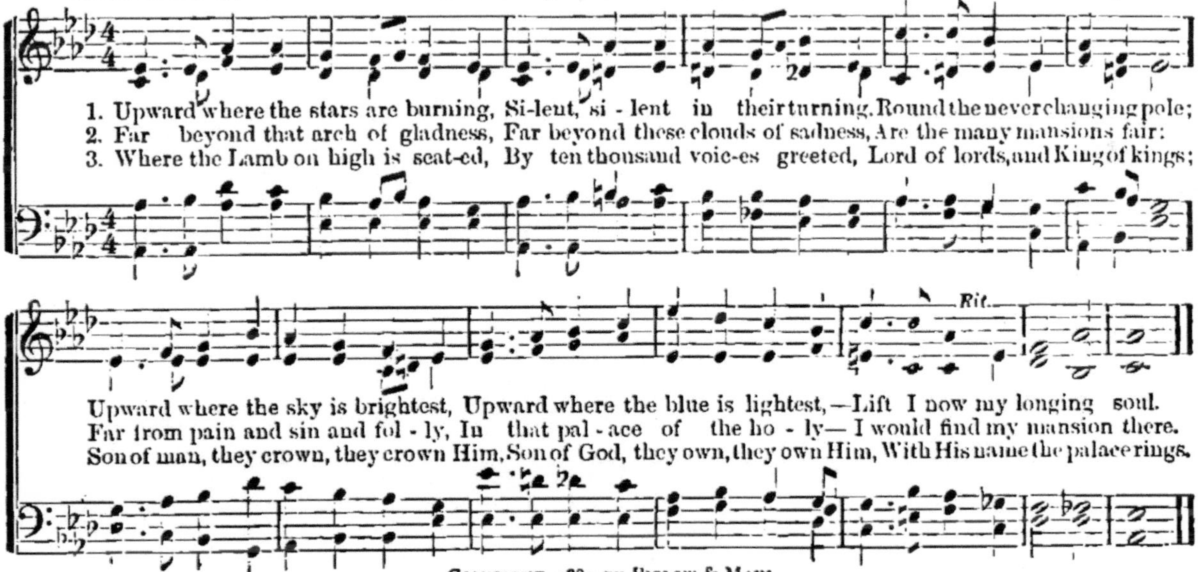
1. Upward where the stars are burning, Si-lent, si - lent in their turning, Round the neverchanging pole;
2. Far beyond that arch of gladness, Far beyond these clouds of sadness, Are the many mansions fair:
3. Where the Lamb on high is seat-ed, By ten thousand voic-es greeted, Lord of lords, and King of kings;
Upward where the sky is brightest, Upward where the blue is lightest,—Lift I now my longing soul.
Far from pain and sin and fol - ly, In that pal - ace of the ho - ly— I would find my mansion there.
Son of man, they crown, they crown Him, Son of God, they own, they own Him, With His name the palace rings.
Rit.

128 Come to the Great Physician.

They that are whole need not a physician, but they that are sick.—LUKE 5: 31.

MRS. E. C. ELLSWORTH. R. LOWRY.

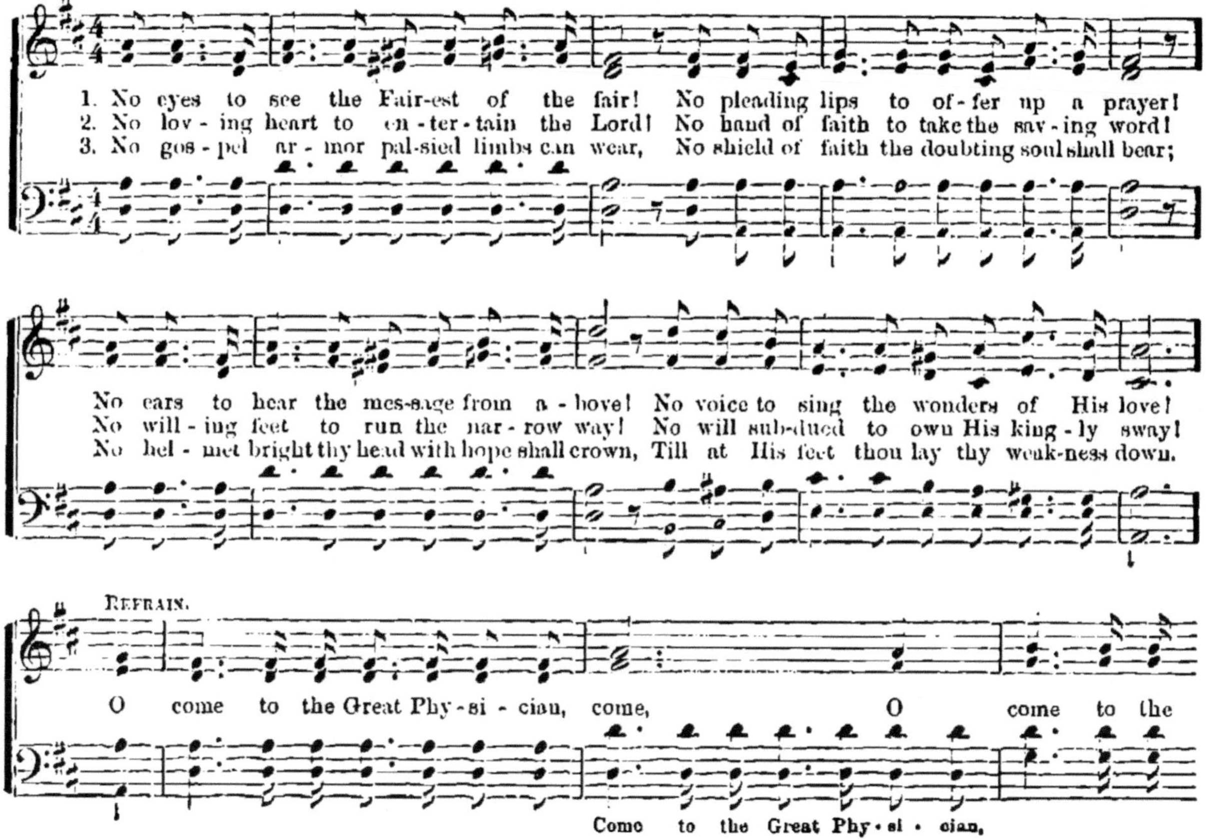
1. No eyes to see the Fair-est of the fair! No pleading lips to of-fer up a prayer!
2. No lov-ing heart to en-ter-tain the Lord! No hand of faith to take the sav-ing word!
3. No gos-pel ar-mor pal-sied limbs can wear, No shield of faith the doubting soul shall bear;
No ears to hear the mes-sage from a-bove! No voice to sing the wonders of His love!
No will-ing feet to run the nar-row way! No will sub-dued to own His king-ly sway!
No hel-met bright thy head with hope shall crown, Till at His feet thou lay thy weak-ness down.
REFRAIN.
O come to the Great Phy-si-cian, come, O come to the
Come to the Great Phy-si-cian,

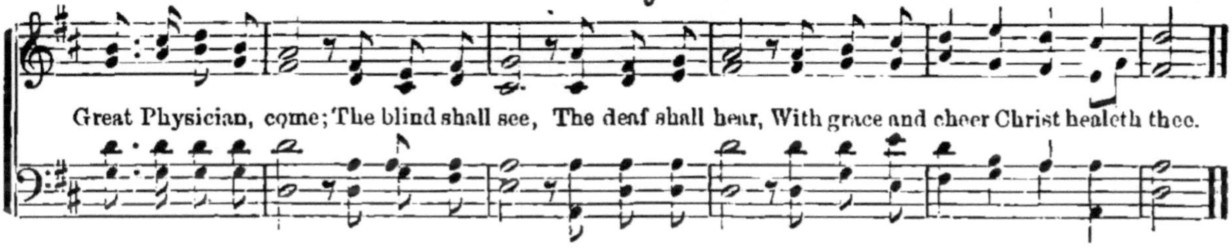
Great Physician, come; The blind shall see, The deaf shall hear, With grace and cheer Christ healeth thee.

Bring in the Tithes.

D. W. H. *Bring ye all the tithes into the storehouse.*—Mal. 19: 5. W. H. Doane.

1. Bring in the tithes to the storehouse, Thus saith the King of kings; He who is guarding His children Under His mighty wings.
2. Bring in the tithes to the storehouse, Prove, and His word believe; He will bestow you a blessing, More than ye can re-ceive.
3. Bring in the tithes to the storehouse, Bring them in faith sincere; Worship the Lord with gladness, Serve Him with holy fear.
D. S.—Come with your gifts to the al-tar. Lay then be-fore His throne.
Fine.
Refrain.
Bring in the tithes, Bring in the tithes, Bring in the tithes to the storehouse;
D. S.

By permission.

130 Hear the Master call for Reapers.

Wm. Stevenson. *The laborers are few.*—Matt. 9: 37. R. Lowry.

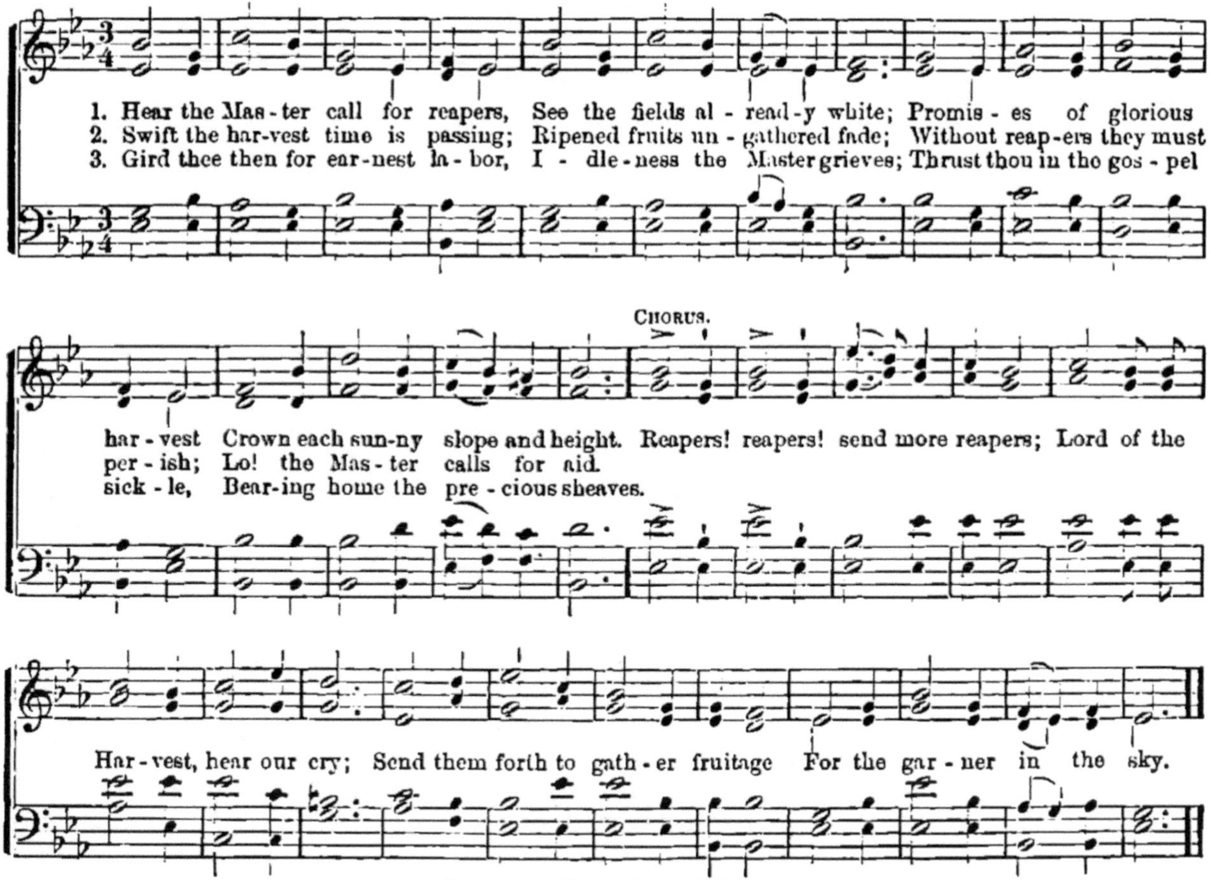

1. Hear the Mas - ter call for reapers, See the fields al - read - y white; Promis - es of glorious
2. Swift the har - vest time is passing; Ripened fruits un - gathered fade; Without reap - ers they must
3. Gird thee then for ear - nest la - bor, I - dle - ness the Master grieves; Thrust thou in the gos - pel
har - vest Crown each sun - ny slope and height.
per - ish; Lo! the Mas - ter calls for aid.
sick - le, Bear - ing home the pre - cious sheaves.
Chorus.
Reapers! reapers! send more reapers; Lord of the Har - vest, hear our cry; Send them forth to gath - er fruitage For the gar - ner in the sky.

SAVIOUR, LIKE A SHEPHERD.

1 Saviour, like a Shepherd lead us,
Much we need Thy tenderest care;
In Thy pleasant pastures feed us,
For our use Thy folds prepare;
Blessed Jesus,
Thou hast bought us, Thine we are.

2 Thou hast promised to receive us,
Poor and sinful though we be;
Thou hast mercy to relieve us,
Grace to cleanse, and power to free;
Blessed Jesus,
We will early turn to Thee.

3 Early let us seek Thy favor,
Early let us do Thy will;
Blessed Lord and only Saviour,
With Thy love our bosoms fill;
Blessed Jesus,
Thou hast loved us, love us still.

Mrs. Dorothy Ann Thrupp.

BOYLSTON.

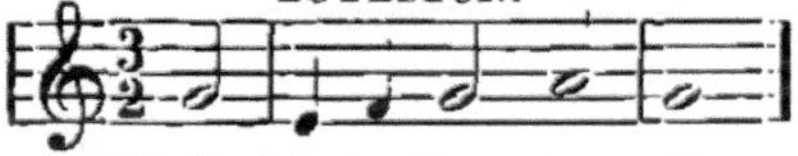

1 Did Christ o'er sinners weep?
And shall our cheeks be dry?
Let floods of penitential grief
Burst forth from every eye.

2 The Son of God in tears
The wondering angels see;
Be thou astonished, O my soul;
He shed those tears for thee.

3 He wept that we might weep;
Each sin demands a tear;
In heaven alone no sin is found,
And there's no weeping there.

Rev. B. Beddome.

MORE LOVE TO THEE.

1 More love to Thee, O Christ,
More love to Thee!
Hear Thou the prayer I make
On bended knee;
This is my earnest plea,
More love, O Christ, to Thee,
More love to Thee!

2 Once earthly joy I craved,
Sought peace and rest;
Now Thee alone I seek,
Give what is best;
This all my prayer shall be,
More love, O Christ, to Thee,
More love to Thee!

3 Then shall my latest breath
Whisper Thy praise;
This be the parting cry
My heart shall raise;
This still its prayer shall be—
More love, O Christ, to Thee,
More love to Thee!

Mrs. Elizabeth Prentiss.

Prayer for the Holy Spirit.

1 O Holy Spirit, come,
And Jesus' love declare;
O tell us of our heavenly home,
And guide us safely there.

2 Our unbelief remove,
By Thine almighty breath;
O work the wondrous work of love,
The mighty work of faith.

3 Come with resistless power,
Come with almighty grace;
Come with the long expected shower,
And fall upon this place.

Oswald Allen.

JESUS PAID IT ALL.

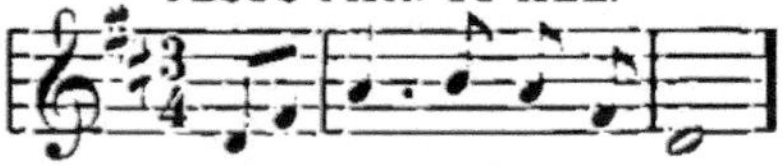

1 Redeeming work is done,
The debt of sin is paid;
The precious Lamb of God,
My sacrifice is made.
REF.—Jesus paid it all:
All to Him I owe;
Sin had left a crimson stain;
He washed it white as snow.

2 I'll bow at Jesus' feet,
And plead His grace so free;
I'll wash me in His blood,
That blood was shed for me.

3 Yes, Jesus paid it all;
To Him the glory be;
His love my pardon speaks,
And grace has set me free.

Fanny J. Crosby.

TALMAR.

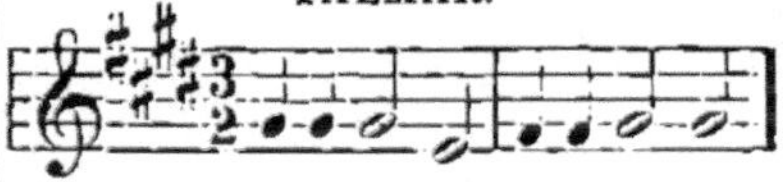

1 One there is, above all others,
Well deserves the name of Friend;
His is love beyond a brother's,
Costly, free, and knows no end.

2 Which of all our friends, to save us,
Could or would have shed His blood?
But our Jesus died to have us
Reconciled in Him to God.

3 O for grace our hearts to soften!
Teach us, Lord, at length, to love;
We, alas! forget too often
What a friend we have above.

Rev. John Newton.

132 Let the Saviour in.

JOSEPHINE POLLARD. *Behold, I stand at the door and knock.*—REV. 3 : 20. MRS. JOSEPH F. KNAPP.

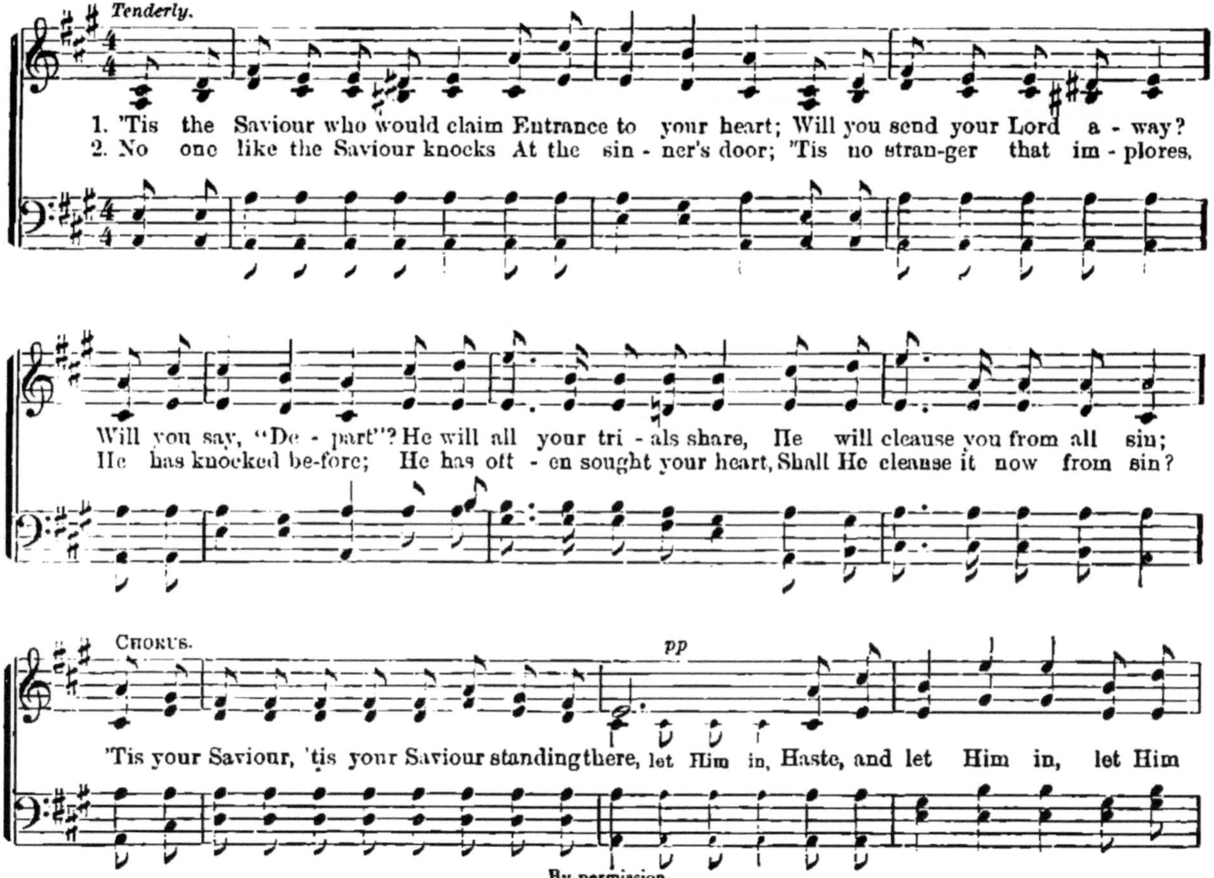

Tenderly.
1. 'Tis the Saviour who would claim Entrance to your heart; Will you send your Lord a - way?
2. No one like the Saviour knocks At the sin - ner's door; 'Tis no stran-ger that im - plores,
Will you say, "De - part"? He will all your tri - als share, He will cleanse you from all sin;
He has knocked be-fore; He has oft - en sought your heart, Shall He cleanse it now from sin?
CHORUS.
pp
'Tis your Saviour, 'tis your Saviour standing there, let Him in, Haste, and let Him in, let Him

By permission.

pp
Rit.
in, let Him in, Lest He turn a - way, let Him in.

3.

O how can you bid Him wait
Till another day,
When already Jesus weeps
At the long delay?
'Twas for you that Jesus died,
And 'tis you He longs to win;
Cho.—'Tis your Saviour, &c.

'Tis not Far to Jesus.

Fanny J. Crosby. *Thou art near, O Lord.*—Ps. 119. 151. W. H. Doane.

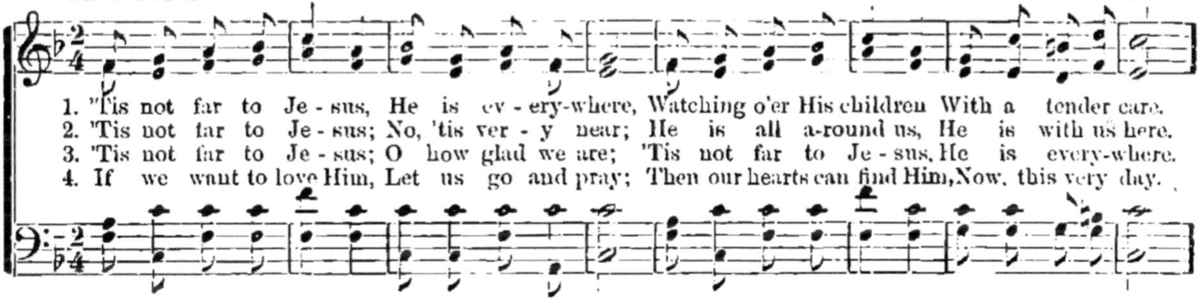
1. 'Tis not far to Je - sus, He is ev - ery-where, Watching o'er His children With a tender care.
2. 'Tis not far to Je - sus; No, 'tis ver - y near; He is all a-round us, He is with us here.
3. 'Tis not far to Je - sus; O how glad we are; 'Tis not far to Je - sus, He is every-where.
4. If we want to love Him, Let us go and pray; Then our hearts can find Him, Now, this very day.

Refrain.
Early if we seek Him, Ear-ly we shall find Him; 'Tis not far to Je - sus, He is ev ery-where.

Follow On.

Rev. W. O. Cushing. *If any man will serve me, let him follow me.*—John 12: 26. R. Lowry.

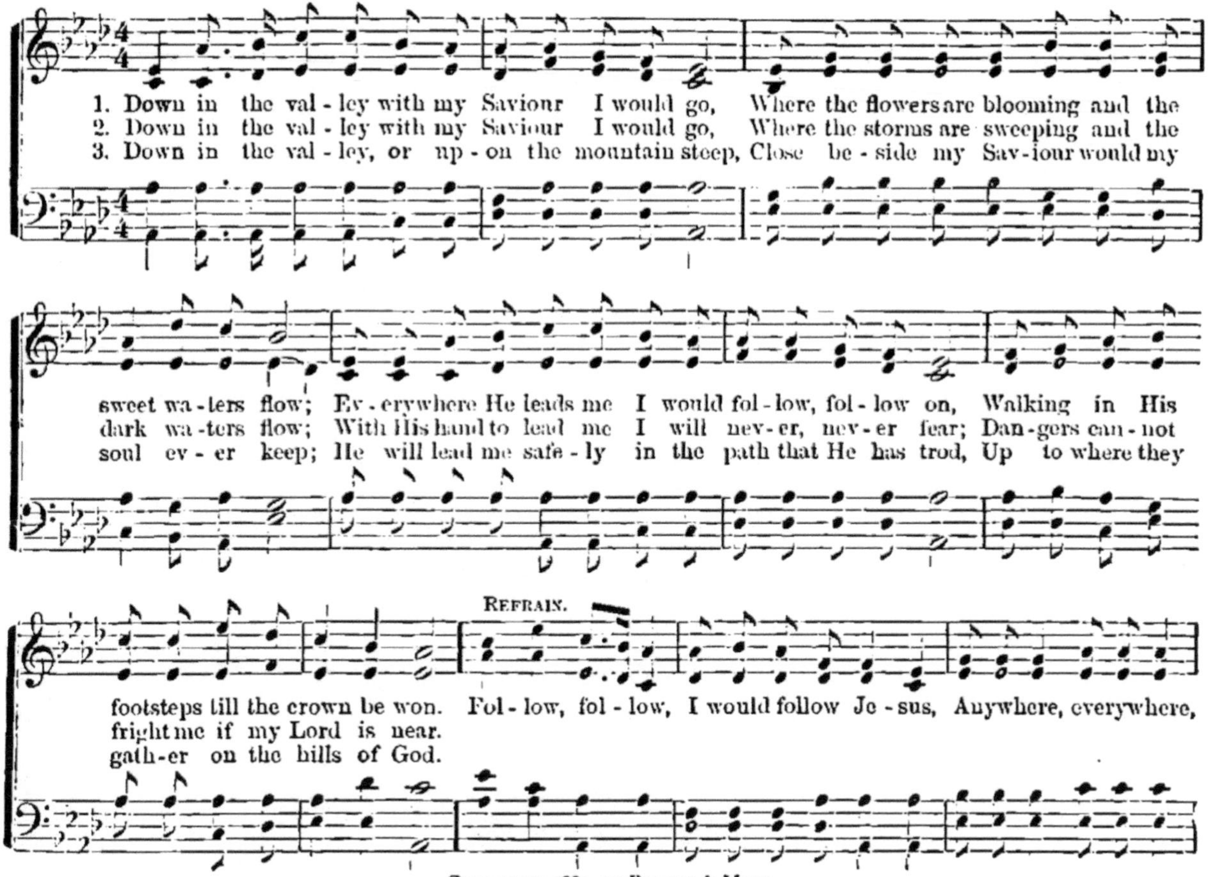
1. Down in the val - ley with my Saviour I would go, Where the flowers are blooming and the sweet wa - ters flow; Ev - erywhere He leads me I would fol - low, fol - low on, Walking in His footsteps till the crown be won.
2. Down in the val - ley with my Saviour I would go, Where the storms are sweeping and the dark wa - ters flow; With His hand to lead me I will nev - er, nev - er fear; Dan - gers can - not fright me if my Lord is near.
3. Down in the val - ley, or up - on the mountain steep, Close be - side my Sav - iour would my soul ev - er keep; He will lead me safe - ly in the path that He has trod, Up to where they gath - er on the hills of God.
Refrain.
Fol - low, fol - low, I would follow Je - sus, Anywhere, everywhere,

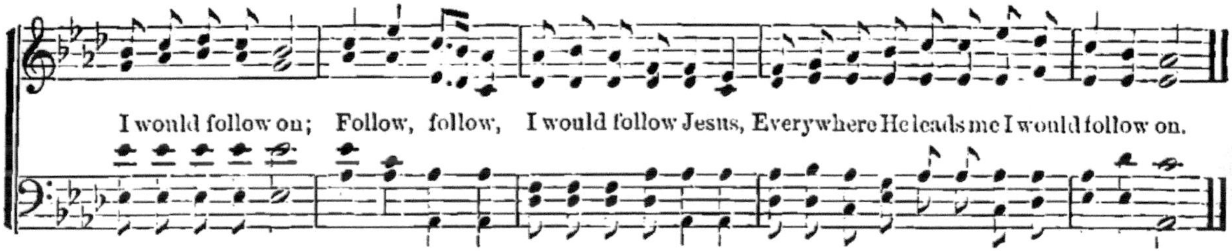
I would follow on; Follow, follow, I would follow Jesus, Everywhere He leads me I would follow on.

Here we Meet.

W. S. *Old men and children.*—Ps. 148 : 12. Wm. Stevenson.

1. Here we meet, Friends we greet, Glad we take our plac - es, While are found,
2. God a - bove, Full of love, Sent His Son to save us; We will raise

All a - round, Hap - py, smil - ing faces.
Loudest praise For the life He gave us.

3 Every day We will pray
For His grace to guide us;
He will care, Break each snare,
In His bosom hide us.

4 Love His cause, Keep His laws,
Doubt or leave Him never;
By and by, Up on high,
Reign with Him for ever.

Poor Wanderer, Come.

C. L. Clifford. *He wandereth abroad.*—Job 15: 23. W. H. Doane.

May be sung as a Solo.

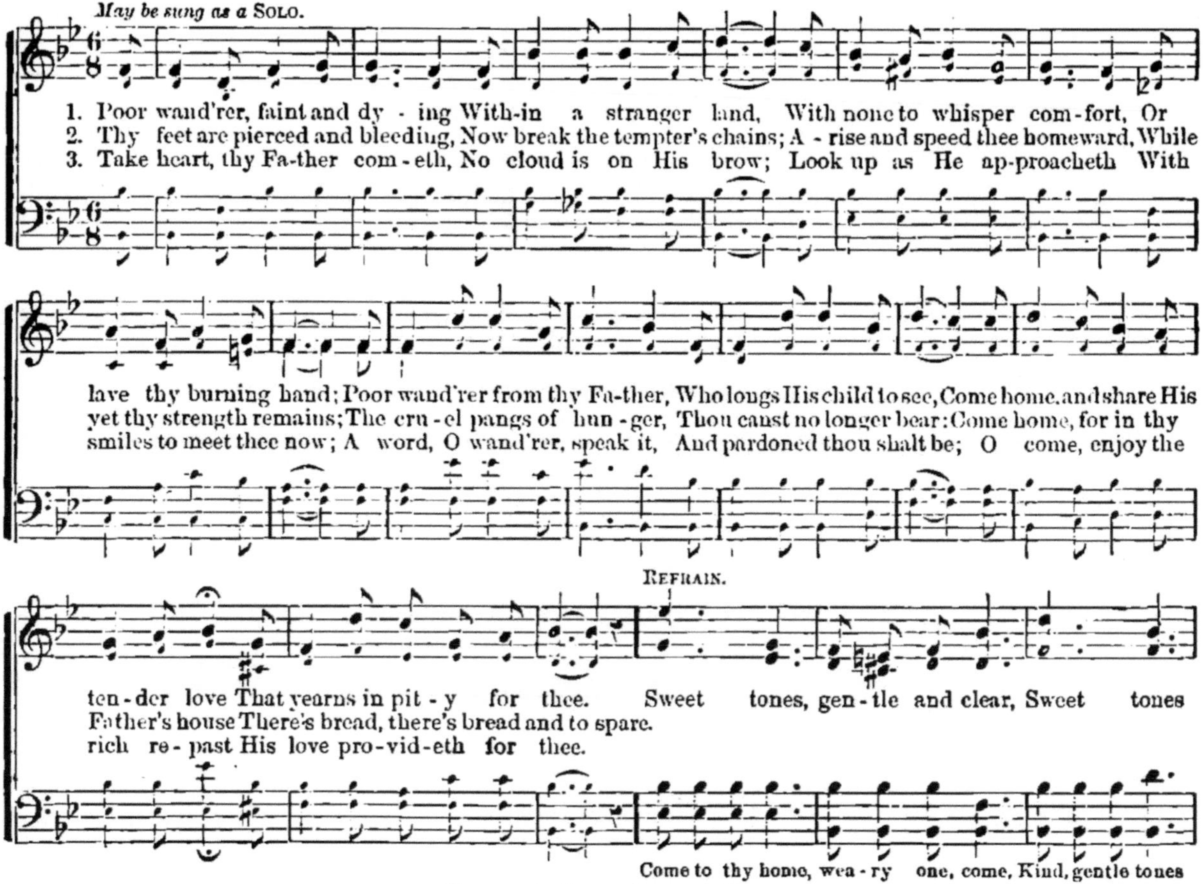

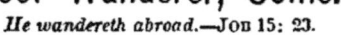

1. Poor wand'rer, faint and dy - ing With-in a stranger land, With none to whisper com-fort, Or
2. Thy feet are pierced and bleeding, Now break the tempter's chains; A - rise and speed thee homeward, While
3. Take heart, thy Fa-ther com - eth, No cloud is on His brow; Look up as He ap-proacheth With
lave thy burning hand; Poor wand'rer from thy Fa-ther, Who longs His child to see, Come home, and share His
yet thy strength remains; The cru - el pangs of hun - ger, Thou canst no longer bear: Come home, for in thy
smiles to meet thee now; A word, O wand'rer, speak it, And pardoned thou shalt be; O come, enjoy the
Refrain.
ten - der love That yearns in pit - y for thee. Sweet tones, gen - tle and clear, Sweet tones
Father's house There's bread, there's bread and to spare.
rich re - past His love pro-vid-eth for thee.
Come to thy home, wea - ry one, come, Kind, gentle tones

float on thine ear; O per-ish-ing soul, their warning o-bey, Come home, come quickly to-day.

How can my Footsteps Fail?

FANNY J. CROSBY. *Thy rod and thy staff they comfort me.*—Ps. 23: 4. HUBERT P. MAIN.

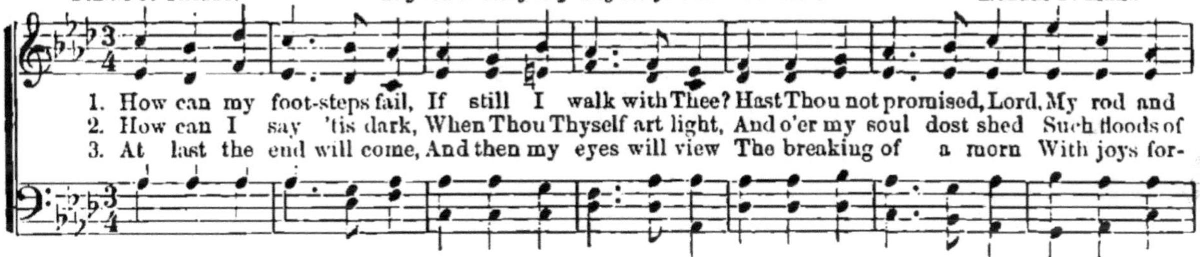
1. How can my foot-steps fail, If still I walk with Thee? Hast Thou not promised, Lord, My rod and
2. How can I say 'tis dark, When Thou Thyself art light, And o'er my soul dost shed Such floods of
3. At last the end will come, And then my eyes will view The breaking of a morn With joys for-

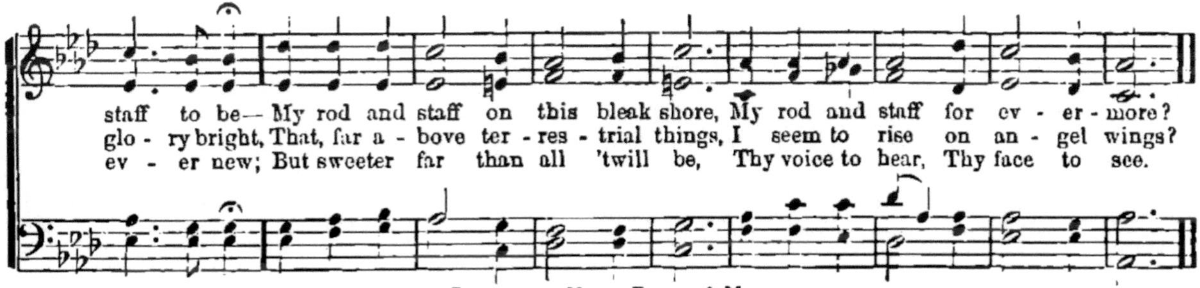
staff to be— My rod and staff on this bleak shore, My rod and staff for ev-er-more?
glo-ry bright, That, far a-bove ter-res-trial things, I seem to rise on an-gel wings?
ev-er new; But sweeter far than all 'twill be, Thy voice to hear, Thy face to see.

138 Come to the Saviour To-day.

Wm. Stevenson. *All things are ready.*—Matt. 22: 4. R. Lowry.

1. O come to the Sav - iour to - day, He waits to be gra - cious and kind; To
2. O come to the Sav - iour to - day, Nor lin - ger in doubt and in fear; This
3. O come to the Sav - iour to - day, Ye wea - ry ones, lad - en and sore; Your
seek Him no longer de - lay, And pardon and peace you shall find. O come...... to - day, O
moment the summons o - bey, 'Tis Je - sus who bids you draw near.
burdens on Him you may lay, And find a sweet rest ev - er-more.
Chorus.
Come to the Saviour
come...... to - day; He waits to be gracious, no longer delay; O come to the Saviour to - day.
Come to the Saviour

DENNIS.

1 Blest be the tie that binds
Our hearts in christian love;
The fellowship of kindred minds
Is like to that above.

2 Before our Father's throne
We pour our ardent prayers;
Our fears, our hopes, our aims are one,
Our comforts and our cares.

3 We share our mutual woes,
Our mutual burdens bear;
And often for each other flows
The sympathizing tear.

Rev. John Fawcett.

Christ our All.

1 Blest be Thy love, dear Lord,
That taught us this sweet way,
To love Thee only for Thyself,
And for that love obey.

2 O Thou, our soul's chief hope,
We to Thy mercy fly;
Where'er we are, Thou canst protect,
Whate'er we need, supply.

3 Whether we sleep or wake,
To Thee we both resign;
By night we see, as well as day,
If Thy light on us shine.

4 Whether we live or die,
Both we submit to Thee;
In death we live, as well as life,
If Thine in death we be.

John Austin.

HENDON.

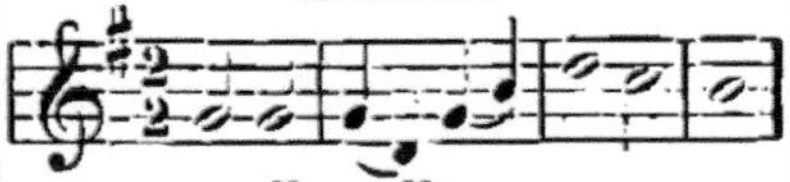

New Year.

1 Bless, O Lord, the opening year
To each soul assembled here;
Clothe Thy word with power divine,
Make us willing to be Thine.

2 Shepherd of Thy blood-bought sheep,
Teach the stony heart to weep;
Let the blind have eyes to see,
See themselves, and look to Thee.

3 Where Thou hast Thy work begun,
Give new strength the race to run;
Scatter darkness, doubts, and fears,
Wipe away the mourner's tears.

4 Bless us all, both old and young;
Call forth praise from every tongue;
Let the whole assembly prove
All Thy power and all Thy love.

Rev. John Newton.

HORTON.

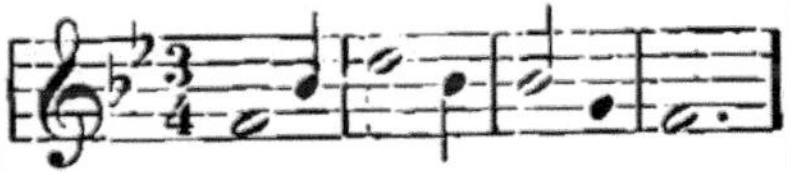

Thine Forever.

1 Thine forever; God of love,
Hear us from Thy throne above;
Thine forever may we be,
Here and in eternity.

2 Thine forever; Lord of life,
Shield us thro' our earthly strife;
Thou, the Life, the Truth, the Way,
Guide us to the realms of day.

3 Thine forever; O how blest,
They who find in Thee their rest!
Saviour, Guardian, heavenly Friend,
O defend us to the end.

4 Thine forever; Thou our Guide,
All our wants by Thee supplied,
All our sins by Thee forgiven,
Lead us, Lord, from earth to heaven.

Mrs. Mary Fawler Maude.

WHAT A FRIEND.

1 What a Friend we have in Jesus,
All our sins and griefs to bear!
What a privilege to carry
Everything to God in prayer!
O what peace we often forfeit,
O what needless pain we bear—
All because we do not carry
Everything to God in prayer.

2 Have we trials and temptations?
Is there trouble anywhere?
We should never be discouraged,
Take it to the Lord in prayer;
Can we find a Friend so faithful,
Who will all our sorrows share?
Jesus knows our every weakness,
Take it to the Lord in prayer.

3 Are we weak and heavy laden,
Cumbered with a load of care?
Precious Saviour, still our refuge,—
Take it to the Lord in prayer;
Do thy friends despise, forsake thee?
Take it to the Lord in prayer;
In His arms He'll take and shield thee,
Thou wilt find a solace there.

Anon.

Lovely Zion.

Mrs. F. J. Alstyne. *How amiable are thy tabernacles, O Lord.*—Ps. 84: 1. W. H. Doane.

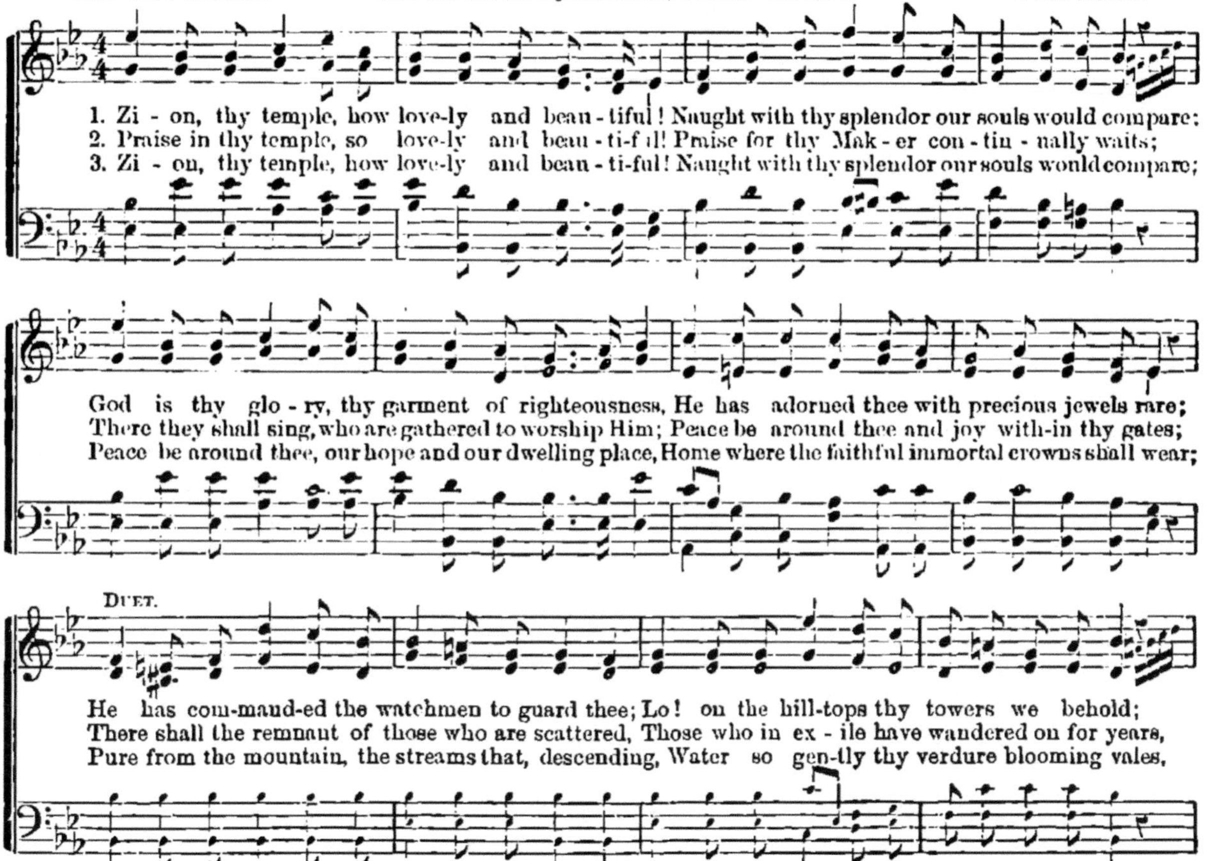
1. Zi - on, thy temple, how love-ly and beau - tiful! Naught with thy splendor our souls would compare;
2. Praise in thy temple, so love-ly and beau - ti-ful! Praise for thy Mak - er con - tin - ually waits;
3. Zi - on, thy temple, how love-ly and beau - ti-ful! Naught with thy splendor our souls would compare;
God is thy glo - ry, thy garment of righteousness, He has adorned thee with precious jewels rare;
There they shall sing, who are gathered to worship Him; Peace be around thee and joy with-in thy gates;
Peace be around thee, our hope and our dwelling place, Home where the faithful immortal crowns shall wear;
Duet.
He has com-mand-ed the watchmen to guard thee; Lo! on the hill-tops thy towers we behold;
There shall the remnant of those who are scattered, Those who in ex - ile have wandered on for years,
Pure from the mountain, the streams that, descending, Water so gen-tly thy verdure blooming vales,

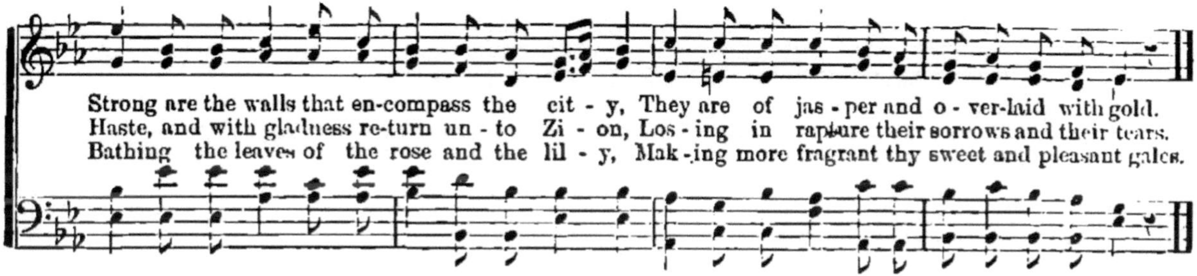
Strong are the walls that en-compass the cit - y, They are of jas - per and o - ver-laid with gold.
Haste, and with gladness re-turn un - to Zi - on, Los - ing in rapture their sorrows and their tears.
Bathing the leaves of the rose and the lil - y, Mak - ing more fragrant thy sweet and pleasant gales.

The Children's Saviour.

Rev. W. St. Hill Bourne. *Suffer the little children to come unto me.*—Mark. 10: 14. John Stainer, Mus. Doc.

1. Christ, who once a - mong us As a child did dwell, Is the children's Sav-iour, And He loves us well;
2. Though we may not see Him, For a lit - tle while, We shall know He holds us, Oft - en feel His smile;
3. Je - sus, our good Shepherd, Lay-ing down Thy life, Lest Thy sheep should perish In the cru-el strife,
If we trust His prom - ise, He will let us rest In His arms for - ev - er, Lean - ing on His breast.
Death will be to slum - ber In that sweet em-brace, And we shall a - wak - en To be - hold His face.
Help us to re - mem - ber All Thy love and care, Trust in Thee, and love Thee, Always, every-where.

Young Pilgrims.

Mrs. Lydia Baxter. ——*my songs in the house of my pilgrimage.*—Ps. 119: 54. Wm. B. Bradbury.

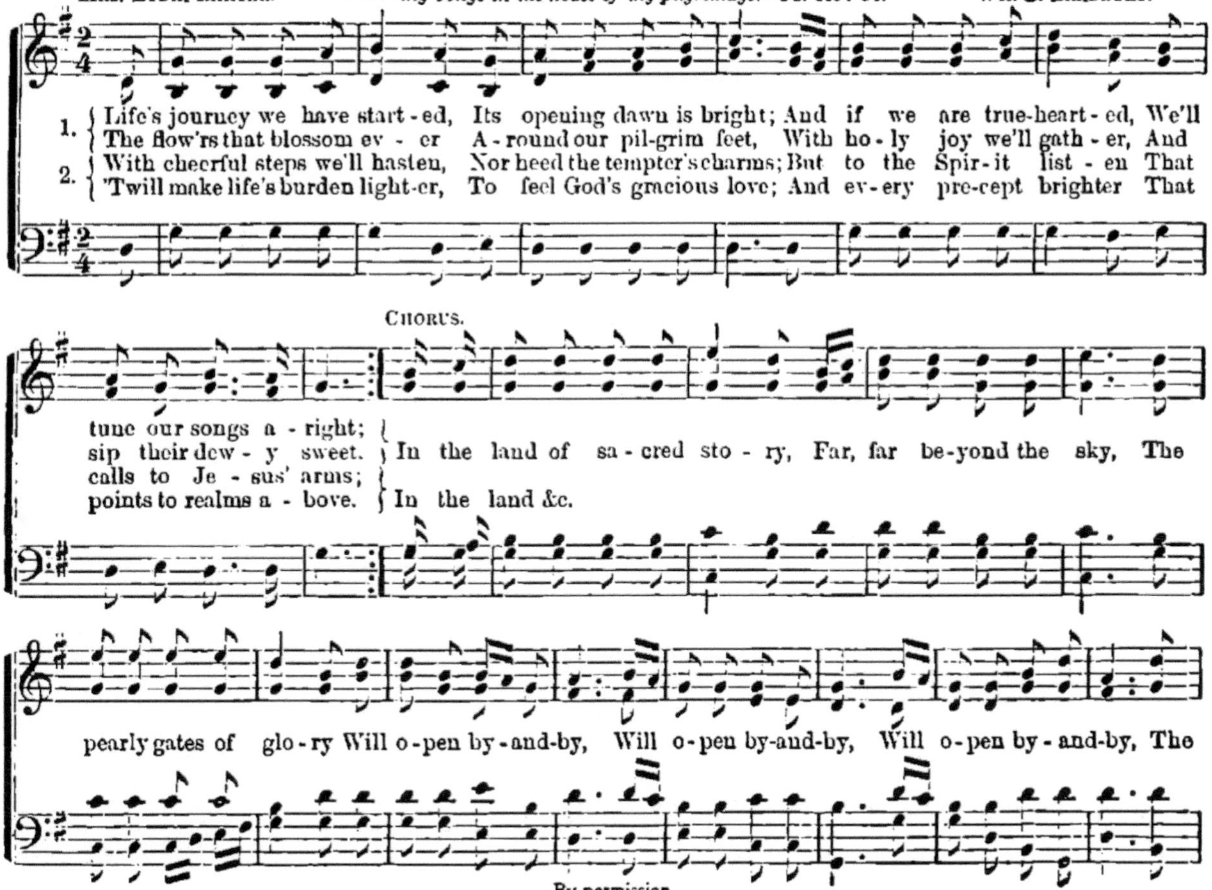
1. Life's journey we have start-ed, Its opening dawn is bright; And if we are true-heart-ed, We'll tune our songs a-right;
The flow'rs that blossom ev-er A-round our pil-grim feet, With ho-ly joy we'll gath-er, And sip their dew-y sweet.
2. With cheerful steps we'll hasten, Nor heed the tempter's charms; But to the Spir-it list-en That calls to Je-sus' arms;
'Twill make life's burden light-er, To feel God's gracious love; And ev-ery pre-cept brighter That points to realms a-bove.
Chorus.
In the land of sa-cred sto-ry, Far, far be-yond the sky, The
In the land &c.
pearly gates of glo-ry Will o-pen by-and-by, Will o-pen by-and-by, Will o-pen by-and-by, The

By permission.

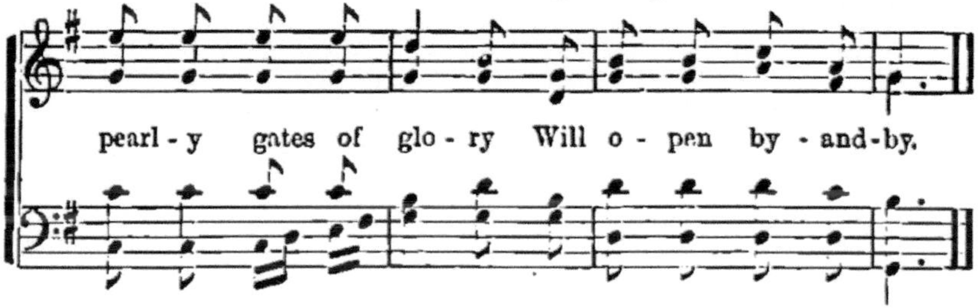
pearl - y gates of glo - ry Will o - pen by - and - by.

3 His holy book will ever
Our onward footsteps guide,
Until we reach our Saviour,
And rest us at His side;
And when we meet our Jesus,
Our tears all wiped away,
We'll take the harp He gives us,
And shout and sing for aye.

Awake Thou, O Sleeper.

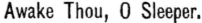

MRS. E. C. ELLSWORTH. *Awake, thou that sleepest.*—EPH. 5: 14. R. LOWRY.

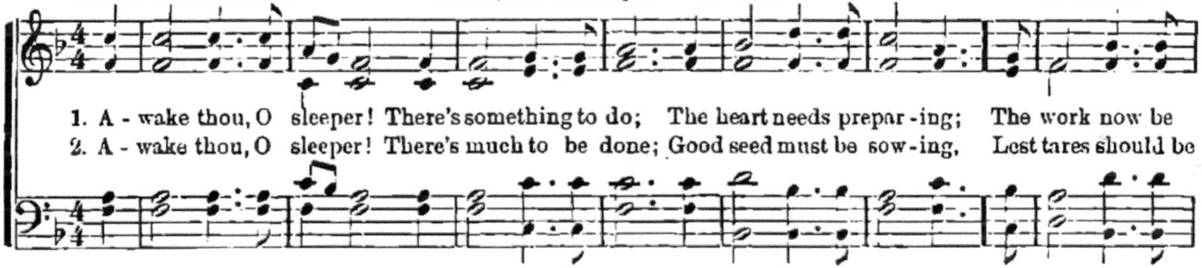
1. A - wake thou, O sleeper! There's something to do; The heart needs prepar - ing; The work now be
2. A - wake thou, O sleeper! There's much to be done; Good seed must be sow - ing, Lest tares should be

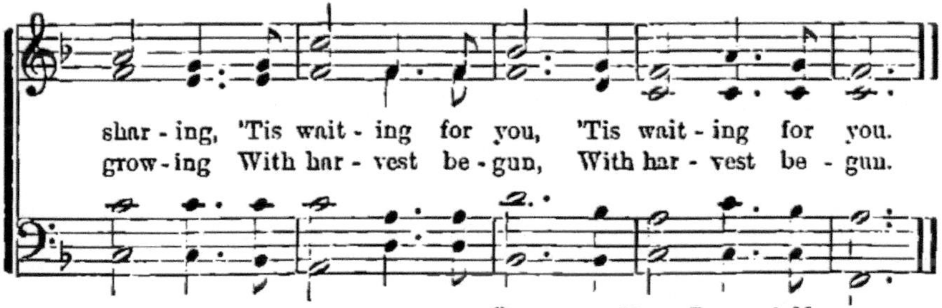
shar - ing, 'Tis wait - ing for you, 'Tis wait - ing for you.
grow - ing With har - vest be - gun, With har - vest be - gun.

3 Awake thou, O sleeper!
The morning is spent;
The day now is hasting,
And time quickly wasting,
The time God has lent.

4 Awake thou, O sleeper!
Yes, up and away;
The light now is waning,
But one hour remaining;
How short is the day!

144

Sound the Alarm.

F. J. C. *Sound an alarm.* —Joel 2: 1. W. H. Doane.

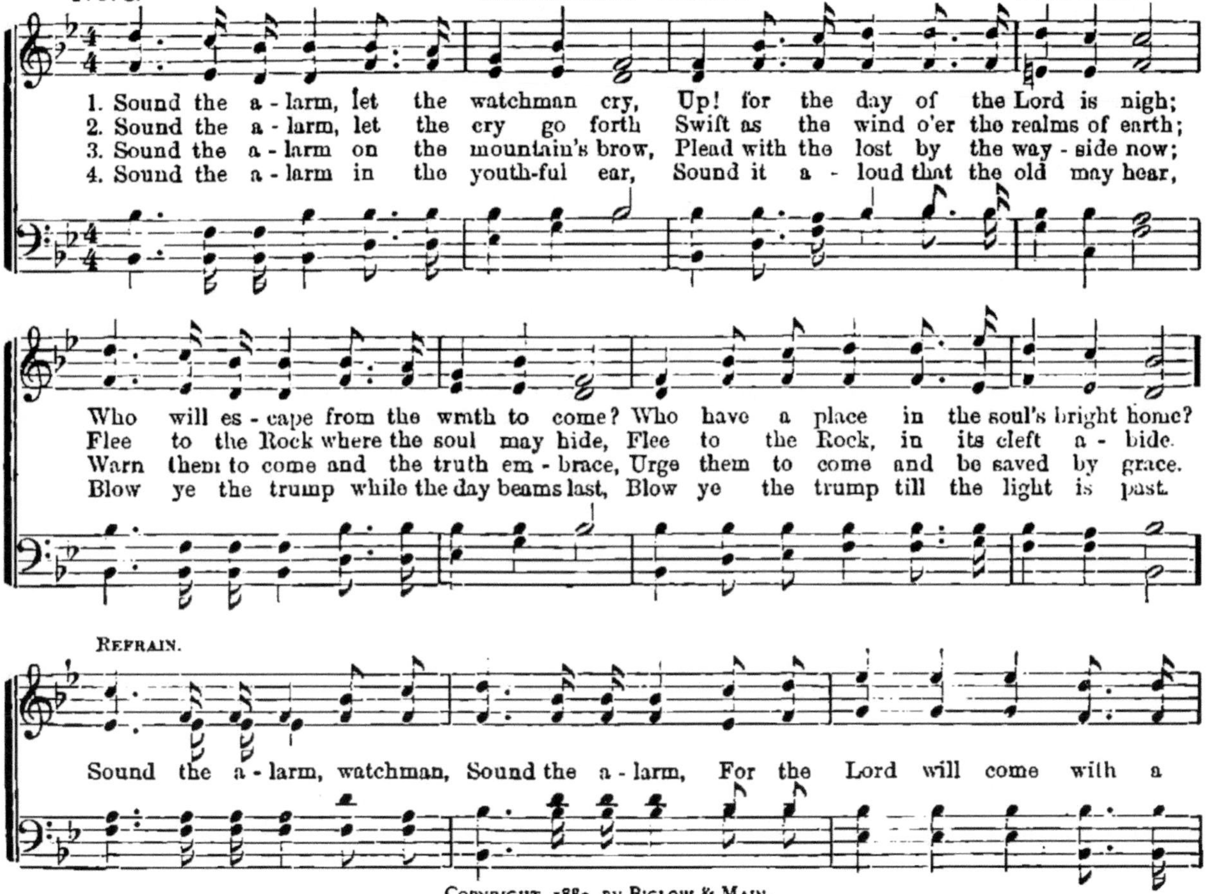
1. Sound the a - larm, let the watchman cry, Up! for the day of the Lord is nigh;
2. Sound the a - larm, let the cry go forth Swift as the wind o'er the realms of earth;
3. Sound the a - larm on the mountain's brow, Plead with the lost by the way - side now;
4. Sound the a - larm in the youth-ful ear, Sound it a - loud that the old may hear,
Who will es - cape from the wrath to come? Who have a place in the soul's bright home?
Flee to the Rock where the soul may hide, Flee to the Rock, in its cleft a - bide.
Warn them to come and the truth em - brace, Urge them to come and be saved by grace.
Blow ye the trump while the day beams last, Blow ye the trump till the light is past.
Refrain.
Sound the a - larm, watchman, Sound the a - larm, For the Lord will come with a

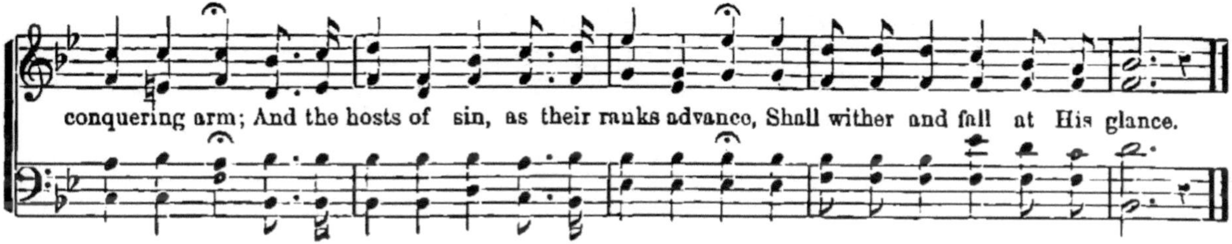
conquering arm; And the hosts of sin, as their ranks advance, Shall wither and fall at His glance.

Who is there like Thee?

There is none upon earth that I desire beside thee.—Ps. 73 : 25.

J. Anastasius Freylinghausen. R. Lowry.

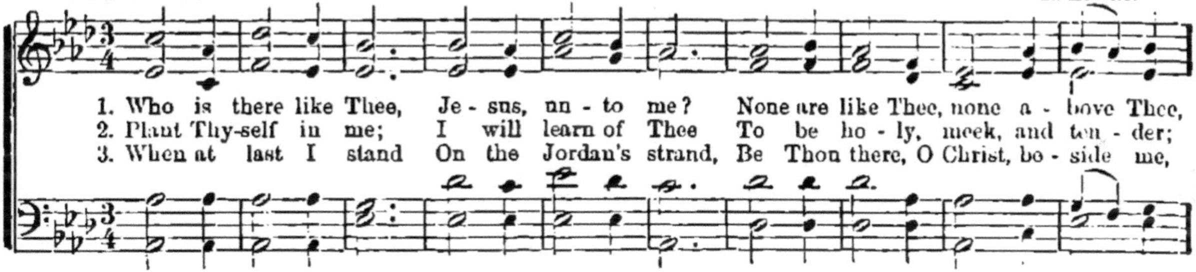
1. Who is there like Thee, Je - sus, un - to me? None are like Thee, none a - bove Thee,
2. Plant Thy-self in me; I will learn of Thee To be ho - ly, meek, and ten - der;
3. When at last I stand On the Jordan's strand, Be Thou there, O Christ, be - side me,

Thou art al - to - geth - er love - ly; None on earth have we, None in heaven, like Thee.
Wrath, and pride, and self, sur - ren - der; Nothing shouldst Thou see But Thy - self in me.
Thro' the gloom - y wa - ters guide me; Take me then to be Ev - er, Lord, with Thee.

146 Just on the Border.

JESSIE CLYDE. *Until we have passed thy borders.*—NUM. 20: 17. W. H. DOANE.

1. Just on the border now we are standing, Watching the dear ones gliding a - way;
2. Just on the border, O there is comfort! Yonder our Saviour smiles from the shore;
3. Just on the border, let us take courage; Others are crossing hopeful and strong;
4. Faith in her gladness brings us from Canaan Clusters of fruitage, garlands of flowers;
Just on the border waiting the boatman Gently to bear us safe o'er the spray.
Waving us onward, lovingly, kindly, Home where the weary sorrow no more.
Over the water smooth as a mirror, List to their triumph wafted in song.
Joy for our sorrow, praise for our weeping, Garments of glory soon will be ours.
REFRAIN.
Soon in the harbor joyful we'll anchor, Anchor where Jesus welcomes the blest;
Soon in the harbor

Rall.
There will our tri - - als slumber for - ev - er. Calmed like the tempest sweetly to rest.
There will our tri - als

Saviour, to Thy Mercy Seat.

WM. STEVENSON. *Draw near with a true heart.*—HEB. 10 : 22. R. LOWRY.

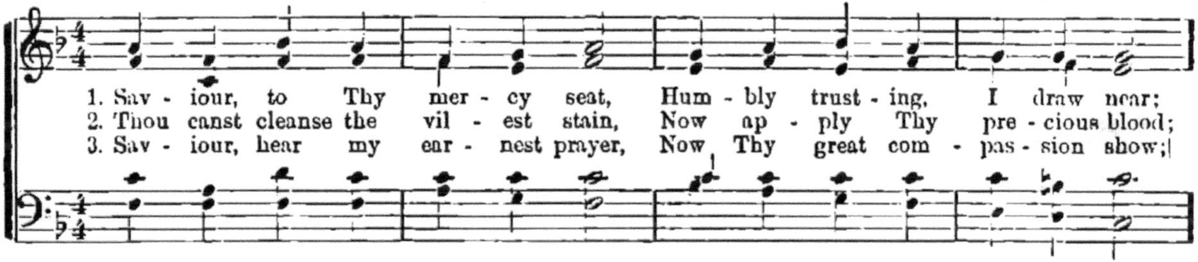
1. Sav - iour, to Thy mer - cy seat, Hum - bly trust - ing, I draw near;
2. Thou canst cleanse the vil - est stain, Now ap - ply Thy pre - cious blood;
3. Sav - iour, hear my ear - nest prayer, Now Thy great com - pas - sion show;

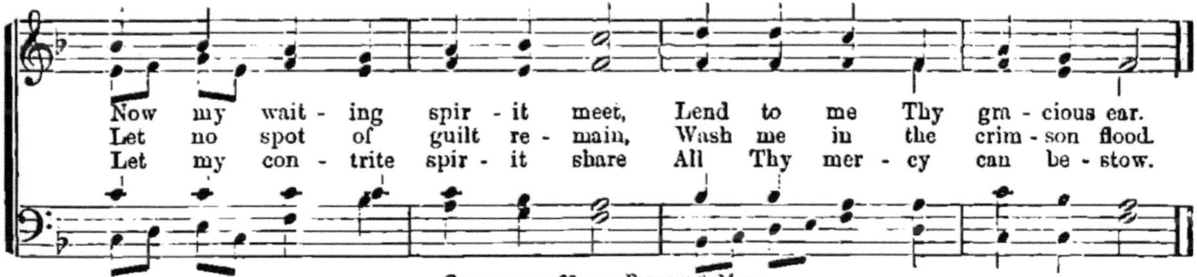
Now my wait - ing spir - it meet, Lend to me Thy gra - cious ear.
Let no spot of guilt re - main, Wash me in the crim - son flood.
Let my con - trite spir - it share All Thy mer - cy can be - stow.

148 Shall we all Meet?

Words arranged. *I go to prepare a place for you.*—John 14: 2. Ira D. Sankey.

1. Shall we all meet at home in the morn - ing, On the shores of the bright crys - tal sea,
With the loved ones who long have been wait - ing? What a meet-ing in-deed it will be!
2. Shall we all meet at home in the morn - ing, And from sor-row for-ev - er be free?
Shall we join in the songs of the ran - somed? What a meet-ing in-deed it will be!
3. Shall we all meet at home in the morn - ing, Our bless-ed Redeem - er to see?
Shall we know and be known by our loved ones? What a meet-ing in-deed it will be!
Chorus.
Gath - ered home, gath - ered home, On the shore of the bright crys - tal sea!
Gathered home, gathered home,

Gath-ered home, gath-ered home,...... With our loved ones for-ev - er to be!
Gathered home. gathered home.

I Love Thee.

MRS. ANNIE S. HAWKS. *Thou knowest that I love thee.*—JOHN 21: 17. R. LOWRY.

1. I love Thee, O Lord, I be-lieve in Thy word; I love Thee, I love Thee, I love Thee, my Lord.
2. By day and by night, In the vale, on the height, In tu - mult or si - lence, Thou art my de-light.
3. But ear nev - er heard Sweeter song, sweeter word, Than this I am singing: Thou lovest me, Lord.
4. This song I can sing Till my spir - it takes wing; 'Tis me that Thou lov-est, My Saviour and King.
REFRAIN.
How sweet to love Thee, And near Thee to be! But sweeter, far sweeter, That Thou lov-est me.

By permission.

150 Closer, Dear Lord, to Thee.

Chas. H. Gabriel. *Peace be to him * * * that is near.*—Isa. 57: 19. W. H. Doane.

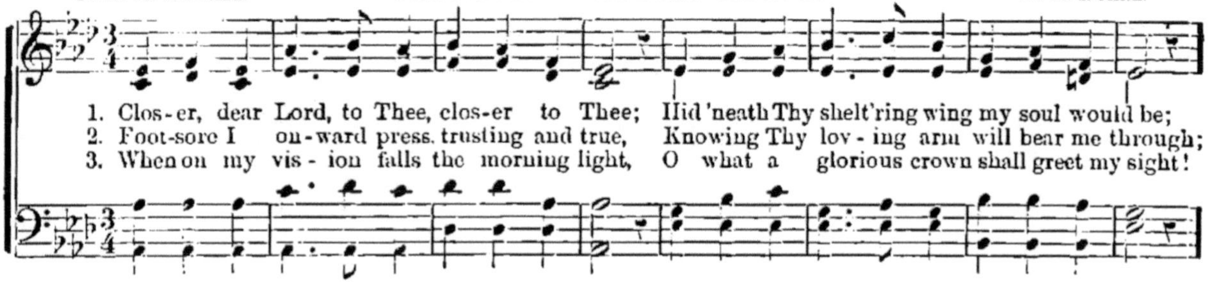
1. Clos-er, dear Lord, to Thee, clos-er to Thee; Hid 'neath Thy shelt'ring wing my soul would be;
2. Foot-sore I on-ward press, trusting and true, Knowing Thy lov-ing arm will bear me through;
3. When on my vis-ion falls the morning light, O what a glorious crown shall greet my sight!

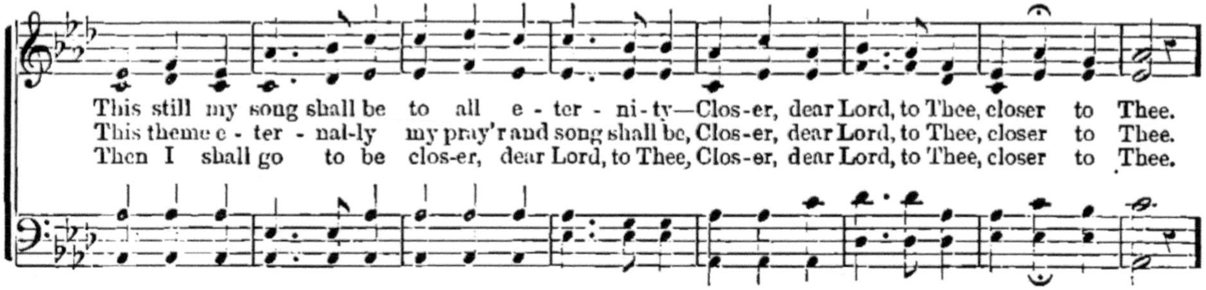
This still my song shall be to all e-ter-ni-ty—Clos-er, dear Lord, to Thee, closer to Thee.
This theme e-ter-nal-ly my pray'r and song shall be, Clos-er, dear Lord, to Thee, closer to Thee.
Then I shall go to be clos-er, dear Lord, to Thee, Clos-er, dear Lord, to Thee, closer to Thee.

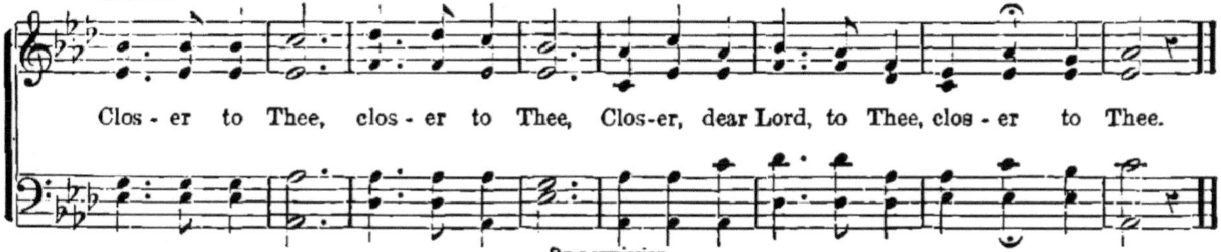
Refrain
Clos-er to Thee, clos-er to Thee, Clos-er, dear Lord, to Thee, clos-er to Thee.

By permission.

RESCUE THE PERISHING.

1 Rescue the perishing,
Care for the dying,
Snatch them in pity from sin and the grave;
Weep o'er the erring one,
Lift up the fallen,
Tell them of Jesus, the mighty to save.
CHO.—Rescue the perishing,
Care for the dying;
Jesus is merciful,
Jesus will save.

2 Though they are slighting Him,
Still He is waiting,
Waiting the penitent child to receive;
Plead with them earnestly,
Plead with them gently,
He will forgive if they only believe.

3 Down in the human heart,
Crushed by the tempter,
Feelings lie buried that Christ can restore:
Touched by a loving heart,
Wakened by kindness,
Chords that were broken will vibrate once more.

Fanny J. Crosby.

LEBANON.

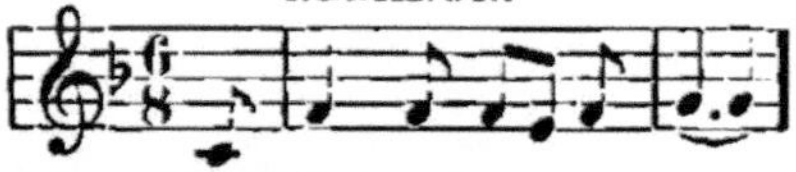

1 I was a wandering sheep,
I did not love the fold;
I did not love my Shepherd's voice,
I would not be controlled;
I was a wayward child,
I did not love my home;
I did not love my Father's voice,
I loved afar to roam.

2 The Shepherd sought His sheep,
The Father sought His child;
They followed me o'er vale and hill,
O'er deserts waste and wild;
They found me nigh to death,
Famished, and faint, and lone;
They bound me with the bands of love,
They saved the wandering one.

3 Jesus my Shepherd is;
'Twas He that loved my soul;
'Twas He that washed me in His blood,
'Twas He that made me whole;
'Twas He that sought the lost,
That found the wandering sheep;
'Twas He that brought me to the fold—
'Tis He that still doth keep.

Dr. H. Bonar.

BROWN.

1 In all my Lord's appointed ways
My journey I'll pursue;
"Hinder me not," ye much loved saints,
For I must go with you.

2 Through duties and through trials too,
I'll go at His command;
"Hinder me not," for I am bound
To my Immanuel's land.

3 And when my Saviour calls me home,
Still this my cry shall be—
"Hinder me not!" come, welcome, death,
I'll gladly go with thee.

John Ryland, D. D.

WE SHALL MEET.

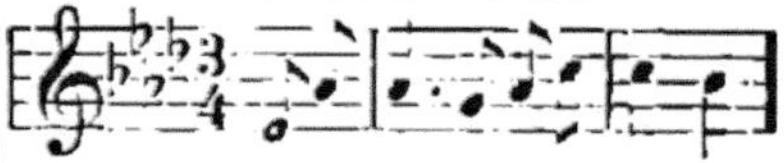

1 We shall meet beyond the river,
By and by, by and by;
And the darkness will be over,
By and by, by and by;
With the toilsome journey done,
And the glorious battle won,
We shall shine forth as the sun,
By and by, by and by.

2 We shall strike the harps of glory,
By and by, by and by;
We shall sing redemption's story,
By and by, by and by;
And the strains for evermore
Shall resound in sweetness o'er
Yonder everlasting shore,
By and by, by and by.

3 Wearing robes of snowy whiteness,
By and by, by and by;
And with crowns of dazzling brightness,
By and by, by and by,—
Then, our storms and perils passed,
And with glory ours at last,
We'll possess the kingdom vast,
By and by, by and by.

John Atkinson, D. D.

152

Never Falter.

Mrs. Ella Dale. *Take courage and do.*—2 Chron. 19: 11. W. H. Doane.

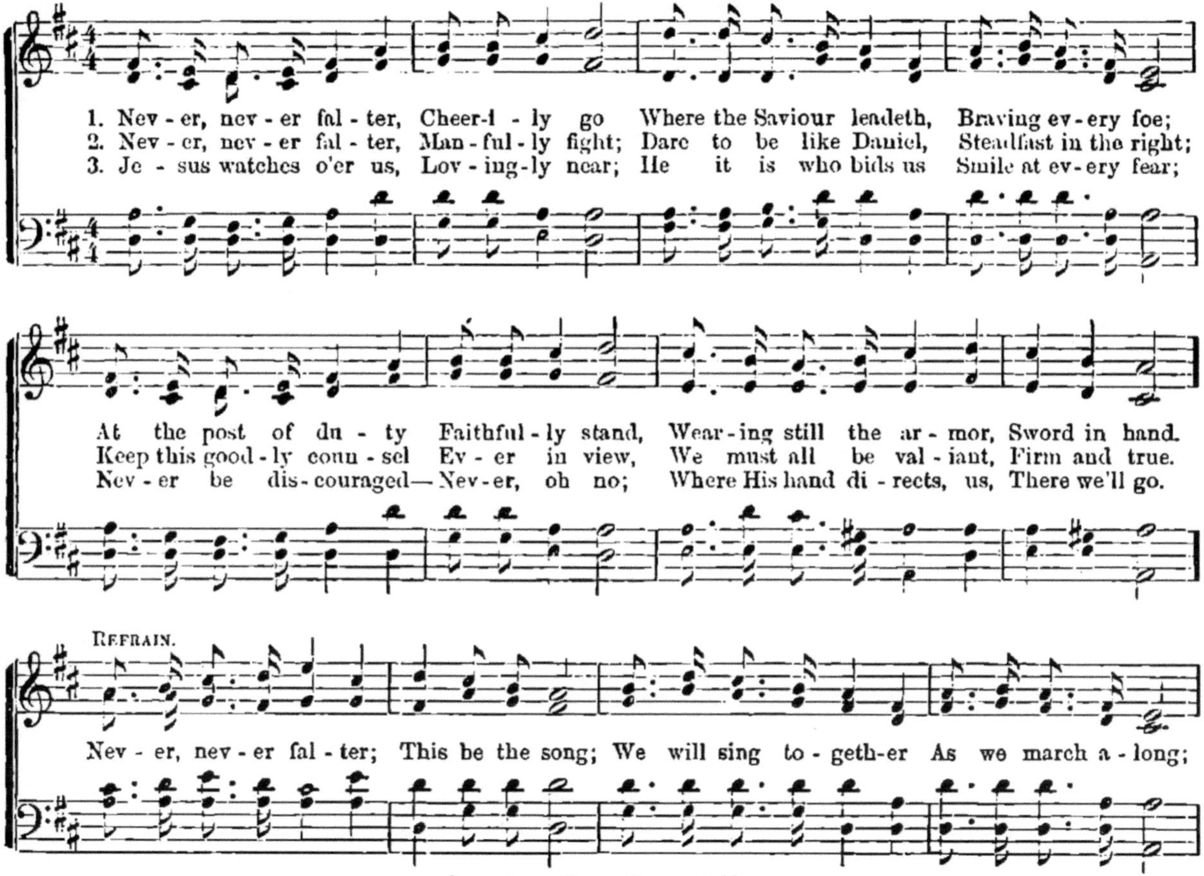
1. Nev - er, nev - er fal - ter, Cheer-i - ly go Where the Saviour leadeth, Braving ev - ery foe;
2. Nev - er, nev - er fal - ter, Man - ful - ly fight; Dare to be like Daniel, Steadfast in the right;
3. Je - sus watches o'er us, Lov - ing - ly near; He it is who bids us Smile at ev - ery fear;
At the post of du - ty Faithful - ly stand, Wear - ing still the ar - mor, Sword in hand.
Keep this good - ly coun - sel Ev - er in view, We must all be val - iant, Firm and true.
Nev - er be dis - couraged—Nev - er, oh no; Where His hand di - rects, us, There we'll go.
Refrain.
Nev - er, nev - er fal - ter; This be the song; We will sing to - geth - er As we march a - long;

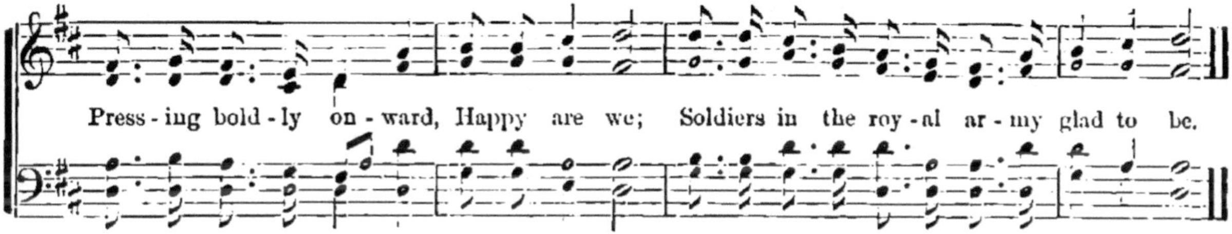
Press - ing bold - ly on - ward, Happy are we; Soldiers in the roy - al ar - my glad to be.

Yes, we Part.

J. DENHAM SMITH. *The grace of our Lord Jesus Christ be with you all.*—REV. 22: 21. R. LOWRY.

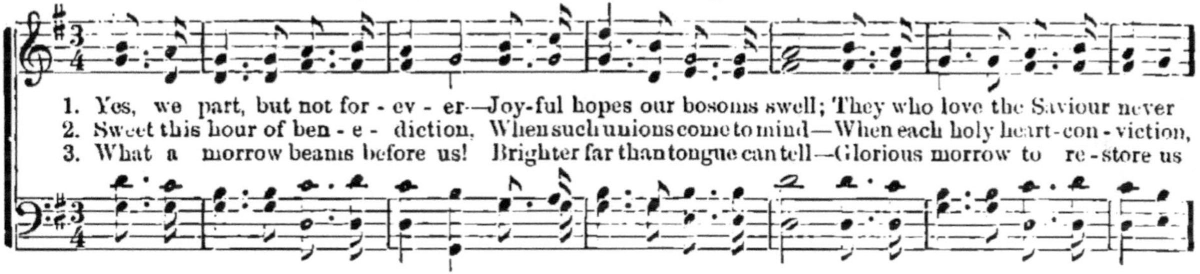
1. Yes, we part, but not for - ev - er—Joy-ful hopes our bosoms swell; They who love the Saviour never
2. Sweet this hour of ben - e - diction, When such unions come to mind—When each holy heart-con - viction,
3. What a morrow beams before us! Brighter far than tongue can tell—Glorious morrow to re - store us

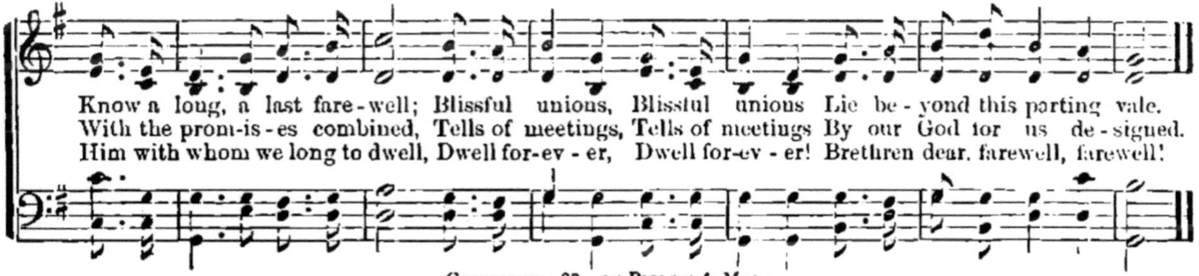
Know a long, a last fare - well; Blissful unions, Blissful unions Lie be - yond this parting vale.
With the prom-is - es combined, Tells of meetings, Tells of meetings By our God for us de - signed.
Him with whom we long to dwell, Dwell for-ev - er, Dwell for-ev - er! Brethren dear, farewell, farewell!

154

Happy Song.

Mrs. Lydia Baxter. *Thou art my trust from my youth.*—Ps. 71: 5. Wm. B. Bradbury.

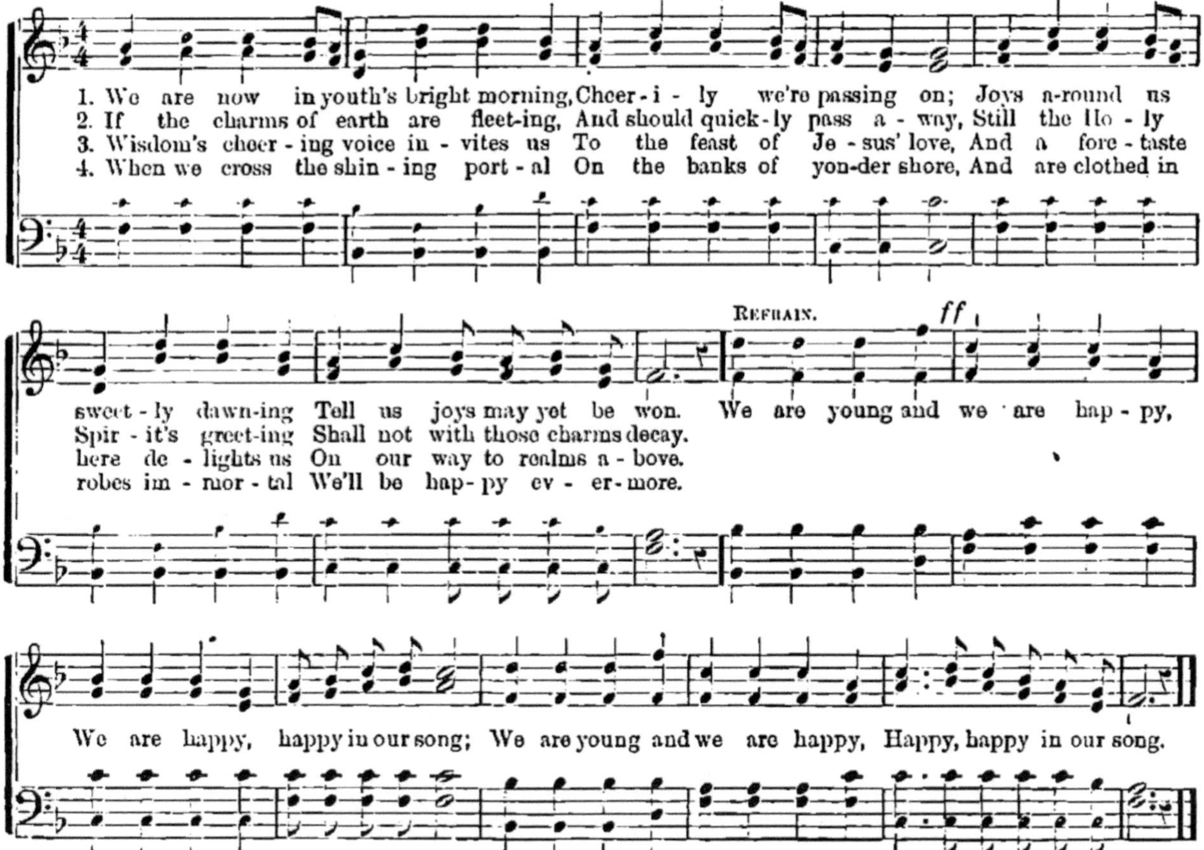
1. We are now in youth's bright morning, Cheer - i - ly we're passing on; Joys a-round us sweet - ly dawn-ing Tell us joys may yet be won.
2. If the charms of earth are fleet-ing, And should quick - ly pass a - way, Still the Ho - ly Spir - it's greet-ing Shall not with those charms decay.
3. Wisdom's cheer - ing voice in - vites us To the feast of Je - sus' love, And a fore - taste here de - lights us On our way to realms a - bove.
4. When we cross the shin - ing port - al On the banks of yon-der shore, And are clothed in robes im - mor - tal We'll be hap - py ev - er - more.
Refrain.
ff
We are young and we are hap - py, We are happy, happy in our song; We are young and we are happy, Happy, happy in our song.

By permission.

Drawing Nearer my Home.

Fanny J. Crosby. *Now is our salvation nearer than when we believed.*—Rom. 13: 11. W. H. Doane.

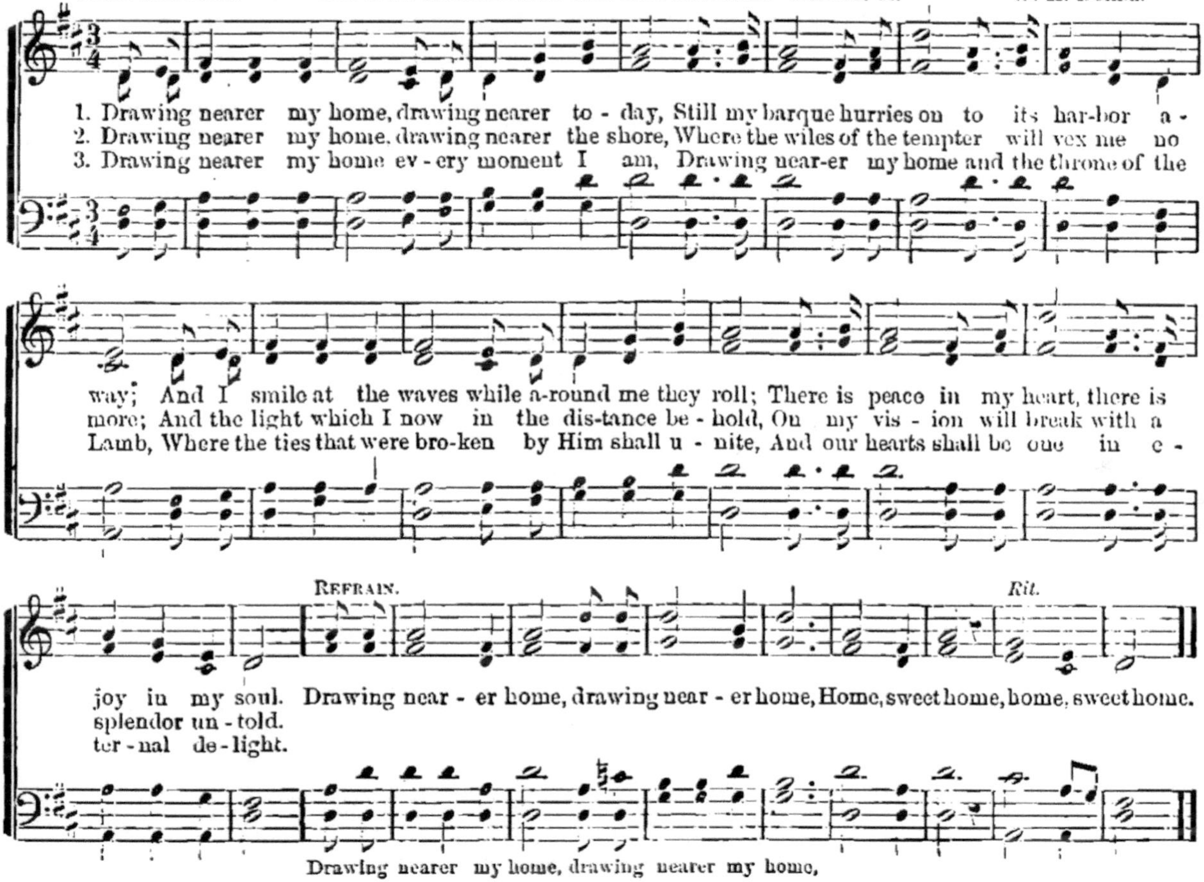
1. Drawing nearer my home, drawing nearer to - day, Still my barque hurries on to its har-bor a - way; And I smile at the waves while a-round me they roll; There is peace in my heart, there is joy in my soul.
2. Drawing nearer my home, drawing nearer the shore, Where the wiles of the tempter will vex me no more; And the light which I now in the dis-tance be - hold, On my vis - ion will break with a splendor un - told.
3. Drawing nearer my home ev - ery moment I am, Drawing near-er my home and the throne of the Lamb, Where the ties that were bro-ken by Him shall u - nite, And our hearts shall be one in e - ter - nal de - light.
Refrain.
Drawing near - er home, drawing near - er home, Home, sweet home, home, sweet home.
Rit.
Drawing nearer my home, drawing nearer my home,

By permission.

156 Sinner, why in Darkness?

WM. STEVENSON. *I would hasten my escape from the windy storm and tempest.*—Ps. 55: 8. R. LOWRY.

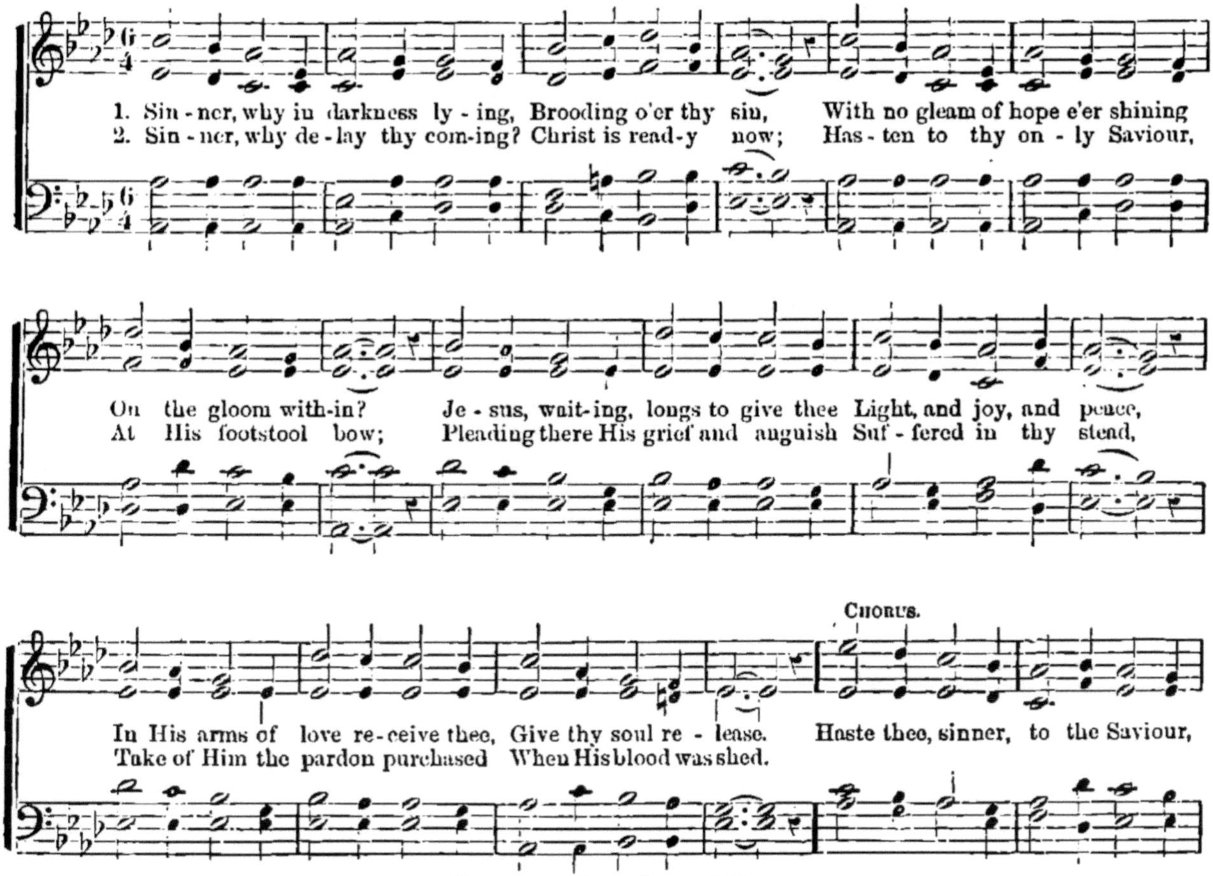
1. Sin - ner, why in darkness ly - ing, Brooding o'er thy sin, With no gleam of hope e'er shining
2. Sin - ner, why de - lay thy com-ing? Christ is read-y now; Has - ten to thy on - ly Saviour,
On the gloom with-in? Je - sus, wait-ing, longs to give thee Light, and joy, and peace,
At His footstool bow; Pleading there His grief and anguish Suf - fered in thy stead,
In His arms of love re-ceive thee, Give thy soul re - lease.
Take of Him the pardon purchased When His blood was shed.
CHORUS.
Haste thee, sinner, to the Saviour,

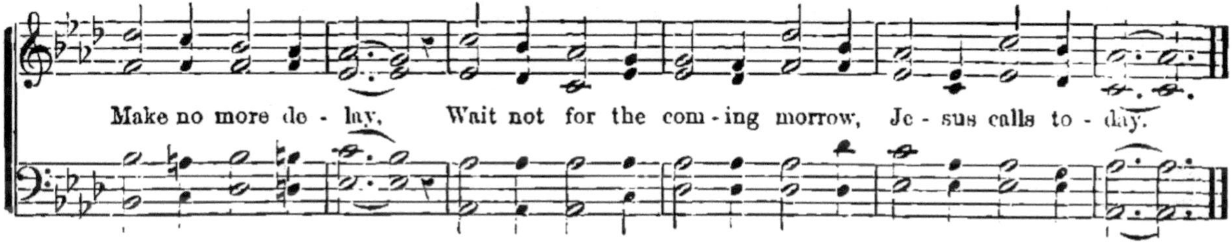
Make no more de - lay, Wait not for the com - ing morrow, Je - sus calls to - day.

Cease, ye Mourners.

W. Bengo Collyer, D. D. *Thy rod and thy staff, they comfort me.*—Ps. 23: 4. F. Mendelssohn-Bartholdy.

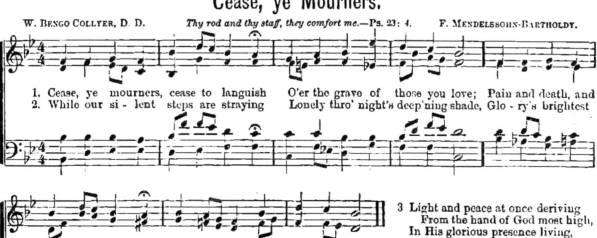

1. Cease, ye mourners, cease to languish O'er the grave of those you love; Pain and death, and
2. While our si - lent steps are straying Lonely thro' night's deep'ning shade, Glo - ry's brightest

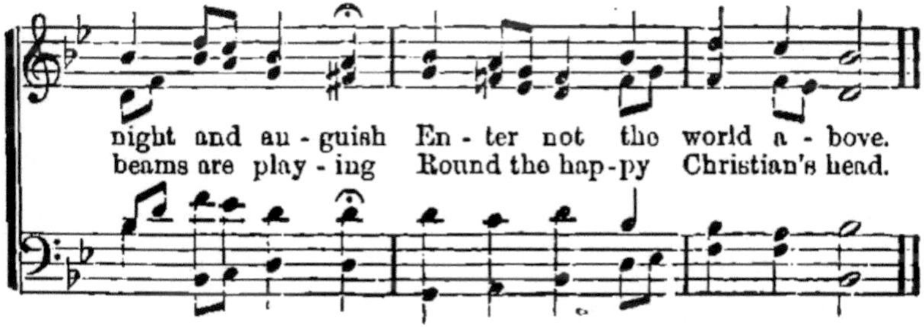
night and an - guish En - ter not the world a - bove.
beams are play - ing Round the hap - py Christian's head.

3 Light and peace at once deriving
From the hand of God most high,
In His glorious presence living,
They shall never, never die.

4 Now, ye mourners, cease to languish
O'er the grave of those you love;
Far removed from pain and anguish,
They are chanting hymns above.

158 Jesus on the Shore.

Fanny J. Crosby. *Jesus stood on the shore.*—John 21: 4. W. H. Doane.

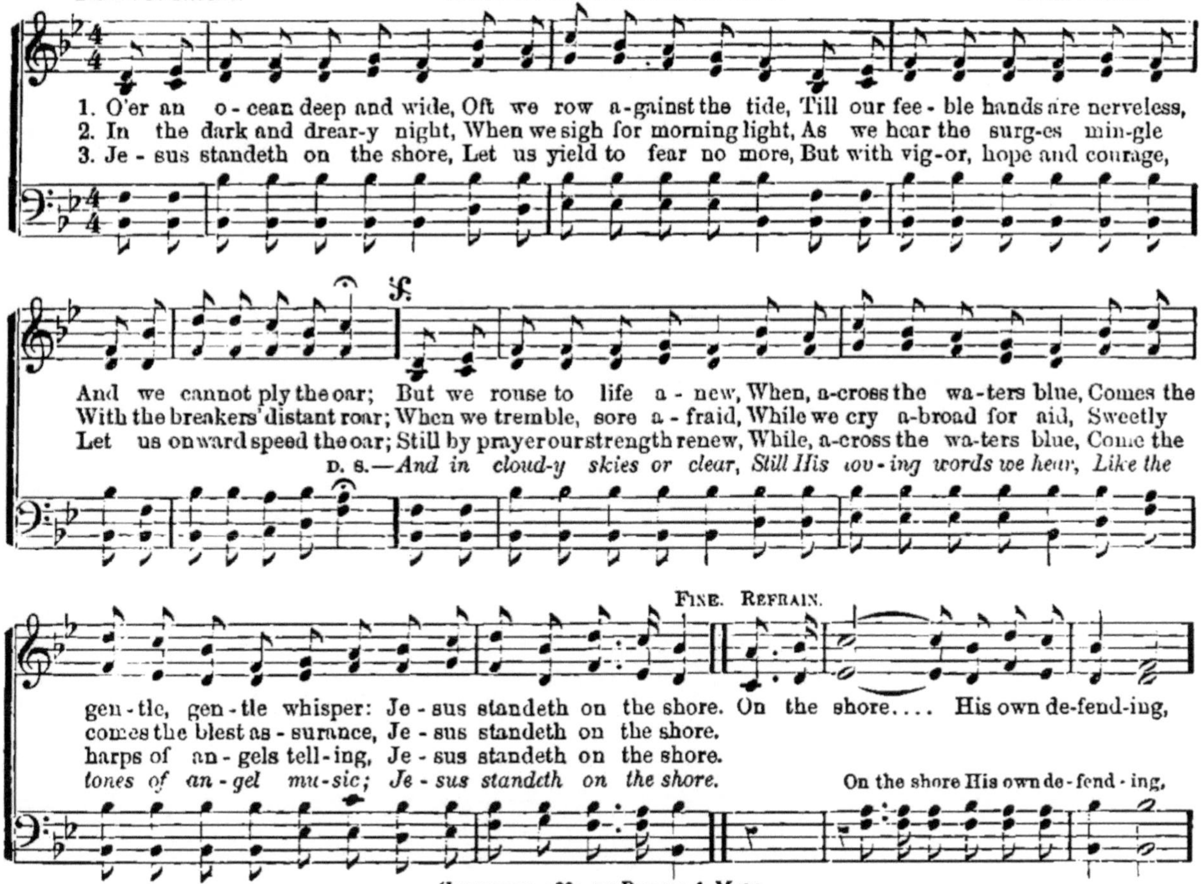
1. O'er an o - cean deep and wide, Oft we row a-gainst the tide, Till our fee - ble hands are nerveless,
2. In the dark and drear-y night, When we sigh for morning light, As we hear the surg-es min-gle
3. Je - sus standeth on the shore, Let us yield to fear no more, But with vig-or, hope and courage,
And we cannot ply the oar; But we rouse to life a - new, When, a-cross the wa-ters blue, Comes the
With the breakers' distant roar; When we tremble, sore a - fraid, While we cry a-broad for aid, Sweetly
Let us onward speed the oar; Still by prayer our strength renew, While, a-cross the wa-ters blue, Come the
D. S.—And in cloud-y skies or clear, Still His lov - ing words we hear, Like the
Fine. Refrain.
gen - tle, gen - tle whisper: Je - sus standeth on the shore. On the shore.... His own de-fend-ing,
comes the blest as - surance, Je - sus standeth on the shore.
harps of an - gels tell - ing, Je - sus standeth on the shore.
tones of an - gel mu - sic; Je - sus standeth on the shore.
On the shore His own de - fend - ing,

Jesus on the Shore. Concluded.

D. S.
In their need...... His aid ex - tend-ing, Je-sus standeth our protector, Till the voyage of life is o'er;
In their need His aid ex - tend - ing,

Jesus saw Me.

LAURA ELMER. *So Jesus had compassion on them.*—MATT. 20: 34. R. LOWRY.

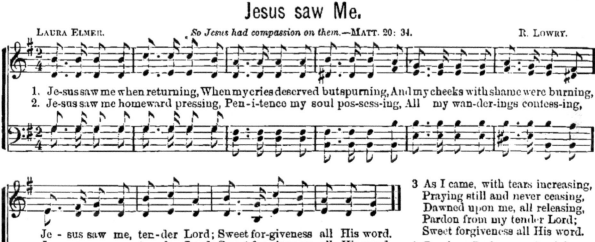

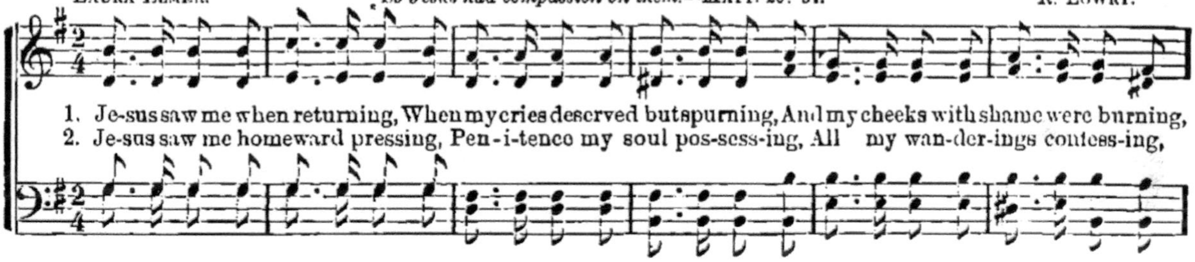
1. Je-sus saw me when returning, When my cries deserved but spurning, And my cheeks with shame were burning,
2. Je-sus saw me homeward pressing, Pen-i-tence my soul pos-sess-ing, All my wan-der-ings confess-ing,

Je - sus saw me, ten-der Lord; Sweet for-giveness all His word.
Je - sus saw me, ten-der Lord; Sweet for-giveness all His word.

3 As I came, with tears increasing,
Praying still and never ceasing,
Dawned upon me, all releasing,
Pardon from my tender Lord;
Sweet forgiveness all His word.

4 Gracious Saviour, so forgiving,
My poor heart, so unbelieving,
Found at last its rest, receiving
Pardon from my tender Lord;
Sweet forgiveness all His word.

160 Yield not to the Tempter.

A. W. French. *Blessed is the man that endureth temptation.*—James 1: 12. J. H. Tenney.

1. Yield not to the tempter; Pass by, and be free; For yielding is ru - in And sorrow for thee;
2. Yield not to the tempter; Turn quickly a - way; Go, mingle with hon-or In life's busy fray;
3. Yield not to the tempter; Be firm and be true; And God, in your weakness, Your strength shall renew;
Why should you now barter The jewel of youth, With shame for your honor, And wrong for the truth?
Fall not from your station, What - ev - er it be; Keep clear from the danger That beckons to thee.
To Him your pe - ti - tion Send upward a - gain, That you may be ev - er A man among men.
Chorus.
Yield not to the tempter; Pass by, and be free; For yielding is ru - in And sorrow for thee.

By permission.

Cast thy Burden on the Lord.

REV. ROWLAND HILL. *He shall sustain thee.*—Ps. 55: 22. R. LOWRY.

1. Cast thy burden on the Lord, On - ly lean up - on His word; Thou shalt soon have cause to bless
2. He sustains thee by His hand, He en - a - bles thee to stand; Those whom Jesus once hath loved,
3. Heav'n and earth may pass away, His free grace shall not de - cay; He hath promised to ful - fill
His un-changing faith-ful - ness.
From His grace are nev - er moved.
All the pleasure of His will.
REFRAIN.
On the Lord, on the Lord, Cast thy burden on the
On the Lord, on the Lord,
Lord; On the Lord,...... on the Lord,........ Cast thy bur - den on the Lord.
Cast thy bur-den on the Lord, on the Lord,

162 A Home and Crown.

Fanny J. Crosby | *Ye shall receive a crown of glory.*—1 Pet. 5: 4. | W. H. Doane.

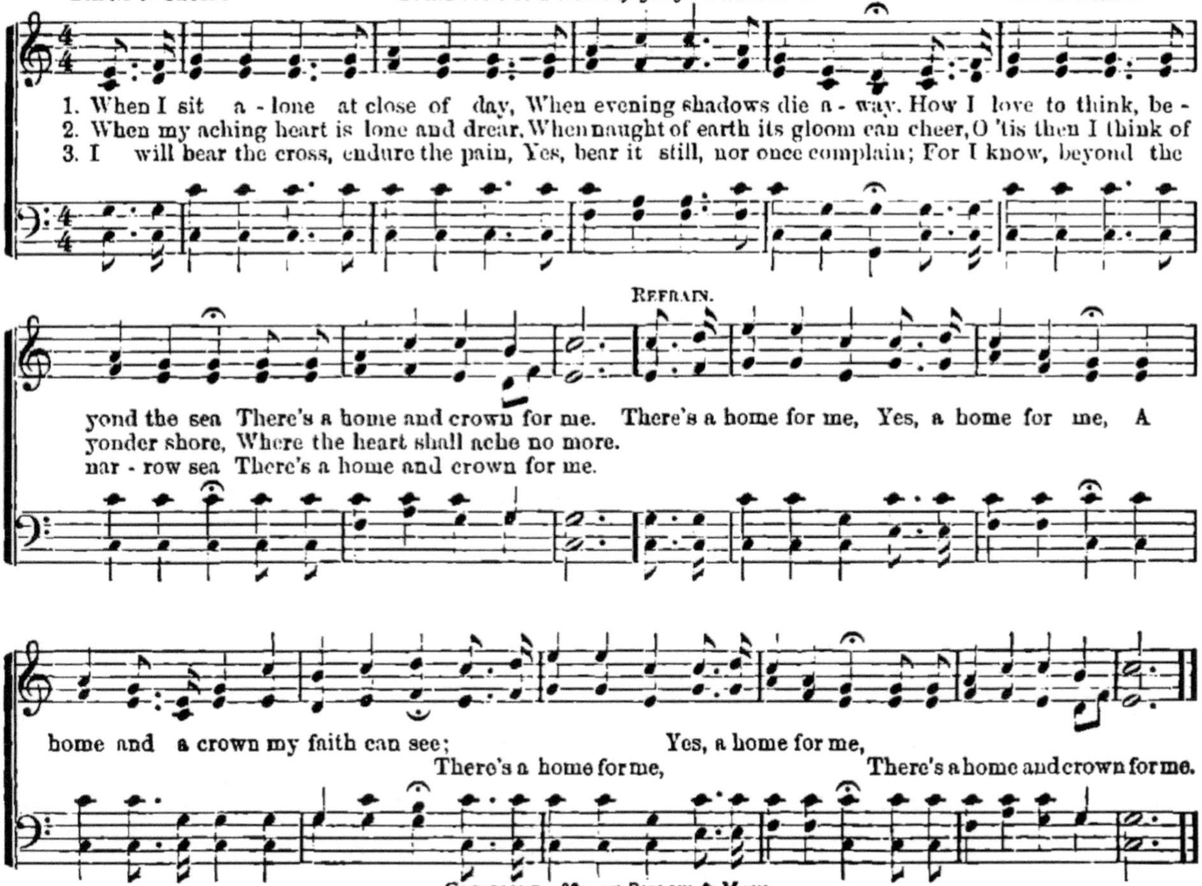
1. When I sit a - lone at close of day, When evening shadows die a - way, How I love to think, be - yond the sea There's a home and crown for me.
2. When my aching heart is lone and drear, When naught of earth its gloom can cheer, O 'tis then I think of yonder shore, Where the heart shall ache no more.
3. I will bear the cross, endure the pain, Yes, bear it still, nor once complain; For I know, beyond the nar - row sea There's a home and crown for me.
Refrain.
There's a home for me, Yes, a home for me, A home and a crown my faith can see; There's a home for me, Yes, a home for me, There's a home and crown for me.

DUNDEE.

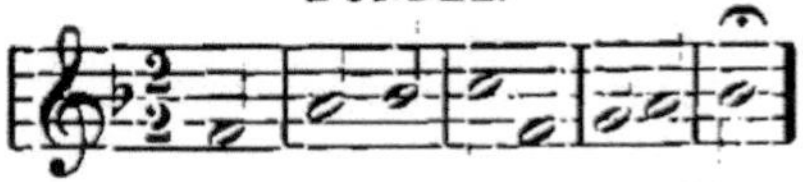

1 Alas! and did my Saviour bleed?
And did my Sovereign die?
Would He devote that sacred head
For such a worm as I?

2 Was it for crimes that I had done
He groaned upon the tree!
Amazing pity! grace unknown!
And love beyond degree!

3 Well might the sun in darkness hide,
And shut His glories in,
When Christ, the mighty Maker, died
For man, the creature's sin.

4 Thus might I hide my blushing face
While His dear cross appears,
Dissolve my heart in thankfulness,
And melt mine eyes to tears.

5 But drops of grief can ne'er repay
The debt of love I owe;
Here, Lord, I give myself away;
'Tis all that I can do.

Isaac Watts, D. D.

NOTHING BUT THE BLOOD.

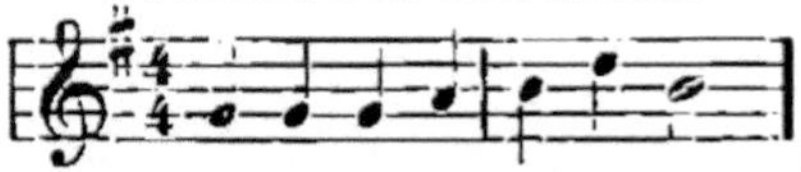

1 What can wash away my stain?
Nothing but the blood of Jesus;
What can make me whole again?
Nothing but the blood of Jesus.

REF.—O precious is the flow
That makes me white as snow:
No other fount I know,
Nothing but the blood of Jesus.

2 For my cleansing this I see—
Nothing but the blood of Jesus;
For my pardon this my plea—
Nothing but the blood of Jesus.

3 Nothing can for sin atone—
Nothing but the blood of Jesus;
Naught of good that I have done—
Nothing but the blood of Jesus.

4 This is all my hope and peace—
Nothing but the blood of Jesus;
This is all my righteousness—
Nothing but the blood of Jesus.

5 Now by this I'll overcome—
Nothing but the blood of Jesus;
Now by this I'll reach my home—
Nothing but the blood of Jesus.

6 Glory! glory! thus I sing—
Nothing but the blood of Jesus;
All my praise for this I bring—
Nothing but the blood of Jesus.

Rev. R. Lowry.

NETTLETON.

1 Come, Thou Fount of every blessing,
Tune my heart to sing Thy grace;
Streams of mercy, never ceasing,
Call for songs of loudest praise;
Teach me some melodious sonnet,
Sung by flaming tongues above;
Praise the mount—O fix me on it,
Mount of God's unchanging love.

2 Here I raise my Ebenezer;
Hither by Thy help I'm come;
And I hope, by Thy good pleasure,
Safely to arrive at home:
Jesus sought me when a stranger,
Wandering from the fold of God;
He, to save my soul from danger,
Interposed His precious blood.

3 O to grace how great a debtor
Daily I'm constrained to be!
Let that grace, Lord, like a fetter,
Bind my wandering heart to Thee;
Prone to wander, Lord, I feel it,
Prone to leave the God I love;
Here's my heart, Lord, take and seal it,
Seal it from Thy courts above.

Rev. R. Robinson.

Birth of Christ.

1 Hark! what mean those holy voices,
Sweetly sounding thro' the skies?
Lo! th'angelic host rejoices;
Heavenly hallelujahs rise;
Hear them tell the wondrous story,
Hear them chant in hymns of joy:
"Glory in the highest, glory!
Glory be to God Most High!

2 "Peace on earth, good will from heaven,
Reaching far as man is found;
Souls redeemed, and sins forgiven!
Loud our golden harps shall sound.
Christ is born, the great Anointed;
Heaven and earth His praises sing;
O receive whom God appointed
For your Prophet, Priest, and King!"

Rev. John Cawood

164 Blessed are They that Mourn.

Josephine Pollard. *—for they shall be comforted.*—Matt. 5: 4. Henry Tucker.

1. The tears that fall from eyes That mourn earth's pleasures fled, Are like the dew that falls On
2. 'Tis those who mourn for sin, And weep re-pent-ant tears, Who see a light break thro' Each
3. For ev-ery wound He can The sovereign balm ap-ply; For ev-ery pain He finds The
sum-mer flow-ers dead: They raise no sweet per-fume, No fu-ture joy be-speak; No
cloud that in-ter-feres; And when their wea-ry feet To Je-sus have been led, Then
heal-ing rem-e-dy: Go, tell thy griefs to Him Who once for sin-ners bled, And,
lov-ing hand will dry Those tears that wet the cheek.
shall their hearts re-joice; "They shall be com-fort-ed!"
lean-ing on His breast, Thou shalt be com-fort-ed!
Refrain.
"Bless-ed are they that mourn,"

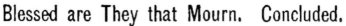

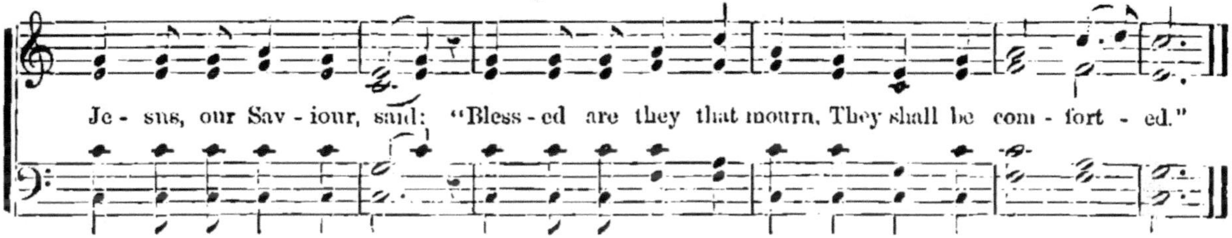
Je - sus, our Sav - iour, said: "Bless - ed are they that mourn, They shall be com - fort - ed."

Home in Glory.

FANNY J. CROSBY. *In my Father's house are many mansions.*—JOHN 14: 2. R. LOWRY.

1. A lit - tle while, and then for me The things that are will cease to be, And what I
2. When I shall find that calm re - pose Be - yond the tide of mor - tal woes, The part - ed
3. A lit - tle while, and I shall say Farewell to each re - volv - ing day, And like a

now but dim - ly see Will brightly shine in glo - ry.
vail will then dis - close My home with Christ in glo - ry.
bird speed on my way To reach my home in glo - ry.
Will brightly shine in glory.

4 I sing of heaven, and love the song;
A little while—'twill not be long—
And I shall join the ransomed throng
Within the gates of glory.

5 I'll sing His love thro' endless days,
Nor shall the brightest angel's praise
Excel the rapture of my lays,
When safe at home in glory

No Passport.

MRS. KATE SMILEY. *Whence camest thou?*—GEN. 16: 8. W. H. DOANE.

This may be sung as Solo, or Quartette and Chorus.

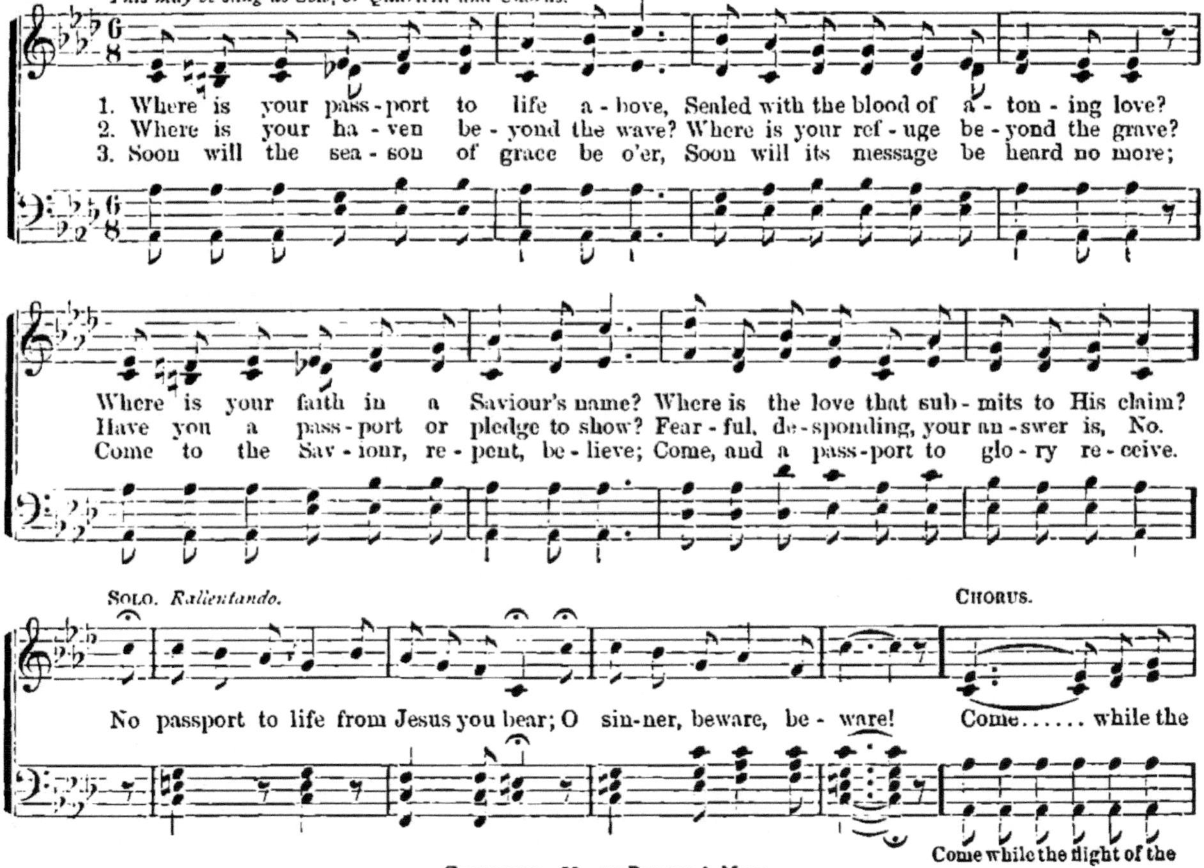
1. Where is your pass-port to life a-bove, Sealed with the blood of a-ton-ing love?
2. Where is your ha-ven be-yond the wave? Where is your ref-uge be-yond the grave?
3. Soon will the sea-son of grace be o'er, Soon will its message be heard no more;
Where is your faith in a Saviour's name? Where is the love that sub-mits to His claim?
Have you a pass-port or pledge to show? Fear-ful, de-sponding, your an-swer is, No.
Come to the Sav-iour, re-pent, be-lieve; Come, and a pass-port to glo-ry re-ceive.
SOLO. Rallentando.
CHORUS.
No passport to life from Jesus you bear; O sin-ner, beware, be-ware!
Come...... while the
Come while the light of the

flight..... of the Spir - - it is stayed,........ Come........ while the
Spir-it is stayed, Come while the flight of the Spir - it is stayed, Come while the sen - tence, the
sen - - tence of death..... is de - layed; Come to the cross, Now there is hope,
sentence of death, Come while the sentence of death is delayed;
Je - sus will save you now; Come to the cross, Now there is hope, He will save you now.

168 O Blest was the Hour.

Josephine Pollard. —*made whole from that very hour.*—Matt. 15: 28. Edward A. Perkins.

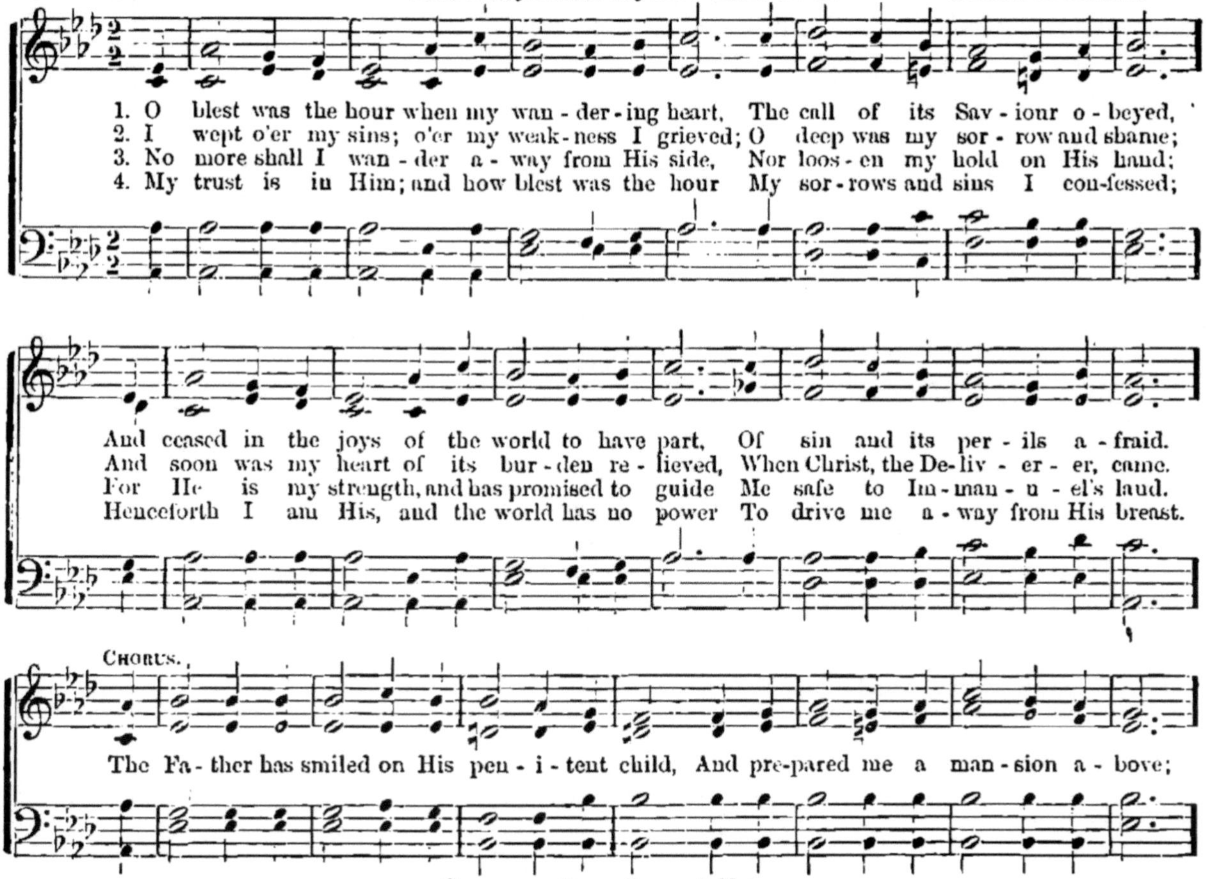
1. O blest was the hour when my wan - der - ing heart, The call of its Sav - iour o - beyed,
2. I wept o'er my sins; o'er my weak - ness I grieved; O deep was my sor - row and shame;
3. No more shall I wan - der a - way from His side, Nor loos - en my hold on His hand;
4. My trust is in Him; and how blest was the hour My sor - rows and sins I con-fessed;
And ceased in the joys of the world to have part, Of sin and its per - ils a - fraid.
And soon was my heart of its bur - den re - lieved, When Christ, the De - liv - er - er, came.
For He is my strength, and has promised to guide Me safe to Im - man - u - el's land.
Henceforth I am His, and the world has no power To drive me a - way from His breast.
Chorus.
The Fa - ther has smiled on His pen - i - tent child, And pre-pared me a man - sion a - bove;

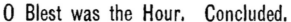

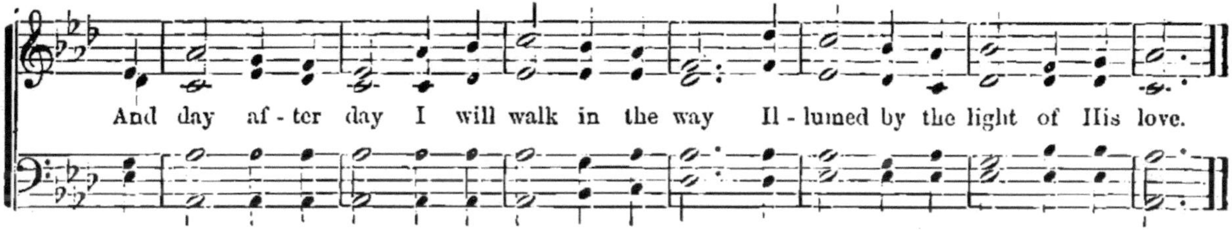
And day af - ter day I will walk in the way Il - lumed by the light of His love.

Reach Me thy Hand.

MRS. ELLEN H. GATES. *With a true heart, in full assurance of faith.—HEB. 10: 22.* W. H. DOANE.

1. Reach me thy hand, my child, Help - less and lone-ly; Thro' the drear and des - ert wild,
2. Reach me thy hand, my child, Home - less and friendless, Un - to me now rec - on-ciled,
3. Reach me thy hand, my child, What can be - tide thee, If the Saviour, meek and mild,
'Tis I, and I on - ly, Can safe - ly con - duct thee, Can safe - ly con - duct thee.
Thy bliss shall be end - less In mansions e - ter - nal, In man - sions e - ter - nal.
Is walk - ing be - side thee, And lov - ing thee al - ways, And lov - ing thee al - ways?

By permission.

170 Come unto Me.

—and I will give you rest.—Matt. 11: 29.

R. Lowry.

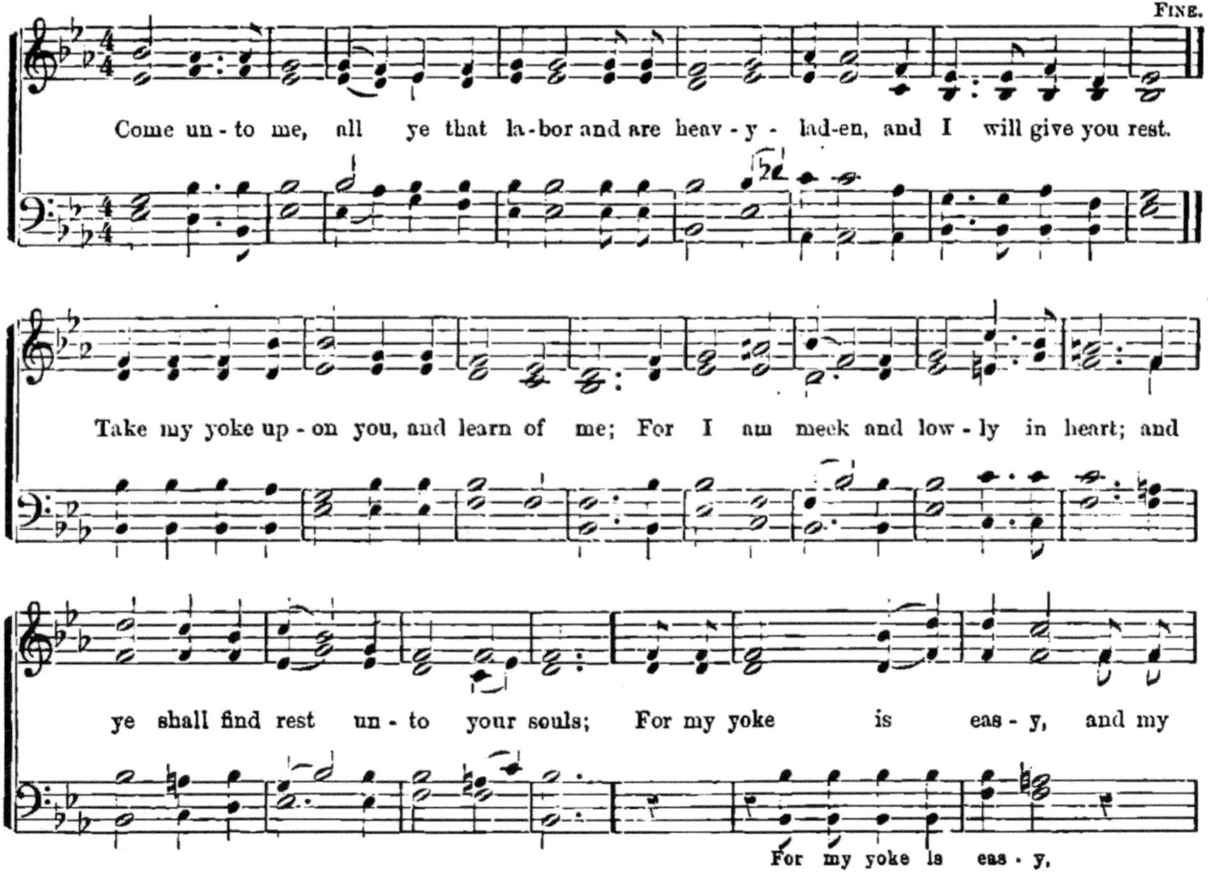
Fine.
Come un - to me, all ye that la-bor and are heav - y - lad-en, and I will give you rest.
Take my yoke up - on you, and learn of me; For I am meek and low - ly in heart; and
ye shall find rest un - to your souls; For my yoke is eas - y, and my
For my yoke is eas - y,

D.C.
bur - den is light, For my yoke is eas - y, and my bur - den is light.
and my bur-den is light, For my yoke is eas - y.

Father of All.

CHRISTOPHER WORDSWORTH, D. D. *Our Father which art in heaven.*—MATT. 6: 9. HENRY JOHN GAUNTLETT.

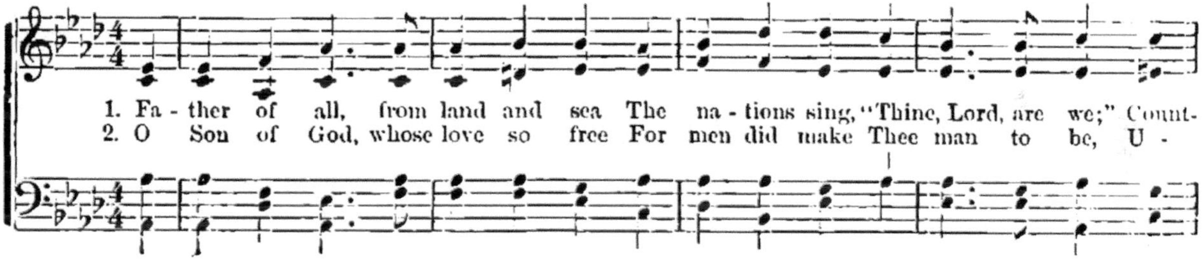
1. Fa - ther of all, from land and sea The na - tions sing, "Thine, Lord, are we;" Count-
2. O Son of God, whose love so free For men did make Thee man to be, U -

less in num - ber, but in Thee May we be one.
nit - ed to our God in Thee May we be one.

3 O Trinity in Unity,
One only God, in Persons Three,
Dwell ever in our hearts; like Thee
May we be one.

4 So when the world shall pass away,
May we awake with joy and say,
"Now in the bliss of endless day
We all are one."

172 Stand, Firmly Stand!

REV. E. A. HOFFMAN. *Stand fast in one spirit.*—PHIL. 1: 27. J. H. TENNEY.

1. Stand, firm-ly stand! A no-ble, val-iant band; For temp'rance and the right, Your forc-es all u-nite,
2. Stand, firm-ly stand! U-nit-ed heart and hand; Press no-bly, bold-ly on, Till vic-to-ry is won,
3. Stand, firm-ly stand! De-fend our blessed land From ev-'ry sub-tle foe, From ev-'ry tide of woe;
And cast in-to the strife The strength of all your life.
Till notes of triumph thrill O'er ev-'ry vale and hill.
Stand bravely in your might, Stand bravely for the right.
CHORUS.
Stand, firm-ly stand! Stand, firm-ly stand!
Stand, firm-ly stand for the righ
On, brave-ly on!
firm-ly stand for the right,

By permission.

Stand, Firmly Stand! 173

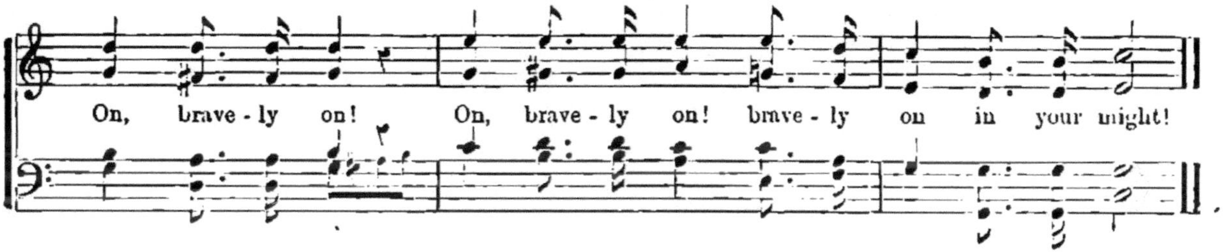
On, brave - ly on! On, brave - ly on! brave - ly on in your might!

Let Him Teach Thee.

L. M. E. *Him shall he teach.*—Ps. 25: 12. W. H Doane.

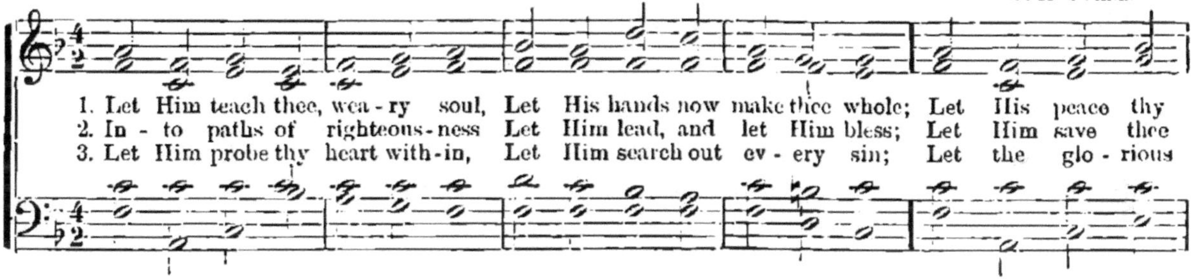
1. Let Him teach thee, wea - ry soul, Let His hands now make thee whole; Let His peace thy
2. In - to paths of righteous - ness Let Him lead, and let Him bless; Let Him save thee
3. Let Him probe thy heart with - in, Let Him search out ev - ery sin; Let the glo - rious

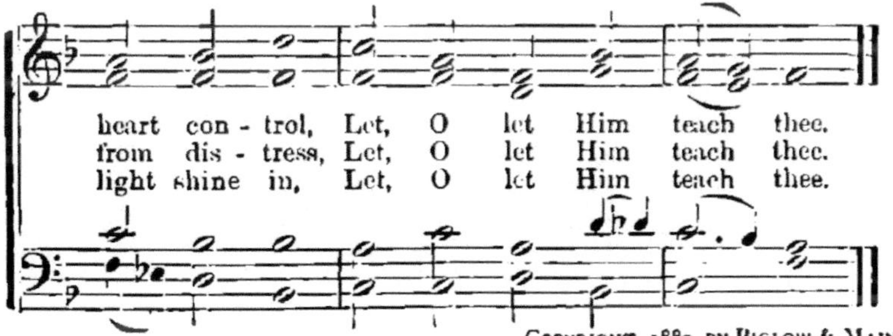
heart con - trol, Let, O let Him teach thee.
from dis - tress, Let, O let Him teach thee.
light shine in, Let, O let Him teach thee.

4 Let Him like a shepherd feed,
Let Him gently, gently lead;
He'll not break the bruised reed,
Let, O let Him teach thee.

5 Let Him give thee songs at night,
Let Him make the darkness light;
Let Him set thy spirit right—
Let, O let Him teach thee.

The Believer's Standing.

Geo. C. Needham. *This grace wherein we stand.*—Rom. 5: 2. C. C. Williams.

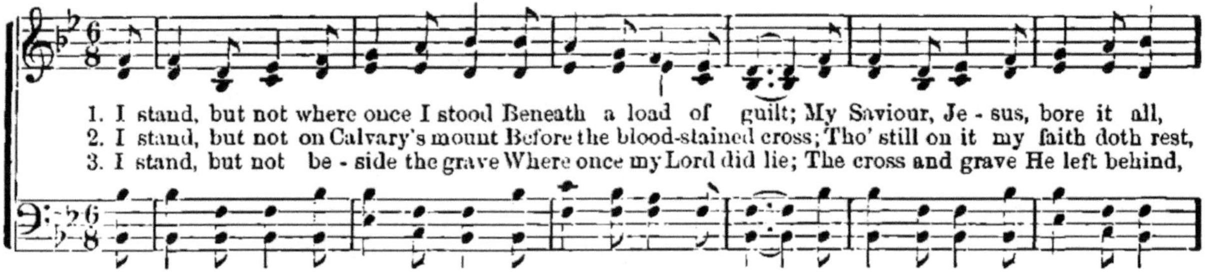
1. I stand, but not where once I stood Beneath a load of guilt; My Saviour, Je - sus, bore it all,
2. I stand, but not on Calvary's mount Before the blood-stained cross; Tho' still on it my faith doth rest,
3. I stand, but not be - side the grave Where once my Lord did lie; The cross and grave He left behind,

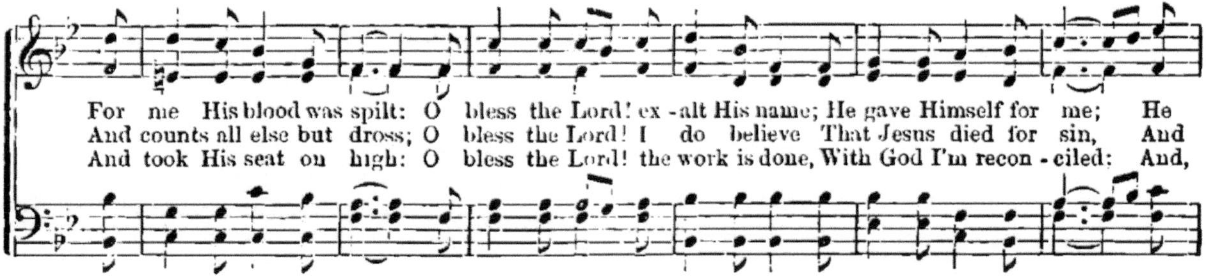
For me His blood was spilt: O bless the Lord! ex - alt His name; He gave Himself for me; He
And counts all else but dross; O bless the Lord! I do believe That Jesus died for sin, And
And took His seat on high: O bless the Lord! the work is done, With God I'm recon - ciled: And,

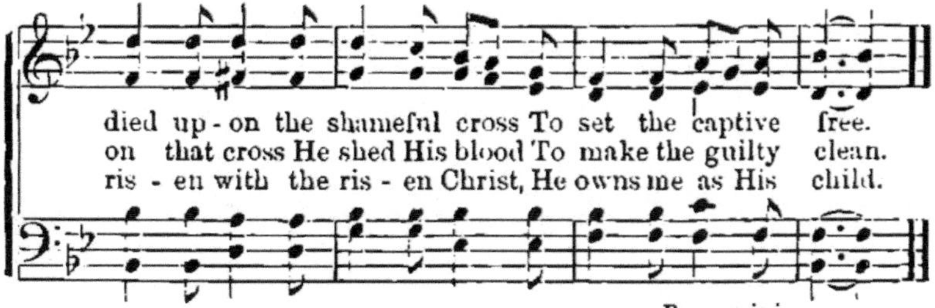
died up - on the shameful cross To set the captive free.
on that cross He shed His blood To make the guilty clean.
ris - en with the ris - en Christ, He owns me as His child.

4.
I stand e'en now within the vail,
In union with my Lord,
Beyond the power of death and hell;
I know it from His word;
O bless the Lord! assured thereby,
In Him we are complete;
We walk by faith, but soon, in sight,
Our glorious King will greet.

By permission.

The Race set before us.

Mrs. E. C. Ellsworth. *Let us run with patience the race set before us.—Heb. 12: 1.* R. Lowry.

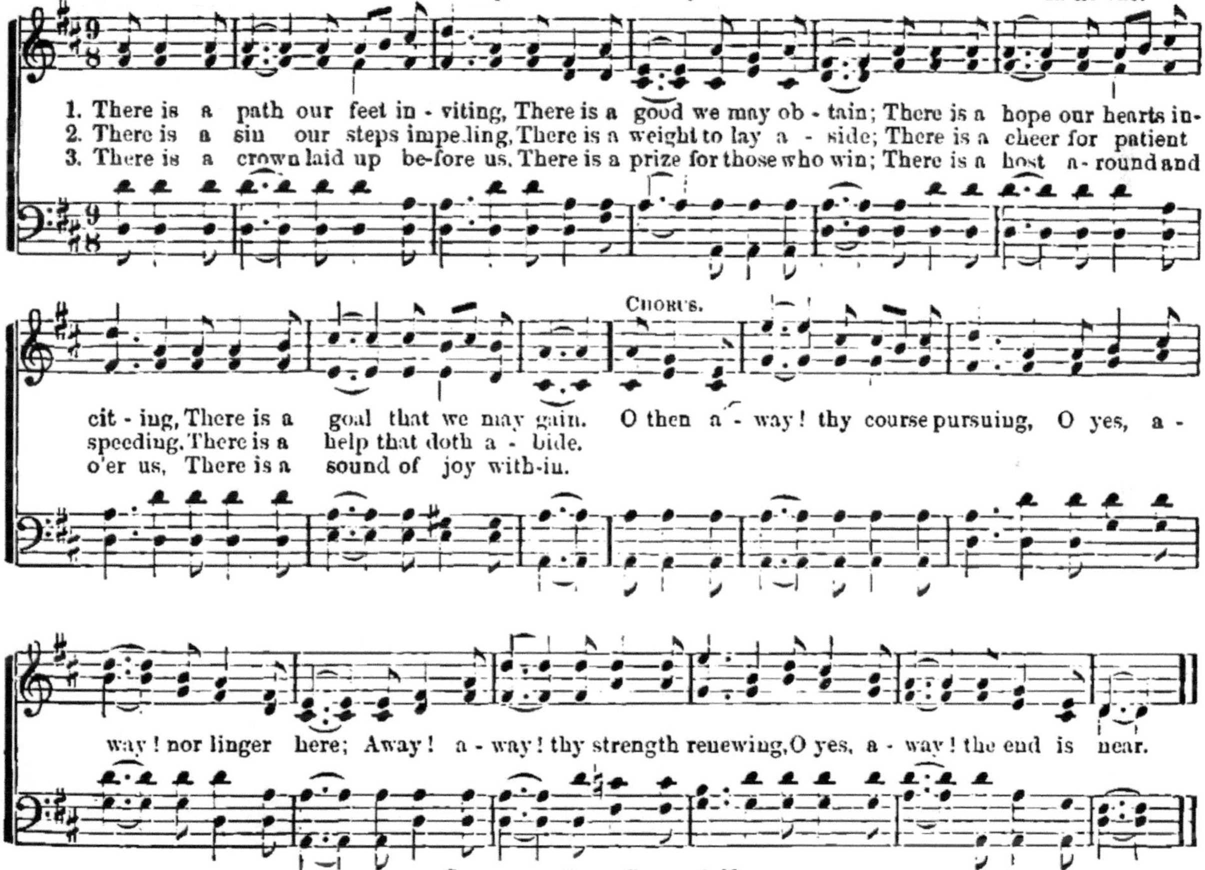
1. There is a path our feet in - viting, There is a good we may ob - tain; There is a hope our hearts in-
2. There is a sin our steps impe.ling, There is a weight to lay a - side; There is a cheer for patient
3. There is a crown laid up be-fore us, There is a prize for those who win; There is a host a-round and
cit - ing, There is a goal that we may gain.
speeding, There is a help that doth a - bide.
o'er us, There is a sound of joy with-in.
Chorus.
O then a - way! thy course pursuing, O yes, a - way! nor linger here; Away! a - way! thy strength renewing, O yes, a - way! the end is near.

176 The Lord is our Refuge.

FANNY J. CROSBY. *A refuge in times of trouble.*—Ps. 9: 9. HENRY TUCKER.

1. The Lord is our Ref - uge; ye na - tions of earth, His won-der - ful good-ness pro-claim; Ex -
2. The Lord is our Ref - uge; His peo - ple of old, How long in the des - ert He fed; And
3. The Lord is our Ref - uge; go, sound it a-broad, Sal - va - tion is boundless and free; And
alt and a - dore Him with glad-ness and mirth, Sing praise to His ex - cel - lent name.
still thro' the jour - ney of life we be - hold The ta - ble His mer - cy has spread.
earth shall be full of the glo - ry of God As wa - ters that cov - er the sea.
D. S.—chang-es to morn-ing the dark-ness of night, And calls us a - way to His rest.
FINE.
CHORUS.
The Lord is our Ref - uge, the Rock of our strength, The Arm of the weak and op-pressed; He
D. S.

The Angels' Song.

R. L. *A multitude of the heavenly host, praising God.*—Luke 2: 13. R. Lowry.

With energy
1. Rolling downward thro' the midnight, Comes a glorious burst of heavenly song; 'Tis a chorus full of sweetness, And the singers are an an - gel throng.
2. Wondering shepherds see the glory, Hear the word the shining ones declare; At the manger fall in wor - ship, While the music fills the quivering air.
3. Christ the Saviour, God's Anointed, Comes to earth our fearful debt to pay— Child of Mary, Man of Sorrows, Lamb of God that takes our sin a-way.
Chorus.
"Glo-ry, glo - ry in the highest! On the earth good-will and peace to men!" Down the a - ges send the ech-o; Let the glad earth shout a-gain.
Glory, glory, glory
ages, down the ages

By permission.

178 Shout Hallelujah.

FANNY J. CROSBY.

Hosanna! blessed is the King of Israel.—JOHN 12: 13.

W. H. DOANE.

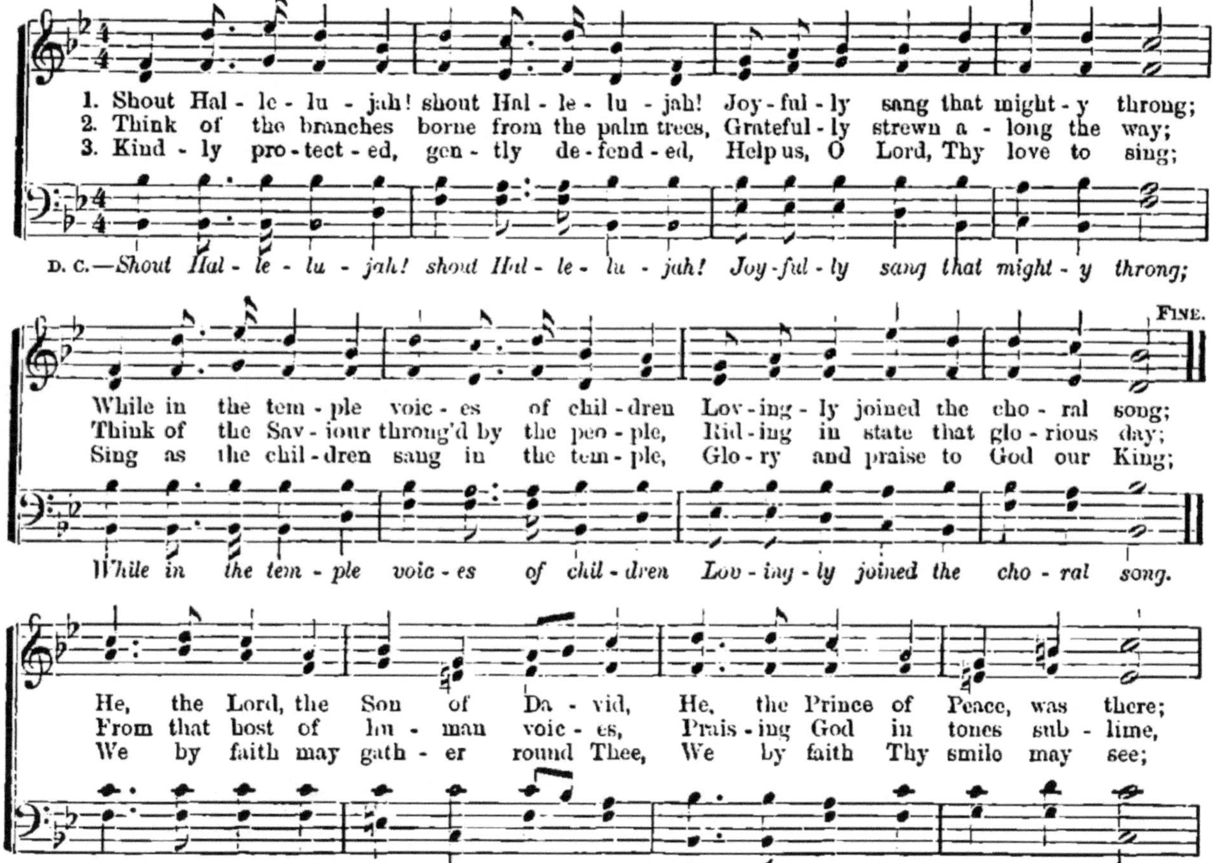
1. Shout Hal - le - lu - jah! shout Hal - le - lu - jah! Joy - ful - ly sang that might - y throng;
2. Think of the branches borne from the palm trees, Grateful - ly strewn a - long the way;
3. Kind - ly pro - tect - ed, gen - tly de - fend - ed, Help us, O Lord, Thy love to sing;
D. C.—Shout Hal - le - lu - jah! shout Hal - le - lu - jah! Joy - ful - ly sang that might - y throng;
FINE.
While in the tem - ple voic - es of chil - dren Lov - ing - ly joined the cho - ral song;
Think of the Sav - iour throng'd by the peo - ple, Rid - ing in state that glo - rious day;
Sing as the chil - dren sang in the tem - ple, Glo - ry and praise to God our King;
While in the tem - ple voic - es of chil - dren Lov - ing - ly joined the cho - ral song.
He, the Lord, the Son of Da - vid, He, the Prince of Peace, was there;
From that host of hu - man voic - es, Prais - ing God in tones sub - lime,
We by faith may gath - er round Thee, We by faith Thy smile may see;

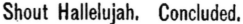

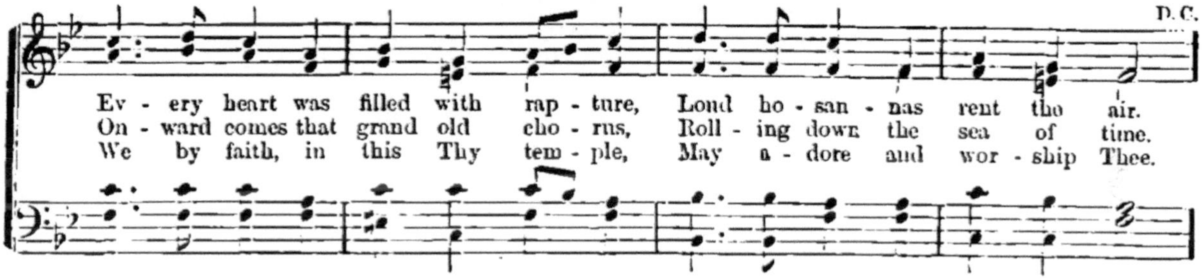
D. C.
Ev - ery heart was filled with rap - ture, Loud ho - san - nas rent the air.
On - ward comes that grand old cho - rus, Roll - ing down the sea of time.
We by faith, in this Thy tem - ple, May a - dore and wor - ship Thee.

Draw near, O Lord.

R. L. *Draw nigh unto my soul.*—Ps. 69: 18. R. Lowry.

1. Draw near, O Lord, draw near, And bless Thy saints to - day; O scat - ter ev - ery
2. Be - fore Thy gra - cious feet Our con - trite spir - its bow; We bold - ly seek Thy

doubt and fear, And grant us peace, we pray.
mer - cy - seat, And plead Thy prom - ise now.

3 Let not our grievous sin
Conceal Thy loving face;
Thou knowest what our lives have been;
We hope but in Thy grace.

4 Then at Thy feet, O Lord,
We find our meet employ;
We wait for Thy sweet pard'ning word,
To fill our hearts with joy.

180 Though your Sins.

Fanny J. Crosby. W. H. Doane.

Though your sins be as scarlet.—Isa. 1: 18.

Gently. Duet.
1st.
2nd.
Trio.
1. Tho' your sins be as scarlet, They shall be as white as snow, as snow: Tho' your sins be as scar-let,
2. Hear the voice that entreats you, O re - turn ye un - to God, to God: Hear the voice that entreats you,
3. He'll for-give your transgressions And remember them no more, no more: He'll forgive your transgressions
Quartet.
f
pp
Duet.
They shall be as white as snow; Tho' they be red . . . . . like crimson, They shall be as wool: Tho' your sins be as
O re-turn ye un - to God: He is of great . . . . . compassion, And of wondrous love; Hear the voice that en-
And remember them no more: Look unto me, ... ye people, Saith the Lord your God; He'll forgive your trans-
Tho' they be red like
Quartet.
Ritard. . . . .
scar - let, Tho' your sins be as scar - let, They shall be as white as snow, They shall be as white as snow.
treats you, Hear the voice that entreats you, O re - turn ye un - to God, O re - turn ye un-to God.
gressions, He'll for-give your transgressions And re-member them no more, And remember them no more.

By permission.

Temperance Bells.

W. S. *To knowledge, temperance.*—2 Pet. 1: 6. Wm. Stevenson.

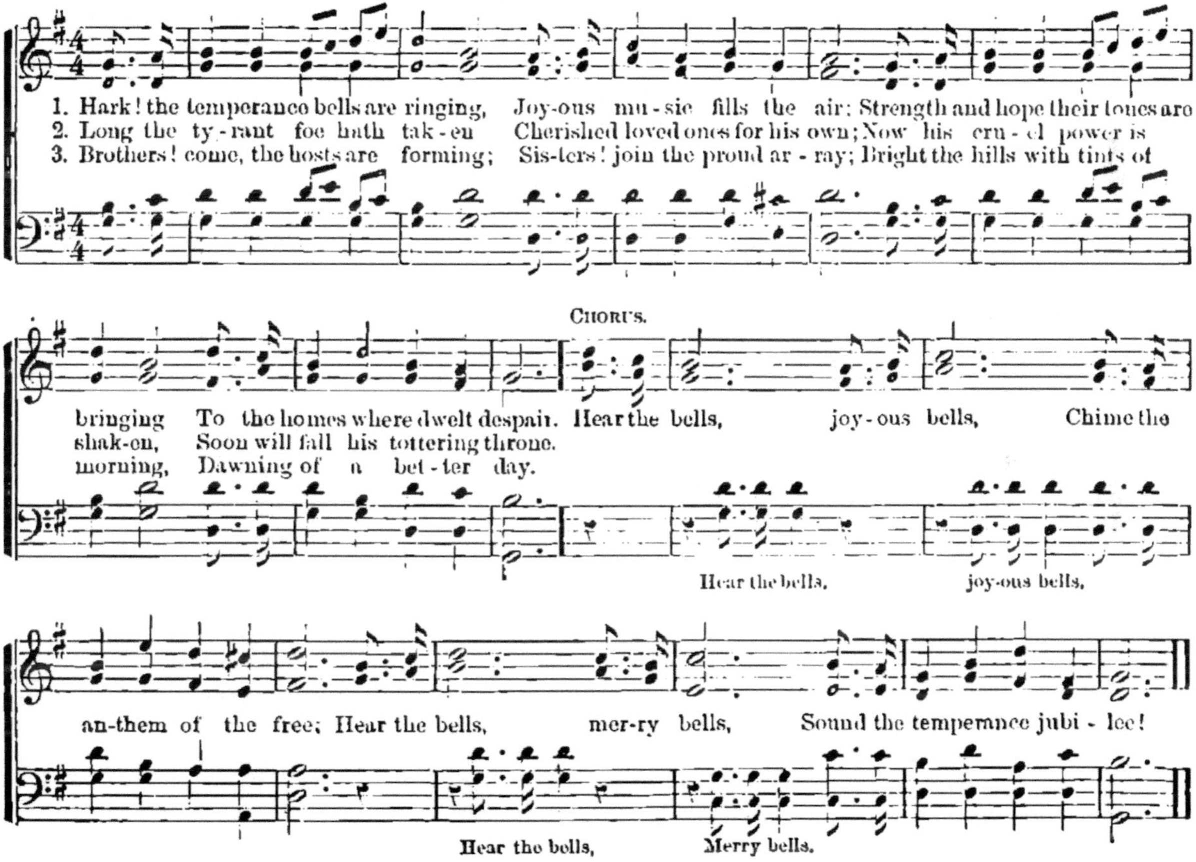
1. Hark! the temperance bells are ringing, Joy-ous mu-sic fills the air; Strength and hope their tones are bringing To the homes where dwelt despair.
2. Long the ty-rant foe hath tak-en Cherished loved ones for his own; Now his cru-el power is shak-en, Soon will fall his tottering throne.
3. Brothers! come, the hosts are forming; Sis-ters! join the proud ar-ray; Bright the hills with tints of morning, Dawning of a bet-ter day.
Chorus.
Hear the bells, joy-ous bells, Chime the an-them of the free; Hear the bells, mer-ry bells, Sound the temperance jubi-lee!
Hear the bells, joy-ous bells,
Hear the bells, Merry bells.

182 We'll Try to do More.

ROSE MATTHEWS. *The righteous giveth and spareth not.*—PROV. 21 : 26. W. H. DOANE.

(SOLO, DUET & CHORUS.)

1st voice.
2d voice.
1. Say, what do you owe to the Saviour For all He has suffered for you? O, what have you done for His glo - ry, And what are you will - ing to do?
2. O, what will you give to the Saviour? His love you can nev - er re - pay: But what will you give to the Sav - iour, Say, what will you give Him to - day?
3. God keep you in peace, O my brother, Your helper, your strength, and your guide; God comfort your heart, O my sis - ter, And bear you in peace o'er the tide;
Duet.
We owe Him our time and our tal - ents, Our service, our lives, and our store; Tho' lit - tle we've done for His glo - ry, In future we'll try to do more.
We'll give as His mer - cy hath blessed us, We'll give from our basket and store; Tho' lit - tle we've done for His glo - ry, Thro' grace we will try to do more.
O bliss, when our la - bor is end - ed! O bliss, when our journey is o'er! We'll rest in the home of the faithful, And sing of His love ever more.
Refrain.
Thro' grace we will try to do more,.......... Thro' grace we will try to do more,..........
try to do more, try to do more;

By permission.

Tho' lit - tle we've done for His glo - - - ry, In fu - ture we'll try to do more.
glo - ry, we own,

The Day is Past and Over.

Tr. by J. M. Neale, D. D. *Thou shalt not be afraid of the terror by night.*—Ps. 91 : 5. R. Lowry.

1. The day is past and o - ver; All thanks, O Lord, to Thee; I pray Thee now that sin - less The
2. The toils of day are o - ver; I raise the hymn to Thee, And ask that free from per - il The
3. Be Thou my soul's Preserv - er, For Thou a - lone dost know How ma - ny are the dan - gers Thro'

Refrain.

hours of dark may be. O Je - sus, keep me in Thy sight, And guard me thro' the coming night.
hours of dark may be.
which I have to go.

Which Way will you Journey?

FANNY J. CROSBY. *By what way we must go.*—DEUT. 1: 22. W. H. DOANE.

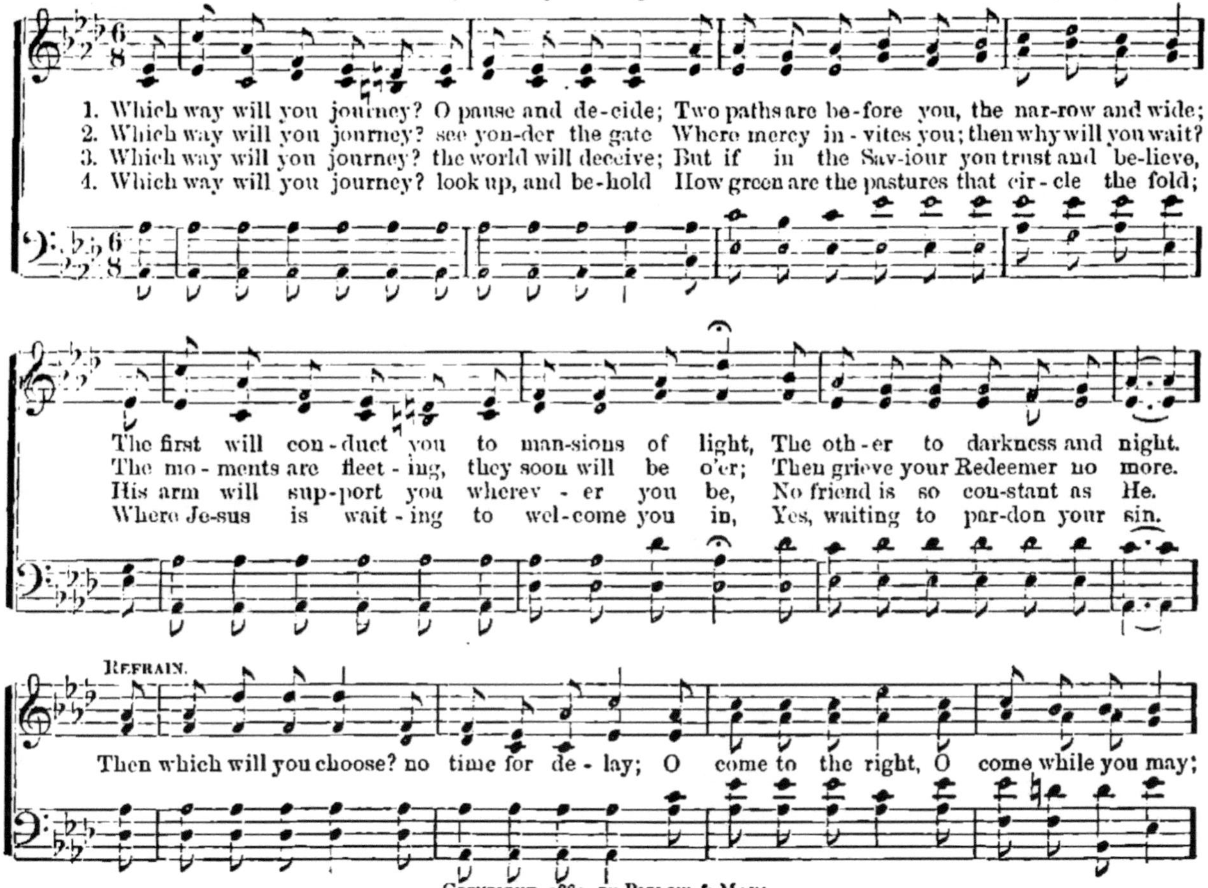
1. Which way will you journey? O pause and de-cide; Two paths are be-fore you, the nar-row and wide;
2. Which way will you journey? see yon-der the gate Where mercy in - vites you; then why will you wait?
3. Which way will you journey? the world will deceive; But if in the Sav-iour you trust and be-lieve,
4. Which way will you journey? look up, and be-hold How green are the pastures that cir - cle the fold;
The first will con-duct you to man-sions of light, The oth - er to darkness and night.
The mo-ments are fleet - ing, they soon will be o'er; Then grieve your Redeemer no more.
His arm will sup-port you wherev - er you be, No friend is so con-stant as He.
Where Je-sus is wait - ing to wel-come you in, Yes, waiting to par-don your sin.
REFRAIN.
Then which will you choose? no time for de - lay; O come to the right, O come while you may;

O come to the path that in glo - ry will end, And make the dear Sav-iour your friend.

Thy Will be Done.

Wm. Stevenson. *Not my will, but thine be done.*—Luke 22: 42. R. Lowry.

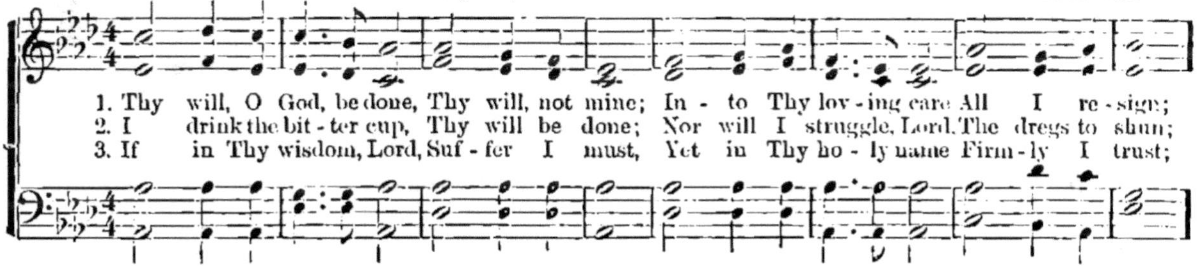
1. Thy will, O God, be done, Thy will, not mine; In - to Thy lov - ing care All I re - sign;
2. I drink the bit - ter cup, Thy will be done; Nor will I struggle, Lord, The dregs to shun;
3. If in Thy wisdom, Lord, Suf - fer I must, Yet in Thy ho - ly name Firm - ly I trust;

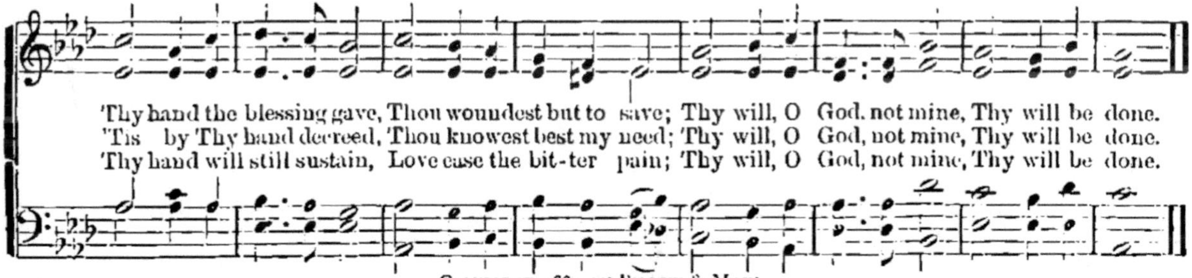
Thy hand the blessing gave, Thou woundest but to save; Thy will, O God, not mine, Thy will be done.
'Tis by Thy hand decreed, Thou knowest best my need; Thy will, O God, not mine, Thy will be done.
Thy hand will still sustain, Love ease the bit - ter pain; Thy will, O God, not mine, Thy will be done.

Offer unto God Thanksgiving.

MRS. KATE SMILEY. *Offer unto God thanksgiving.*—Ps. 50: 14. W. H. DOANE.

1. Of - fer un - to God thanks-giv - ing, Of - fer un - to God thanks-giv - ing, Worship Him with
2. Of - fer un - to God thanks-giv - ing, Of - fer un - to God thanks-giv - ing, Tell of His sal -
gladness in the courts of His house; Of-fer un - to God thanksgiv - ing, Of-fer un - to God thanks-
va - tion and re - joice in His word; Of-fer un - to God thanksgiv - ing, Of-fer un - to God thanks-
D. S.—*Of-fer un - to God thanksgiv - ing, Of - fer un - to God thanks-*
FINE.
SOLO OR QUARTET. *Andante.*
giv - ing, Lift our hearts with mel-o - dy and pay our vows.
giv - ing, Come be - fore Him joy-ful - ly and praise the Lord.
1. Great is He who has
2. Blest are they who de -
giv - ing, Lift our hearts with mel - o - dy and pay our vows.

Offer unto God Thanksgiving. Concluded.

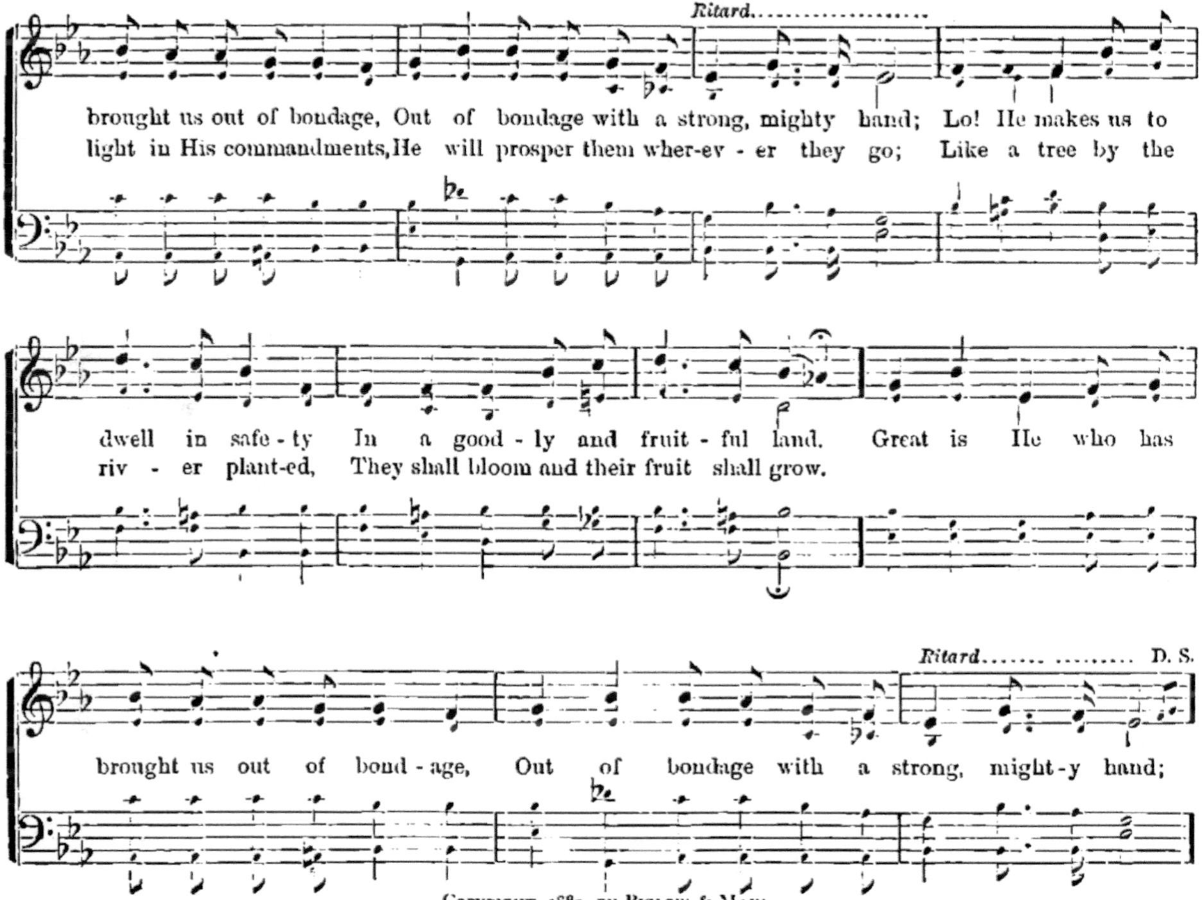
Ritard.
brought us out of bondage, Out of bondage with a strong, mighty hand; Lo! He makes us to
light in His commandments, He will prosper them wher-ev - er they go; Like a tree by the
dwell in safe - ty In a good - ly and fruit - ful land. Great is He who has
riv - er plant-ed, They shall bloom and their fruit shall grow.
Ritard. D. S.
brought us out of bond - age, Out of bondage with a strong, might - y hand;

PLEYEL'S HYMN.

1 Jesus! Master! hear me cry.
Save me, heal me, with a word;
Fainting, at Thy feet I lie,
Thou my whispered plaint hast heard.

2 Jesus! Master! mercy show;
Thou art passing near my soul;
Thou my inward grief dost know,
Thou alone canst make me whole.

3 Jesus! Master! as of yore
Thou didst make the blind man see,
Light upon my soul restore;
Jesus! Master! heal Thou me.

Anna Shipton.

Gracious Spirit.

1 Gracious Spirit, Love Divine,
Let Thy light within me shine;
All my guilty fears remove,
Fill me full of heaven and love.

2 Speak Thy pardoning grace to me,
Set the burdened sinner free,
Lead me to the Lamb of God,
Wash me in His precious blood.

3 Life and peace to me impart,
Seal salvation on my heart,
Breathe Thyself into my breast,
Earnest of immortal rest.

4 Let me never from Thee stray,
Keep me in the narrow way,
Fill my soul with joy divine,
Keep me, Lord, forever Thine.

John Stocker.

GREENVILLE.

Holy Spirit Invoked.

1 Holy Source of consolation,
Life and light Thy grace imparts;
Visit us in Thy compassion,
Guide our minds and fill our hearts;
Heavenly blessings without measure
Thou canst bring us from above;
Lord, we seek that heavenly treasure,
Wisdom, holiness, and love.

2 Dwell within us, blessed Spirit;
Where Thou art no ill can come;
Bless us now through Jesus' merit,
Reign in every heart and home;
Saviour, lead us to adore Thee,
While Thou dost prolong our days;
Then, with angel hosts before Thee,
May we worship, love, and praise.

Rev. B. W. Noel.

BOYLSTON.

Dependence on the Holy Spirit.

1 'Tis God the Spirit leads
In paths before unknown;
The work to be performed is ours,
The strength is all His own.

2 Supported by His grace,
We still pursue our way;
And hope at last to reach the prize,
Secure in endless day.

3 'Tis He that works to will,
'Tis He that works to do;
His is the power by which we act,
His be the glory too.

Rev. B. Beddome.

ARLINGTON.

1 Am I a soldier of the cross?
A follower of the Lamb?
And shall I fear to own His cause,
Or blush to speak His name?

2 Must I be carried to the skies
On flowery beds of ease,
While others fought to win the prize,
And sailed through bloody seas?

3 Sure I must fight, if I would reign;
Increase my courage, Lord;
I'll bear the toil, endure the pain,
Supported by Thy word.

4 Thy saints in all this glorious war,
Shall conquer, though they die;
They view the triumph from afar,
With faith's discerning eye.

Isaac Watts, D.D.

Doxology.

8, 7, 4.

Lord, dismiss us with Thy blessing,
Fill our hearts with joy and peace;
Let us each, Thy love possessing,
Triumph in redeeming grace;
O refresh us,
Traveling through this wilderness.

John Fawcett, D. D.